DWELLING IN POSSIBILITY

Dwelling

IN POSSIBILITY

~

Searching for the Soul of Shelter

~

HOWARD MANSFIELD

BAUHAN PUBLISHING

PETERBOROUGH · NEW HAMPSHIRE

2013

Library of Congress Cataloging-in-Publication Data

Mansfield, Howard.
Dwelling in possibility : searching for the soul of shelter / Howard Mansfield. -- First [edition].
   pages cm
Includes bibliographical references.
ISBN 978-0-87233-167-9 (alk. paper)
1. Architecture, Domestic--Psychological aspects. I. Title.
NA7125.M36 2013
728.01'9--dc23
                    2013022593

Books by Howard Mansfield (www.howardmansfield.com)
Cosmopolis
In the Memory House
Skylark
The Same Ax, Twice
The Bones of the Earth
Turn & Jump

Editor
Where the Mountain Stands Alone

For Children
Hogwood Steps Out

Cover Painting: "Under the Hill" by Frankie Brackley Tolman
www.frankiebrackleytolman.com

BAUHAN
PUBLISHING LLC
PO BOX 117 PETERBOROUGH NEW HAMPSHIRE 03458
603-567-4430
WWW.BAUHANPUBLISHING.COM

Manufactured in the United States of America

In memory of Christina Ward

In Kyoto
Hearing the cuckoo,
I long for Kyoto
— Basho

CONTENTS

House Hunting

In a boom market, a boom fever, we were hunting for a house. We had been hunting for months. A house on the market had the life of a mayfly, a day or two and it was sold. This was not a beginner's market. The houses went by at a dazzling speed, as if they were on a racetrack. We looked at many houses, even houses that were dead on description, dying in the phrase off the real estate agent's lips.

Pulling up to a house, the agent would say, "That's your driveway." (Oh so clever, slipping possessive ownership right in.) "And that's the driveway to the sandpit."

"Sandpit?"

"Oh, it's not big and he only works on the weekends."

At that point we should have said no—No thank you. We don't want to live next to a sandpit. But into the house we went. In the boom we had to look at what came along.

As we arrived at another house, she would say: "And he's just cleared all the trees!" This was delivered as good news, as if to say: "Good news! You won't have to despoil the land yourself!" The new house sat naked on its muddy lot. The recently felled great trees were stacked like Lincoln Logs awaiting the truck. No thank you.

I'd stay and look around long after it was clear that this was not the house for us (about thirty seconds). I was caught up in the psychological drama of the house, the hide-and-seek views of the people dwelling there.

My wife was distressed. As an Army brat, she had ping-ponged up and down the East Coast, packing everything up, being torn out of friendships. House hunting brought the anxiety back; she felt it in her stomach.

"Did you see that?" I'd say.

"Yeah, awful house," she'd say.

"Yes—but did you see all those photos of the guy around the house? Here's a guy with a wife and a newborn and all the photos are of him. Not one of the baby—or wife. Odd. And did you see those stock-picking tables and tips posted by his desk? He's going to be broke. Broke and divorced." He was, the agent told us, a failed stockpicker who needed to sell. (What the real estate agents call a "motivated seller.") "What's the next house we're going to see?"

Coming out of another house, my wife would say, "Well, that was bad."

"Yes, but did you see that little red furnace? It was imported from Sweden. It burns wood, coal, oil, gas, tofu, Stephen King paperbacks. You could heat your house through January with just a few copies of *The Shining*. That's a great furnace."

The most fascinating houses we saw were a topographical map of a family's inner turmoil, their unsettled psyche. In one house the family had walked out. There were still cereal boxes on the table and bits of furniture about. The house had sat like this for years, the agent had warned us as we drove up the hill. But she couldn't have prepared us for the feeling of indecision that hung in the air. It was like walking in on a stale family argument. As best as I can recall, two brothers had inherited the house and just couldn't agree about what to do.

The house had more serious problems than this. It had been built in two sections; the original house in around 1830 and an addition fifty years later. It sat on the side of a hill, and each section, like the brothers, was going its own way: 1830 heading north and 1880 falling south, downhill.

We'd brought along an architect friend to look at it. He didn't mince words. "It's a derelict," he said. Well, said my wife, what about this fence?—an aging white picket fence she was standing next to. "This?" he answered—and pulled the gatepost right out of the ground. "It's a derelict." Next house.

∼

The houses we saw had curb-appall—the opposite of curb appeal.

Houses choked for light and air.

Houses with failing septic fields—the telltale signs of cinnamon apple cider bubbling on the stove, and a suspiciously strong affection for potpourri or scented candles that just happened to be lighted in every room.

Tiny houses attached to huge barns. Little houses adrift on twenty rough acres. Big houses on wedges of land, a pie sliver of the old farm, cut up by a developer. Move here and have your heart ripped out.

Undernourished new houses so flimsy that you could put your foot through the particle-board sheathing and the vinyl siding and out in the world. Eggshell thin walls—but not as strong as a real eggshell.

Houses fallen from grace and houses fallen from non-grace. Houses melting before your eyes. Beautiful, ruined places. There was the old farmhouse that was diminished by renovation. On the table was a photo album of how it had been, how we wished it still was. In the photos the family is working hard with the best intentions, removing the barn, deleting the special spirit of the place, leaving the house with a green AstroTurf rug and a wagon-wheel chandelier and funky brickwork. The house still reached out to the missing barn, a phantom limb.

There was the house built in 1809 with a great ridgepole made from one tree. Below were two floors of crumbling plaster, a moody ruin. The attic told of good beginnings; the rest of the house had decayed, the plaster walls dissolving in the rain when the family let the roof go. And there was the gutted Victorian abandoned midway. It needed so much work that I could see us living in a tent in what had been the front parlor.

When the market boiled over in a frenzy, we were priced out of even these houses. We were shown camps built long ago with a bottle of whiskey or two, salvaged lumber, and a casual respect for the right angle. They were meant only to be camps, little better than tents with some plumbing. Approximate and crude. Over time they were propped up, jacked up, patched, added to, dressed up, fussed over—but camps never learn company manners. They slump back to the earth, the porch following the fall and rise of the ground like a caterpillar, a later addition floating against the old like a boat tied to a dock. The floors were soft with the give of mossy ground.

The asking price for the camps was astounding. "No, really," you wanted to say to the real estate agent. "That's very funny. Ha ha and all, but really isn't there a zero too many in that price?"

～

I liked house hunting. I am fascinated by how houses succeed or fail to shelter us, body and soul. I could go from house to house clear across the country, knock on doors, and ask, Can I come in? Look around? What's your favorite room? Your latest house project? I'd like to see them all.

The sour living rooms behind dirty windows and overgrown shrubs; the small rooms made smaller by dark wood paneling, big fat La-Z-Boy recliners and the large-screen TV.

McMansions where rooms and rooms leak space.

Prim places where the grass is edged, the shrubs are obedient, and inside the couch is under a plastic cover and the cabinet of curios is dusted and gleams at attention.

Houses where the Bible and the baby Jesus are the only ornaments, and guns lie asleep in drawers and cabinets.

Houses that are all noise, as if they are cotton candy spun from the loud, always-on TV and the radio giving traffic reports to the resident who doesn't drive.

Houses that smell from the morning's bacon all day long, where one breakfast seems to compound the next, as if staleness were compounded daily like old-fashioned passbook saving accounts.

Houses that smell of feet, or vaguely like diapers, even though the children are in high school.

Houses you covet, so airy, so modest in their grandeur.

Houses where everything seems to be right. Husband loves wife, cat loves dog, tree loves house, house loves view.

Houses that are worn and comfortable, like an old fielder's mitt, like the sweatshirt and jeans the commuting executive wears on Saturdays.

Houses that are mysterious in their blandness. The rooms of furniture set out as expected, as prescribed, but you know no one really lives there. Where's the real life? This is a front. You want to see/don't want to see the private rooms.

Houses that are walled in with photos of children, grandchildren, nieces, and grandnieces. The walls of diplomas hanging like battle ribbons.

Houses that you pass a hundred days, a thousand days, maybe every day of your life, and no one enters. Even the lawn seems to be self-mowing, the mail self-removing.

Houses that command a hill; houses that play hide-and-seek behind trees and shrubs.

Houses that seem vulnerable, exposed, by a highway exit, on a traffic island, backing to a big store parking lot or railroad tracks, the house a goldfish bowl.

Houses in which terrible things have happened in daylight.

Houses in which nothing has happened, and that seems terrible. Houses where boredom sticks to the walls, yellows the walls like grease from ten thousand meals.

Houses that grow old with their inhabitants—roof and walls, windows, all flaking, peeling, breaking. The house has arthritis. The house is closed to the world.

Houses that spill out toys and bikes and cars and tools and projects, sometimes right to the line of their neighbor's land.

Thousands, millions of houses. You drive past them at 1 a.m., 2 a.m., all those people asleep—snoring, dreaming, all in the dark, trusting in the state that no marauders will come in the night.

~

All houses are mysteries. In all houses we are struggling to live the life we should; we are confined, cluttered, slothful, or ambitious, planning, rebuilding, self-improving. In all houses we are hiding out, from the neighbors, from the world out there, from the world in here, from each other, from ourselves. The domestic is strange. *Unheimlich*, as the Germans say. Not home-like, haunted. The *unheimlich* is intertwined with the *heimlich*, the comfortable and familiar, Freud said. We settle in our routines. We shield them. We need to. We don't want to be found out as being ordinary or extraordinary.

The mystery that holds my attention is that some houses have life—are home, are dwellings—and others don't. Dwelling is an old-fashioned word that we've misplaced.

When we live heart and soul, we dwell. When we belong to a place, we dwell. Possession, they say, is nine-tenths of the law, but it is also what too many houses and towns lack. We are not possessed by our home places. Dwelling has left our buildings. We have "housing" without dwellings. We have Home Depot, but not home. This lost quality of dwelling—the soul of buildings—haunts most of our houses and our landscape.

The philosopher Martin Heidegger wrote an influential essay in which

he says that dwelling is our basic character. Dwelling involves letting things
be, letting the earth be the earth at that spot. Or, as he says, letting things
"presence." A good dwelling defines a place, brings forth the true qualities
of that place. When this happens, he says, we are in touch with the higher
realities, with a spiritual life. "The peak of dwelling is poetry." But "when we
rule things, as modern man does, we are homeless . . . even though we have a
place to live."

"Dwelling, and not atomic energy, is the real, even though hidden as yet,
problem of modern times," he said in the 1950s. "Finding ways for a true
dwelling is more important than harnessing atomic energy."

A more concise definition of dwelling comes from Samuel Mockbee, the
wizard/architect who started Alabama's Rural Studio, in which architecture
students design and build homes for the poorest of the poor. Mockbee said,
"Everyone, rich or poor, deserves a shelter for the soul."

Dwelling is the restoration we seek. We want to build and live in a way
that, though chosen, exists as the right fit, as the only way to build. We want
to inhabit and build without second-guessing, with delight, with old tools
and knowledge that lead us easily step to step. We want our home not to come
from the big home center or the shelter magazines or the zoning code, but to
arise out of the place and the materials. We want to build the only house possible at that spot on earth. As the geographer J. B. Jackson said, "The dwelling is the primary effort of man to create heaven on earth." But this is not a
thought that comes to mind when you're out house hunting. It seems more
like a sentiment that would be stitched in a sampler, as archaic as Home Sweet
Home. Insisting that our shelters should have soul seems naïve, like profess-
ing heart-felt beliefs at a job interview.

In this Flip This House/Flip That House era there is little talk of dwelling.
Meanwhile we go on building anti-dwellings: bad houses, depressing waiting rooms, miles of roadside slop. And all of it with due deliberation, all of
it to code. We build thousands of houses, but only a few homes. With the
world's population projected to double, we will have to build this world all
over again. How can we do that and shelter the soul?

At the gym where I work out, warding off creakiness, I see those home-
decorator, design-in-a-whirlwind shows. All the shows, no matter the channel
or premise, are the same—hope lies in quick fixes, in bold paint schemes,

mirrors, cutesy photo displays, contrived twists of fabric. But the space is just usually bad-dim rooms as narrow as a single bowling alley, rooms in which every door, window, cabinet, and light switch is in the wrong place. This is just renovating deck chairs on the *Titanic*. The shows are about dolling up a house to compensate for how unsheltered people feel. These shows deal only with surfaces. They are working in a long tradition of faux finishes and false fronts. "American architecture is the art of covering one thing with another thing to imitate a third thing which, if genuine, would not be desirable," said the nineteenth-century architect Leopold Eidlitz. The real problem isn't the window treatment or the clutter by the door. The real problem is that too many of our houses are no longer dwellings.

We have shelter from the rain and snow and sun, but our houses aren't sheltering our souls. They aren't nourishing. We treat houses as investments or as social policy problems, as in the statistical Sahara of "the housing problem." The soul starves—we're in our house, but not at home. Our dream houses lack room for us to dream.

All houses are houses of dreams, said Gaston Bachelard, the philosopher-poet of dwelling. We live in houses and so we dream houses. We daydream there and daydream about them. They give us the shelter to enlarge ourselves. They are the vessel in which we go forth into the universe. A good house is a good daydreaming space. It is the universe, he says.

∾

House hunting is a matter of numbers and intuition. The numbers weigh heavily on us—what we can afford, the size of the house, the reputation of the school district. But if we are to be happy in our new home, it's intuition that rules. We know within seconds upon entering a house if it's the place for us. We know when a place makes us feel more alive. (My wife and I followed our intuition, gave up the search, and bought the old house where we were caretakers.)

We are tuned in to the qualities of dwelling, the feeling of home that some houses have and others lack. We can recognize these elusive qualities, and yet we find it very difficult, if not impossible, to create this feeling in our new houses and in our towns and cities.

The architect Christopher Alexander calls this animating spirit "the quality without a name." "The search which we make for this quality, in our own lives, is the central search of any person, and the crux of any individual person's story," Alexander writes. "It is the search for those moments and situations when we are most alive."

Dwelling in Possibility is a search for the soul of shelter. The book looks into our houses, and thus our selves, to rediscover the endangered qualities of homes that offer us the private commons that nurture our dreams.

This book is in three parts:

1 *Dwelling in the Ordinary.* We look at some things that were once ordinary but are now vanishing: the hearth, rooms without clutter, a footpath, and the simplicity of a beloved and hated modern house.

2 *Dwelling in Destruction.* The wars of the last century targeted homes that were far from the battlefield. After World War II, with Europe in ruins, three distinctly different writers sought to restore the safety of home. We also look at the Gulf Coast after Hurricane Katrina to get a sharper sense of how fragile our dwellings are and how strong our commitment is to the idea of home.

3 *Dwelling in Possibility.* How do we court this unnamable "quality without a name"? Where can it be found? We seek out some hints with the aid of the census and an additional set of questions. And we enter into the hidden lives of the most ordinary buildings there are, the many kinds of sheds.

$\sim$

To go house hunting is to dwell in possibility. But what is that possibility? One is that we'll be a new person in a new home. Given a fresh start, our better selves will rise. That's part of the answer. But the real possibility we seek is habit; it's the ordinary. We want room for the mundane. This is not what we ask real estate agents or builders for. We ask for "great rooms" and "upgrades": granite counters, stainless-steel appliances, luxurious "spa bathrooms," home theaters, walk-in closets the size of Wyoming. But we should ask: Give us room for tumult and quiet, for solitude and passing the time with friends. Give us room for ordinary pleasures, for a day well lived. "How to spend a day nobly is the problem to be solved, beside which all the great reforms which are preached seem to me trivial," wrote Ralph Waldo Emerson. We should be hunting for the ordinary.

DWELLING IN THE ORDINARY

I have long been of an Opinion similar to that you express, and think Happiness consists more in small Conveniencies or Pleasures that occur every day, than in great Pieces of good Fortune that happen but seldom to a Man in the Course of his Life.

☛ Benjamin Franklin, letter to Lord Kames,
February 28, 1768

⟫ Pages from an Ice Storm Journal ⟪

I

Ice and Fire

On December 11, 2008, an ice storm hit New England. In New Hampshire 420,000 houses and businesses—55 percent of the state—lost power for as long as two weeks. It was the worst natural disaster in the state's history.

THURSDAY, DECEMBER 11
A slight ticking on the window, low like a sizzle of static beginning or oil just heating up in a pan. The freezing rain has begun. The sky is forecast to fall in with ice, sleet, snow, and rain over the next two days. It's a dark morning in what has been a dark week.

FRIDAY, DECEMBER 12
I awaken at 1 a.m. and turn on the radio—silence. NHPR is off the air. Our lights go out. The battery-backups for the computers begin beeping. I take one of the small flashlights that we've left by the bed and go poke and prod the back-up boxes until they stop the alarm call. I pull all the plugs out of the wall.

Sometime after 2:30 a.m. we're both jostled awake by a cracking thud. The snap of wood, the smash of it landing. It's all in the bass range and this one rocks the house. I get up to look out, but in the dark I can't see.

There's more cracking and thudding, near and far.

We sleep fitfully. At 7 a.m., in a cold house, we arise. Sally is afraid. She is curled tight, a black-and-white ball of border collie, pressed close to my wife, Sy. We play a little with her, tug with her toy, a big, soft red bone.

In the morning light—silver on silver—I first see part of the old ash on the icy ground: one ten-foot-long broken branch. I look out the other side of the house. The silver maple has taken a hit. That was the big thud. A tangle of tree limbs lies on the ground. Sy thinks that maybe an eighth of our favorite tree has sheared off. In the summer we live under this tree as much as possible. Our house is tucked under its elegant upward sweep and the stouter ash.

I'm sick to my stomach. Even as I know that impermanence is our lot, I love this tree. We had it trimmed years ago to take weight off its long arching limbs.

The tree had ducked every storm in the twenty years we've been here, most notably the ice storm of '98.

Another big limb falls nearer the house as I light a fire in the woodstove, and another limb falls from the ash, slamming the porch.

Now our neighbors are stirring. We hear Bobbie and Jarvis's backup generator starting. Sy has brought in a bucket of water and we've eaten breakfast. I sit by the fire, drinking tea and writing. I can work on my computer two hours or so, until the battery runs out. Note to self: order a second battery, a back-up generator for the house, etc.

∼

A lot of cleanup is ahead for us. We'll be at it Saturday morning, once it's safe to be under the trees.

MONDAY, DECEMBER 15—ICE STORM, DAY 4

No power. The trees that fell onto the power lines at the head of our road and at the corner of Route 137 hang there still, making for a one-lane tunnel that cars take turns entering. There's a broken telephone pole hanging in the middle of Route 101 near Temple Mountain, we've been told. Route 101—the major east/west road—has been reduced to one lane there. On Friday one car led a small band of cars through a detour. At each fallen tree blocking the road, the driver would get out and clear the way with his chainsaw. Up near the Harris Center on King's Highway, Bobby Fogg says that he must have cut sixty trees. Route 9 down to Keene is a slalom course of felled trees. Around Dublin Lake there's one inch of ice on the branches, our tree guy Dan and his wife, Marilyn, tell us when they visit. (Tree doctors still make house calls.) Towns to the south—Marlborough, Jaffrey, Rindge—are "a war zone."

So we will not be getting our power back for two or three days and that is an optimistic view. Last night our road agent told me that the utilities have discovered the major feeder lines are severely damaged. And Marilyn said she had heard they were running short of wire.

∼

Our world is upended and reorganized by the disaster. Our lives revolve around feeding the woodstove, bringing in wood, fetching water, and cutting up the maple.

We have done fairly well. The living room is hot and the heat travels upstairs to make the bedroom warm enough. Sy has cooked good meals on the gas stove—fresh eggs from our hens. We have a pile of flashlights and candles.

Our one failing was in not buying a generator. We had discussed it years ago. A good friend has a top-of-the-line generator wired to go on automatically. It has never worked. We know another person with a failed propane model. So that was out. We'd decided against getting a gasoline generator because if the power is out, the gas pumps would be out too, and so it would be useless.

But the gasoline generators around here have been running fine. Seeking a perfect solution, we have a perfect nothing.

∾

Generators have been quite the topic among our neighbors: Who has one and when did he start it? In the classic New England manner, no one offers the information unless asked. To flaunt one's generator would be immodest. We sit in the dark and talk of generating electricity. What kind of generator is best? A generator is the ship that would take us home.

It's been good to hear Bobbie and Jarvis's generator thrumming along. I had a hot shower over there on Saturday night. It was like a little holiday, a visit to a far-off land called electricity.

∾

To be "off the grid" is to lose, by degrees, your citizenship. This was really brought home when I talked by phone with my brother and father who live two hundred miles from here. I heard the television in the background. I'm trying to tell my father about the trees cracking through the night, but he's telling me about what he saw on TV—"the announcer was talking and there were trees cracking right behind him. You should have seen it."

I am reminded of when Sy returned from seeing the mountain gorillas in Rwanda. A friend had seen that same troop on TV. He kept interrupting her. He'd seen it on TV—he'd been there. It was the same thing.

If a tree falls and it's not near your house, it makes no sound. Weather only happens to us.

～

We sat watching the fire on Saturday night. One log had a play of colors that was like lightning in the jungle or like the play of lightning across the earth when seen from space.

The entire fire box glowed red. Along a cleft of one small log that glowed red too, the lights would flash—blue and yellow on the left and yellow-green along the fissure. The flames danced in a regular pattern as they moved along the split. The yellow-green dancing up, rolling down, dancing up. The blue-green flashing at the end. Stunning. We were going to go for a walk, but we just sat watching. Sy said that it looked like the aurora borealis.

Full moon. Bright cold nights, Friday and Saturday.

～

Another spirit is in this house. I felt it when I was upstairs as I closed the doors to chase the heat to the bedroom. There's a tinge of woodsmoke in the house and muted light—shadowy rooms lit only by daylight and moonlight. This house may have felt like this back in the 1880s and 1890s.

～

The question I'm dancing with here is this: What parts of shelter are obscured or liberated by electric power? Obscured: quiet, daylight, and attention to the mundane. Without electricity, the basics of shelter require our attention. We are reintroduced to once-common chores. Each day presents itself with a demanding fullness. Without electricity we are quiet enough, still enough, to see the blue-green flashing of one burning log.

And what is liberated? The house steps away from its primary role as shelter, just as we step away from keeping a fire in the hearth.

～

Basic statistics: As of Monday morning, Public Service of New Hampshire has restored power to one-third of the powerless homes. That leaves 280,000 in the dark. The big ice storm in 1998 blacked out 55,000 customers.

~

We worked intensely to remove the fallen limbs of the silver maple, so like a dead elephant or a whale upon a beach. We worked Saturday from morning to late afternoon and finished up, on Sunday. I sawed steadily. Sy hauled and stacked wood. It's all cut up, cleaned up, and under cover.

~

It was good today to know that all we had to do was cook, bring in wood and water, and that we were able to do that, Sy said. There was no anxiety about unfinished tasks, no doubting about what you were doing. We needed to stay warm. We were.

Tuesday, December 16—Ice Storm, Day 5

We are phototropic creatures. I'm never without a small pocket flashlight. Our kitchen looks like a testing lab for candles. We sit around the fire; to read, we pull chairs to the window. We've lost power during the shortest days of the year. By 4:30 it's dark. Bedtime comes early. We rise and it's still dark. We are living in the dark depths of the ocean.

~

Other neighbors, the Garands, now have a generator—much louder than Bobbie and Jarvis's. Now two generators thrum away.

~

The trees blocking Route 137 and Antrim Road have been removed. At noon a crew was cutting them away from the wires, a guy high up in a bucket leaning over a tangle of trees and wires with a regular chain saw.

The trees fell away and the wires snapped back into their usual position. There are piles of slash on both sides of the road. Newly cut tree stumps lean outward. It looks as if a tornado has been through.

~

We are riding the black-out seesaw. Late yesterday Sy said that the word on Main Street was that power would be restored by Monday night. They said that included us, one mile away. My spirits rose. Shortly afterward I was out in the street and I ran into a friend from around the corner. She had just talked to a utility crew who were nearby. They told her that our road would get power Wednesday, "unless they were called away to an emergency."

~

We trade rumors and stories. It's all word of mouth.

Within twenty miles of here, people are unaffected by the storm. Someone who went to a supermarket said there were two classes of people—the unshaved, unwashed, obviously without power, and those who walked along oblivious, plugged into their routine.

Another friend told us this story: Peterborough's police chief was off duty in plain clothes. He saw a guy selling generators at the corner of routes 101 and 202. He went over to talk to him: Tell me about your generators. . . . Do you have a business card?

He never identified himself as a cop; he didn't have to. He said, I'm going to bring this card to the police station. This town has laws against street vending. There's four ways out of town right where you stand. I suggest that you take one.

The man departed.

And here's a mark of desperation: People are going to the hospital to eat.

~

We gather a "nail soup" supper. Bobbie brings over two quiches to cook in our stove, one for us. We have a gas stove; they have a generator keeping their well pump, furnace, and a few lights on. Would we like to eat it over there? We gladly accept. Sy adds a pie to the dinner. She's been baking constantly to heat the kitchen.

By the time we arrive for dinner, two other friends, Rick and Jody, have been invited. They'll bring spaghetti and bread.

Sitting by the light of an aged Coleman camping lantern, we drink several glasses of wine waiting for Rick and Jody. They arrive with great news: they've just got their power on Main Street. We chide them—the power brokers are here! Don't forget the simple folk in the provinces.

It's a wonderful, loopy, sideways dinner. Normally we'd never eat out on a week night. We'd be glued to our computers. This evening is a gift of found time, another way that the storm has reshuffled our lives.

WEDNESDAY, DECEMBER 17— ICE STORM, DAY 6
Snowing. Colder. Dark this morning. The island of darkness shrinks, but we're still on it. Friends call to tell us they have power. Each of these euphoric calls is delivered like the news of the invention of the electric light itself, each caller another lottery winner. There are utility trucks all over town, crews from the Midwest, Quebec, and down south. They were at our corner yesterday afternoon. A fleet of four or five drove out of our road after 5 p.m. Still, no power.

PSNH reports that it has restored power to 80 percent of those who had lost it. The powerless are now down to eighty thousand. The power company's officials say that they have a list online of towns that will be 95 percent restored. Online. Thanks. On the radio they keep telling us to check the PSNH website. No one seems to have gotten the word that computers and all the rest run on electricity.

So we ride the seesaw. We had thought that power would return last night.

⁓

I move around, a Wi-Fi refugee, working and showering at different houses. At one house I visit, as I sit writing, there's a steady stream of friends and neighbors seeking showers. At each house there is another reason why I can't get my email. I don't usually care about email, but I'm waiting to hear if a publisher has accepted a book.

Yesterday I went to a friend's house to work. Old Street Road and Sand Hill Road in Peterborough were the worst I've seen. Yet another place that looks like a tornado has been through. A telephone pole had snapped and hung in the air; a gray transformer sat on the ground. The yellow blinking traffic light was down, swept to the roadside like parade litter. I drove along Sand Hill cautiously, picking my way around the hanging broken wires, flagged yellow, red, or blue. (No code, likely, just what was on hand.) Went to the Wellness Center at noon, which had just reopened. I steamed, showered, and shaved. Drove back to Hancock, got the mail, and went to the library where I fiddled, trying to get my email, until I was told that Comcast was out of service.

The library was packed with moms chatting in the magazine area. A booming

Polar Express movie played in the next room, a film the librarian had quickly scheduled to help out local families since the schools were closed.

~

Neighbors are checking on each other. Bobbie and Jarvis called the Garands, who are in their 80s. He's a retired shepherd. How were they doing? Oh, fine. They had heat, of course, and they had water. They still had a hand pump at their (c. 1790) house.

A hand pump! We sat by the fire and marveled at the wonders of low tech. You can keep your Next Big Thing, touch-screen, satellite-guided, digital wonder. The last shall be first. Old technology may be out of fashion, but it is only dormant, it's the lifeboat on the big ship.

Lesson learned: be ready to devolve. (And who says that a more complicated system is a higher order?)

~

To sleep at eight, up at six. Dark, dark. Snowing. Get more wood. Get water. Look out—lights on anywhere? It's been a long winter and it's not even Christmas yet.

THURSDAY, DECEMBER 18—ICE STORM, DAY 7

Yesterday at noon we got electricity. I threw the circuit breaker. The entire house whirled into action like an old Wurlitzer jukebox—furnace shuddering alive, fridge regaining its destiny, lights, clocks, the tick and hum of electric motors. The world rushed back in: email, email, email . . . and the light reveals that there's candle wax everywhere.

Our chances weren't looking good earlier in the morning. When Sy was out walking Sally, she had learned that folks just up the road had power. She had found some sort of dividing line, crossing from the unlit to the lit. We began to think that we might be in the unlucky 5 percent who PSNH says may not get power until Christmas or after.

A fleet of white utility trucks from who-knows-where began working on our road. All the men had on cowboy hats. They drove very slowly, sticking their heads out of the windows to look at the wires. That's the diagnostic tool. Unbelievable.

I turned up the heat, lit the hot water heater, closed the refrigerator doors, removed the water buckets, put away candles and scraped up piles of wax, sorted the mail, plugged in all the computers, and waded into the email. There was the good news I had sought. The publisher had accepted my book.

I was a whirlwind. Everyone springs up like Martha Stewart once the lights come back on, Sy says. They race around cleaning up, restarting their lives, and then they collapse.

∼

Big plume of gray-white smoke curling up from the towering burn pile at the dump. At midday the smoke hung over the town. A big front loader pushed at the pile, mostly wet pine branches.

∼

What I learned from this power failure:

1 The perfect is the enemy of the good. Trying for the best, cover-all-contingencies plan, and failing to find that, can leave you with nothing. In other words, half a loaf is a feast in a disaster.

2 You can't prepare for all disasters. This, too, stops you in your tracks. Prepare for what you can. Put that half-solution on your shelves for the emergency.

I have a copy of the FEMA book the town handed out a few years ago: *Are You Ready?* It's a full-course meal of disaster: floods, hurricanes, tornadoes, lightning, winter storms, extreme cold, earthquakes, tsunamis, fire, "hazardous materials incidences," nuclear power plant accidents, and terrorism. One read and you're paralyzed. When the tsunami hits Mount Monadnock I won't be ready.

3 We all have our "Sponge Bob" whining. We can be superior when talking about someone who is deprived of a non-vital, non-necessity. But we all have something we miss. Marilyn told us about a family living next door with three little kids whining, "I want Sponge Bob! Why can't I have Sponge Bob?" I felt that way about the *Sunday New York Times*. I love to read the *Times* on Sunday night. I couldn't have my *Sponge Bob Times*.

∼

And one more lesson:

I've been asking people what they learned. Our friend Elizabeth Marshall

Thomas, wise, eighty years old, and with the insight of a skilled observer who has lived among the Kalahari Bushmen, said, "I wish that we could go back to a time without all these . . . *things*." By "these *things*" she meant everything that makes up our homes today, the entire electric, digital Great Big Beautiful Tomorrow.

Her son and daughter-in-law didn't consider it a likely proposal. They have a lively four-year-old boy who has his own Sponge Bob-type requirements.

I agreed. "That train's left the station," I said, and added: "No, I'm wrong— that station is no longer even there."

∾

So I come back to my question: Does electricity inhibit the spirit of a house? Or can we at last say that electricity *is* the hearth now?

The spirit of a house lives in the hearth, in heat and light. We have shut down the old central fire, the fire linking us back to the first fires. We have spread fire and light through the house. We have lit the darkest corners and the night sky. We have lost mystery; we have lost soul. This is how we live now.

It's not all bad: Hot water, indoor bathrooms, reading late at night. Sitting in a cold, dark house on a winter's night, it's easy to see that these are good things. But we don't stop there. We are crowding ourselves out of our own homes with images and noise. "Reddy Kilowatt" is our hearth. If we stopped denying that, could anything positive come of it?

Saturday, December 20 — Ice Storm, Day 9
Snowing. There's about 8 inches or so, loose, drifty powder.

Storm count—still thirty-three thousand without power. One-third of Peterborough still in the dark. PSNH now says it'll get power to 90 percent by Christmas. The PSNH website lists a few towns where only one or two houses are in the dark—the cruelty of that, of looking out across the way to the electric world.

∾

We took in our first refugees from Peterborough on Thursday. Our friends arrived carrying their laundry and empty water jugs. They looked beleaguered, exhausted. We set them up with a shower and laundry, and Sy made them dinner.

They were buoyed by their visit, but yesterday Red Cross workers came to their house and told them that it will be a long time. How long? They couldn't say.

TUESDAY, DECEMBER 23—ICE STORM, DAY 12

There are still ten thousand households without power and this on a morning when it's seven degrees here and zero or below in other parts of New Hampshire.

A good friend was here for dinner last night and told us stories of her eleven days alone in the dark. On her road an armada of utility trucks arrived with a police escort. The trucks lined the road. It turns out that the power lines up in the woods behind her house had fallen—the ice had toppled three towers. And just down the road, an entire line of poles had gone down. These two spots were a choke hold on their town getting its power back.

A small helicopter buzzed back and forth by the lines, bringing in supplies. A huge moon-rover-like truck was sent in. A truckload of transformers arrived—accompanied by cheers and calls around town.

She too had heard that crews were running out of wire. She said that a neighbor had run into a Hydro Quebec guy—French speaking—at the store, who held out his hands, bowed his head, and said sadly, "We no wire."

~

Peterborough was crazy-busy with everyone zipping around, compressing almost two weeks of Christmas shopping into three days. It was like a chaotic cocktail party. In the space of a few minutes, I spoke with more than a half dozen people I know. And all the talk the same: Do you have power? How long were you out for? (I thought that the local weekly should've printed numbers we could pin on ourselves: 3, 6, 12.) How'd you do? Did you have a generator? Are you getting a generator?

The streets were thick with utility trucks, parked, idling. Troop movements.

~

Every dinner, every encounter has its ice storm story. We were talking to another friend about how her power came on four days before ours. "I feel guilty about that, but not too guilty," she said.

"We were about to kill each other," she explained, referring to the morning the lights came back on.

She and her partner were up all night feeding the fire. They had only a fire-place. It was our friend's turn to get up each hour, but her partner would wake up and tell her how to put the wood in.

"*So why don't you just do it?*" she said at some icy hour of darkness.

The days of the open hearth are often recalled with great sentimental flourish, but the truth is hotter than nostalgia.

WEDNESDAY, DECEMBER 24—ICE STORM, DAY 13

As of this morning, Christmas Eve, about two thousand are without power. That's thirteen days out. Everyone in our town seems to be back after eleven days.

In yesterday's *Monadnock Ledger-Transcript*, PSNH spokesman Martin Murray said, "One of the interesting things is that there is an expectation now from the public for instant, accurate information. That is a product of our times."

Wow, where's he been the last dozen years?

～

The electric hearth. More thoughts on being restored to the plug-in world, to the kingdom of the grid.

  ⊸ Electricity drives the shadows and silences out of a house.

  ⊸ It frees us from weighing each choice—a light, a flush, more heat. It allows us to be ignorant of the weight of these choices.

  ⊸ It allows us to be weightless.

  ⊸ It allows us to live in the world of information and image, shortchanging the here and now.

  ⊸ Is it that we can live only in one kingdom? Quiet or the grid?

  ⊸ We dwell in electricity—we dwell in what it makes possible: noise and image.

～

Stirring moonlit walk with Sy and Sally. Bright out—the snowflakes glowing. Cold night with a slight breeze that, when facing it, numbed your nose.

Not a car passed us. Walking past one house set far across a field, we could see a huge TV inside—a big stamp of colored light. It was like a drive-in movie.

That's what lives there, said Sy. The house is a house for the TV.

II

Smoke and Fire

We once lived with smoke and fire. When we moved indoors, we moved the campfire indoors. In the medieval manor, an open fire burned near the center of a large hall. The smoke was left to rise up to the second story and out a hole in the roof. The fire drew air from open doors. These were spaces that stood at the threshold of inside and outside. A well-known parable of the time compared life to a sparrow flying through a hall, briefly finding shelter from a storm. This is a permeable shelter, like a barn, a place with the qualities of inside/outsideness. This is not "climate-controlled" or "man-made weather," as Willis Carrier first called air-conditioning. This is climate. People were drier and warmer, gathered near a smoky fire in a drafty hall. Birds flew through. This is life, pre-thermostat, double-insulated windows, R-38 insulation.

We read complaints about smoky hearths only once chimneys start coming along, indicating a change in the ideas of comfort, says historian John E. Crowley. Many of these early chimneys were not vertical but cut through the wall at slanting angles, and were likely smoky, too. These fireplaces first appeared in smaller chambers, often in monasteries, even as the hall's open hearth persisted. In time, in an effort to clear the smoke from the hall, the hearth was moved to one side and placed under a hood.

The fireplace replaced the hood. The open fire was now enclosed on three sides. They were usually big fireplaces, more like a fire room. Some fireplaces had benches inside. In Colonial America, the kitchen fireplace could be eight feet wide and three or four feet deep. The cook would walk to the back of the fireplace to use the brick bake oven. (In other designs the brick oven is alongside the big hearth.) Most of the heat went right up the chimney. As in the medieval hall, doors were left open to feed the fire and move the smoke out of the room.

Houses were cold. Snow sifted through the windows, water froze in pitchers, ink froze in inkwells, well-pump handles froze, and wells froze. Empty back chambers kept Thanksgiving pies "fresh and good" until April's violets. Late in spring, sometimes, liquids froze "hard *in*doors."

Diaries of eighteenth- and early nineteenth-century New England portray a cold world punctuated with punishing fires. The hearth in contemporary observation is not the welcoming emblem of home-feeling, the happy family circle bathed in firelight. It is, rather, a big messy beast that must be fed and fed, returns little heat and is prone to lashing out and taking sacrifices. Houses burned down, herbs and flax drying by the hearth caught fire, children fell into fireplaces or were scalded to death by big kettles of water, chimneys burned. The losses from fire run like a swift, tragic river through the old town histories. The hearth is a mercurial god.

The hearth needed discipline. The fireplace shrank, and it disappeared. In the 1790s, Count Rumford designed a shallow, small fireplace that pushed more heat into the room and effectively drew the smoke up the chimney. For the first time a fire would actually warm a room. Rumford's design was brilliant, but it was the last hurrah for the downsized hearth. Woodstoves, gaining acceptance in the 1840s, ended the reign of the campfire. Smoke and fire had been separated and the fire hidden in a cast-iron box.

The cookstove was the biggest change in the nineteenth-century home. It used less wood and was less work—for men who usually cut, split, and brought in the wood. Women's cooking increased, says historian Ruth Cowan. One-pot meals cooked over the open hearth were gone. Women labored baking cakes, some of which required hand-beating for three-quarters of an hour. To care for the stove itself required almost an hour a day to tend fires, sift ashes, and apply blacking to keep it from rusting.

The boxed-fire still held the household in its orbit. Only the kitchen cookstove fire was kept going through the winter, a practice that lasted into the 1930s in the countryside. The rest of the house was cold and dark. A fire would only be set in the sitting room for guests. Candles were a luxury. Much of life was lived in the cold and shadows.

Keeping warm kept the family together—everyone in the kitchen—mom sewing or reading, dad figuring or fixing tools, children doing homework or playing games, aunts, uncles, grandparents all in the mix. It was wonderful, some say—we sang, we told stories, we read the Bible aloud. "My boys are all so musical and the other fellows come in and we all have such a good sing together," recalled one mother. It was horrible, others say—we fought, we got in each other's way. Once warmer weather came, it was a relief to move my spinning wheel away from prying eyes," said one.

Whether they were happy families like all other happy families, or each unhappy in its own way, as in Tolstoy's famous appraisal, all of that joy and grief was condensed into one room. It was a long, long trip through winter.

~

When the flames were encased in a metal box, houses were warmer, but there were laments for the lost fire. Benjamin Franklin kept an open fire in his first famous stove, the Pennsylvania fireplace. He derided German and Scandinavian stoves brought to this country because the fire was hidden.

A home without a hearth just seemed wrong. "Would our Revolutionary fathers have gone barefooted and bleeding over the snows to defend air-tight stoves and cooking ranges?" asked Harriet Beecher Stowe in 1864. "It was the memory of the great open kitchen fire with . . . its roaring, hilarious voice of invitation, its dancing tongues of flames that called to them through the snows of that dreadful winter to keep up their courage, that made their hearts warm and bright with a thousand reflected memories."

Stowe and her sister Catherine were impassioned defenders of the open fire, which was the "nearest to the natural mode of the Creator, who heats the earth and its furniture by the great central fire of heaven." Together they published the bestselling *American Woman's Home* in 1869, setting the model for household advice. Even as they acknowledged the benefits of cookstoves, and described the best designs, they couldn't part with the hearth.

"Better, far better, the old houses of the olden time, with their great roaring fires, and their bedrooms where the snow came in and the wintry winds whistled," wrote Stowe. "Then, to be sure, you froze your back while you burned your face, your water froze nightly in your pitcher, your breath congealed in ice-wreaths on the blankets, and you could write your name on the pretty snow-wreath that had sifted in through the window-cracks. But you woke full of life and vigor, you looked out into whirling snow-storms without a shiver, and thought nothing of plunging through drifts as high as your head on your daily way to school. You jingled in sleighs, you snowballed, you lived in snow like a snow-bird, and your blood coursed and tingled, in full tide of good, merry, real life, through your veins—none of the slow-creeping, black blood which clogs the brain and lies like a weight on the vital wheels!"

Freezing by the fire—now that was living! Edward Everett Hale's mother wouldn't hear of the "poetry" of the open hearth. Put away your nostalgia, she told her son. "You may take the poetry of an open wood fire of the present day, but to me in those early days it was only dismal prose, and I am grateful to have lived in the time of anthracite coal." The open hearth was prose and icy prose at that.

∽

With the loss of the fireplace inhaling vast draughts of air, houses stopped breathing. Chimneys and drafty windows and doors used to circulate the air, but now the air just sat there. Houses were built tighter. Interiors were brighter, hotter, stuffier, and stank from burning coal and coal-gas lights. New technology had been inserted into the ancient house. The open fire was extinguished and with it went generations of accumulated wisdom.

The American Woman's Home is obsessed with ventilation. Good living is good breathing. The Beecher sisters return to the point repeatedly, preaching the necessity of fresh air by way of biology and thermodynamics. In this book of household advice, there are drawings of the lungs and heart, of an experiment with a candle in a glass tube, and there's the basic introductory physics diagrams of thermodynamics with arrows glancing off a surface in the dance of conduction, radiation, and reflection. They quote a "learned physician" (who says "every person, every day, vitiates thirty-three hogsheads of the air") as well as a French physician, a Yale professor, and additional unnamed doctors and studies. "Defective ventilation is one great cause of diseased joints, as well as diseases of the eyes, ears, and skin," they write. "Foul air is the leading cause of tubercular and scrofulous consumption, so very common in our country." The air in houses is "poisonous," "injurious," drier than "the Sahara," and "a slow suicide and murder." Reading *American Woman's Home*, one wants to throw open a window.

"No other gift of God, so precious, so inspiring, is treated with such utter irreverence and contempt in the calculations of us mortals as this same air of heaven," wrote Stowe. "A sermon on oxygen, if we had a preacher who understood the subject, might do more to repress sin than the most orthodox discourse to show when and how and why sin came. A minister gets up in a crowded lecture-room, where the mephitic air almost makes the candles burn blue, and bewails the deadness of the church—the church the while, drugged by the poisoned air, growing sleepier and sleepier, though they feel dreadfully wicked for being so." (As a daughter of the most famous preacher in the land, with seven brothers as preachers, Stowe had been in a few churches.)

The Beecher sisters were suffocating in America's houses. They were not alone. Charles Dickens on his American tour in 1842, conveyed the English preference for a drafty chill. Visiting a state hospital in South Boston, "which was in the best order," he noted: "It had one fault, however, which is common to all American interiors: the presence of the eternal, accursed, suffocating, red-hot demon of a stove, whose breath would blight the purest air under Heaven."

∾

The hearth-centered house came apart in stages—first with woodstoves, then with electricity and central heat. Fire was exiled to a furnace in the cellar. The campfire had learned indoor manners. It had been tamed. Electric motors were now the lungs of the house, circulating heat from the unseen fire. Growing up, I remember looking in through the vent of the old oil furnace in the basement and seeing the surprising eye of fire—the devil's eye, we called it.

Even before electricity, houses were becoming brighter and less smoky. Candles were improved, candlesticks were cheaper, oil lamps were improved, though expensive. Life changed. The main meal was later in the day. Fewer people retired early. They began to unyoke their days from the sun. A chart would show a rapid climb from the one-candle evening to gaslights. In Philadelphia from 1855 to 1895 the average gaslight illumination in the home increased twentyfold. Electricity continued this push for more light. "Evening hours are cheerless" in a poorly lighted house, the electric companies advertised. "Make your house a home." The electric light is the "entering wedge" for more sales, said a General Electric manager. The company sold light fixtures and appliances door-to-door.

Rooms emerged from the shadows; darkness was no longer a presence pooling in corners, backrooms, and on stairs, another inhabitant, a spirit. It was if background and foreground were swept away by the lights. Just as the smoky medieval hall was permeable, this was another kind of permeability. The hours of the day were the hours of the house. Rooms sat in morning light, in late sun, and twilight. Light floods the modern house; the door is shut to the night.

Utopians and feminists saw in electricity the promise of cooperative living—shared cooking and dining, laundry, child care. The first New York apartments did offer dining halls and laundry service, but long before electricity was prevalent, Americans passed on this utopia. Americans want the single home. Electricity wasn't predestined to isolate people, says historian David E. Nye. We used electricity to further atomize American life. We shaped electricity. It's a tool we made in our own image—the image of the American Dream.

~

The electric light and the central furnace freed the family, dispersing men, women and children to their own semiautonomous regions in the home. More heat and light equals more space. Heat was the gravity of the old household. Once the fire is exiled, it's as if gravity is repealed. The size of houses grows steadily as families shrink. Shared dinners are fewer and the happy family is lost in space.

Think of the hearth-centered home as a centripetal force pulling everything to the center. But electricity is centrifugal, throwing everything outward, de-centering life. This interior migration is repeated later in the twentieth century. The family gathered around the radio for Franklin Delano Roosevelt's "fireside chats," the family and neighbors crowded around the first television watching Milton Berle, and then everyone dispersed to a private electronic utopia with televisions, computers, and cell phones in almost every room. Indeed, we now see the same dispersion in the car that we saw in the house. Now the kids are hooked into their video I-V. *Drip drip*: A video screen drops down or is strapped to the back of a seat, or an iPod is piped into the ears. The happy family together, alone. (Or is that alone together?) But first, the fire goes out in the hearth. None of this would happen without losing the fire.

A home without a hearth was unmoored. It was a tent with its central pole removed. Once the hearth is extinguished, just what is a home? The Beechers and many others were campaigning to bring order to the post-hearth home. They were struggling to redefine a place once defined by the hearth.

The new house was weightless—no hauling in wood, no making candles or filling kerosene lamps. Heat and light flowed in at the flick of a switch, just as the advertising promised. "The chief characteristic of our age is man's independence of his immediate surroundings," Charles P. Steinmetz said in 1922. Steinmetz was a pioneering electrical engineer who led the development of alternating current. Today, an architect can write that "climate is an important consideration for any site." Once it was the only consideration. Almost any house can be built any place if you can plug into enough power.

Do we have a moral obligation to live as if the hearth still ruled? Is that behind some of the criticism of television-loving, computer-centric America? We often feel guilty about not being that family gathered around the hearth evening after evening. As late as 1900, houses with central heating often had vestigial mantelpieces framing a radiator, an appliqué of the old hearth. Catalogs offered elaborate mantelpieces, with some models said to display your deep ancestry, and others an "altar . . . for refuge, for love." The fire was gone; the hearth became metaphorical. Homilies of piety replaced fire and smoke.

A revolution has taken place. Fire has journeyed from the center to the cellar. Putting out a campfire that's burned through the millennia is such a significant change that we can divide the history of dwelling between Hearth and Post Hearth. Tell me how you heat your house or make your breakfast and I'll tell you how you dwell.

Our ancestors moved the campfire indoors and they held on to it for centuries, even after better means of heating came along. Reformers, moralists, and scientists preached the comforts of improved chimneys and stoves, and at last the fire was diminished—stuck in the wall, then boxed, and finally hidden downstairs.

Houses were free of smoke and soot. They were brighter and cleaner. And they possessed less spirit. You can read that in the laments of nostalgists. The story can be told in the origins of the words for hearth. *Hearth* is derived from the Old English *heorþ* for the place where the fire is set on the ground. (*Oerþ* in Old English—ground, earth.) Our houses were losing the connection between fire and earth. *Focus* is Latin for hearth. Our houses were losing focus.

The house has been *un-hearthed*. How do we remain at home?

As smoke and fire have left our houses, the household gods are banished, the ancestors diminished, the future truncated by its acceleration.

In the ice storm we lost the ordinary electric hum of our days. The circle of the home contracted around the fire. The old campfire reasserted itself. We were thrown back to an ancient ordinary—chop wood, carry water. This ancient ordinary sleeps in our houses.

⌁ The Age of Clutter ⌁

Our Closets, Ourselves

Want to get rid of the junk around your house? Donna Smallin has "seven simple steps" for you:

Step 1 Put Yourself First (Practice Wellness . . . Pamper Yourself)

Step 2 Live Authentically (Question Everything . . . Create a New Vision)

Step 3 Follow Your Passion (What's Stopping You?)

Step 4 Live Mindfully (Being Here and Now . . . Caring for Family)

Step 5 Gain Financial Freedom (Frugal Grown-up Fun)

Step 6 Lighten Your Load (Unclutter Your Home)

Step 7 Simplify Daily Living (Celebrate Today . . . Nourish Your Soul)

Put down the broom and the box of garbage bags. It's going to be a while before you toss out all the old shoes, magazines, and broken answering machines.

Actually, there are at least forty-two simple steps, judging by the contents page, and perhaps another one hundred simple steps once you delve into the list. "Question Everything," for example, could be quite time consuming. And as for "Caring for Family," well, if you have any time or energy left after that, please phone the U.S. Olympic Committee immediately. (Become an Olympic Athlete, Win the Nobel Peace Prize, the list is endless. Cure Cancer. . . . All that is available to any citizen with a clean garage.)

Seven Simple Steps to Unclutter Your Life promises to lead the reader out of the wilderness of clutter to a happy place where he or she will "find balance in an unbalanced world." That pile of junk is more than a pile of junk—it's you, dear reader. It's telling tales on you. Mind creates the world, say the Buddhists. This mess is us.

⌁

Clutter is an obsession of our era. We have poured our concerns about clutter into almost every shape we know: self-help, recovery support groups (Messies Anonymous, Clutter Diet), meet-up groups, Let Go of Clutter retreats, feng shui, vague Zen aspirations ("Do More With Less in Your Zen Bathroom"), decluttering online in the Second Life world, and television shows where you can watch people throw out junk. There's a Clutter Awareness Week (the third week in March), a Clutter Hoarding Scale, newspaper stories ready to pronounce a national epidemic ("Stuff robbed Dee Wallace of love"), and a tsunami of books soon to be at a flea market near you. "I own several organizing books and this is my favorite," said one reader at Amazon. Another woman, who had surrendered to a professional organizer, confessed to squirreling away boxes of her favorite "decluttering" magazine articles.

It is the Age of Clutter, of walk-in closets and "closet systems," of "clutter busters," decluttering experts, professional organizers, and a thriving "self-storage" industry—some fifty thousand metal shed-bunker facilities renting out more than two billion square feet of space to house stuff. (That odd name, "self-storage," is revealing: people aren't just storing excess; this stuff is a part of their identity.) Some of the newest storage is far grander than sheds, like the $5 million one in a tony New York suburb that looks like a Victorian railroad station.

"Twenty years ago, people were embarrassed and ashamed to admit they needed a professional organizer, let alone to hire one," said Barry Izsak, a former president of the National Association of Professional Organizers. "Today, it's commonplace and, for some, a status symbol. Professional organizing has become chic!" he told the organizers' convention. "Soon, people will not be able to imagine life without professional organizers, just as we now can't imagine life without cell phones, computers, and palm pilots."

~

All clutter books and clutter websites are lists. The shortest lists are reduced to acronyms like SHED or LIFE, for I don't know what. (Okay, I do. SHED: Separate treasures, Heave the rest, Embrace identity from within, and Drive yourself forward. LIFE: Lighten up, Invest in comfort, Forget perfection, and Enhance flow.)

I've been working on my own acronym—SLOB:

Stop! buying junk.

Less! is more.

Out! with it all—husband or wife, if that's what it takes.

Bliss! or Bag it! depending if you're reaching for "awareness" or just want a chance to see your desktop, floor, or chair again.

The basic advice runs something like this:

1 *Poor Cluttered Richard.* If Ben Franklin were alive, Poor Richard would have offered decluttering advice. Popular magazines fill out his role with Yes-you-can! "quick tips," "easy strategies," and "do's and don'ts":

↬ Make a list, make a rule, stick to it.

↬ Pick up your mess, you slob—a word that is never used. Throw it out; donate it.

↬ Make a place for everything.

↬ Less! Less! Less is more. For each item that comes in, throw something out. If you haven't used it in six months, twelve months, toss it. But don't get carried away. "I haven't used my fire extinguisher in 15 years, and I haven't thrown it out," says one clutter coach.

2 *Clutter on the psychologist's couch.* It's not about your stuff, it's about you.

↬ Ask yourself: Why am I holding on to all this stuff? This stuff is not life—it's getting in the way of life. And: You're going to die anyway, no matter how much stuff you've heaped up.

↬ It's like the old middle-school physics experiment to measure "displacement." You take a one-ounce lead weight and gently lower it into a graduated cylinder. How much water does this lead weight displace? How much life does this stuff displace?

3 *You need help.*

↬ Hire a professional organizer.

↬ Join a recovery support group.

↬ Hire a feng shui expert. Get your stuff marching with the earth.

4 *You need more stuff to organize your stuff.* Buy our shelves, containers, labels.

↬ The Clutter World is divided between those who say "Don't organize, discard," and companies like California Closets, the Container Store, and many others who seek to sell us more stuff to solve our clutter problem. *More is less!* What you need is this box, this storage system.

5 *Clean your mind, your outlook, your life.* Clutter stories are pilgrimage stories, a journey through junk to redemption. They're about moving the mountain of consumer trash and bad mental habits. This stuff is smothering you. Toss it all out, and while you're at it, toss out the miserable emotions that have

you going round and round. Clear the stuff and in flows life and love, the stories promise. Let go of the old size-five dresses and never-to-be-finished craft projects and in will flow a lighter, happier you. "Say adios to your disaster zone and hello to a brand-new Zen utopia!" crows a teen magazine.

One day you're in a messy house that is jammed with broken toys and orphaned exercise equipment, and the next day a summer breeze moves through a sun-lit, sparsely furnished, white interior with room for (a thinner) you to sit on your yoga mat and drink green tea as orange-scented candles burn and little feng shui mirrors twinkle. The journey of a thousand miles begins with a yard sale, Chairman Mao might have said.

But first, you must make a list:

- ✧ Clean the clothes closet.
- ✧ Take clothes to Goodwill.
- ✧ Clean out the kitchen drawers, basement, garage. . . .
- ✧ Throw out everything you own.
- ✧ Clean mind, mend soul.
- ✧ Start again. . . .
- ✧ Throw out the old lists.
- ✧ Sit under a tree.
- ✧ Become enlightened.

Of all these decluttering methods, my favorite is "FlyLady's 27-Fling Boogie": Grab twenty-seven things and throw them out. Pick an area and give it fifteen minutes. Get on with it.

∾

Clutter is the cholesterol of the home; it's clogging the hearth. The "Clean Sweep" team from the television show of that name usually hauls away about a half ton of trash from each house that it rescues from clutter. (Which may explain why 23 percent of Americans admit to paying bills late because they can't find them, and why 25 percent of people with two-car garages have to park their cars outside.) "We have too much. We're overhoused, overclothed, overfed, and over-entertained," said Don Aslett, getting right to the point. Aslett would know; he's been poking around houses for fifty years. In college Aslett started what has become one of the country's largest cleaning companies, and his books on clutter helped to establish the genre. People call Aslett, saying, "We don't know how all this stuff got here." Think of it as a whodunit. He solves the mystery and gently interrogates the guilty. Ask yourself: Does this item "enhance your life"? If not, get rid of it.

We're crowding ourselves out of our houses. And it's not just stuff. Work has come home. Home offices are like small, overwhelmed rail yards, heaped with paper and tangled with cords for all the devices associated with a computer (printers, backup hard drives, routers, scanners, backup power, speakers). The computer or desk is often tagged in a flurry of Post-it Notes in an attempt to remember obscure computer prompts. The computer itself presents a virtual heap of emails, text, sound, photo, and video files. Entertainment has come home, too. Television sprawls out to 120 or 240 channels or more. There are more television sets than people in the average home. Adults are looking at screens—TVs, computers, cell phones, even GPS devices—about 8.5 hours a day, according to a study by the Council for Research Excellence. TV ads claim about an hour of each day. The hours spent watching television—seventy-two days out of each year—continue to grow, alongside the rapid rise of watching online videos. Our homes are wide open.

Somewhere in there, between the physical and virtual clutter, we are losing the ordinary qualities of home—the solitude to recollect ourselves, the time for families to talk. (Yet another study has clocked only 14.5 minutes a day of actual conversation between parents and children.) We are losing the "nothing much" that is home. Clutter is choking our shelters. Is there any room left for ourselves in our houses?

∾

A few years back, the fifth-grade class at the Great Brook School produced a handsome booklet about our town, *Hancock Then and Now*, which turned out to be one of those accidental anthropological documents. In front of Charles W. Farmer's house, circa 1875, stands the Farmer family, ten in all. One hundred thirty years later, one woman poses before the house. In front of Hervey Bugbee's house, circa 1860s, there's a rather handsome sporting party of eight, the men and women posing with long croquet mallets. One hundred fifty years later, a family of four with two dogs gathers for the camera. And so the photo census goes: six now two, seven now one, four now two. . . . If you came upon this document lacking any historical context, you might think the population had been ravaged by an epidemic.

In two hundred years we have turned our domestic world upside down. Colonial America was a land of small, crowded houses. Each household had many people, but few possessions. The average family size was seven or eight. Twelve or more people—relations, servants, hired hands, slaves—would live and work in seven hundred square feet or less, notes Jack Larkin, the chief historian at Old Sturbridge Village. Most houses were five hundred square feet or smaller (further reduced in the north when rooms were closed for winter). People slept alone in a bed only in sickness or childbirth. They ate in the room where the family slept, often sharing utensils, passing around one dirty pewter mug, eating out of one pot. Birth, illness, and death all took place in this small house. Home and work were one—but in a quite different way from today. Everyone worked to grow food and make clothing, with a spinning wheel in the kitchen and a loom upstairs. The family was Colonial society, writes historian John Demos. The family was a business, trade school, weekday church, hospital, orphanage, old age home, welfare institute, and even a house of correction—criminals were sometimes sentenced to live as servants.

These houses would offend our senses today. You could say that they were cluttered with smells: chamber pots, lye, manure from the fields on boots, woodsmoke, pipe tobacco, souring milk, ripening cheese, and sweaty inhabitants who didn't bathe. Flies, bedbugs, and lice were common. "Keeping farmhouses clean with broom, bucket, and mop was a losing battle because dirt and grime came in from everywhere—fields, barnyards and pigsties, muddy or dusty roads, open windows, fireplaces," Larkin writes in *Where We Lived.* "Filth and slovenliness were everywhere else, too. The aisles of churches and meetinghouses would be fouled by dogs and chickens that wandered in and out in warm weather. Men in church, even those in choir, chewed and spat tobacco."

At Old Sturbridge Village, the curators try to be scrupulous about presenting an accurate portrayal of the era from 1790 to 1840, but visitors see a much more clean, pleasant smelling, and lightly populated village.

I had long believed that what museum visitors don't understand about

Colonial era houses was how few things people had owned—basic things like bowls, spoons, chairs, shirts, shoes. But the museum-goer also has no idea of how crowded the houses were. With few possessions and more people, it's the inverse of our world. We live in families shrunken to less than 2.6 people per household with an average of 1,200 square feet per person. Larkin compares this to the cramped conditions in 1800: two East Coast towns he surveyed averaged only 90 and 120 square feet per person. We live in ten to fourteen times more space today. That 700-square-foot Colonial house is about the size of the two-car garage on a suburban "Colonial." And since 1970, the American home has grown 60 percent, from an average of 1,500 square feet to about 2,400 square feet today (and people still have to rent storage sheds). We see many old houses once they have been emptied out and slicked up in museums, or we see them in the black-and-white photos taken for the Historic American Buildings Survey. People are almost never in these photos. In the deserted historic survey photos the houses lean and twist evocatively, like bonsai. The photos are like those that Eugene Atget took of Paris early in the morning, surreal, dreamlike in their emptiness.

∽

Probate inventories, those detailed listings of the household contents of the deceased, provide a glimpse of how we got to today's jumble house. Kevin M. Sweeney carefully sifted through nearly eight hundred probate inventories from Wethersfield, Connecticut. The inventories were made between 1639 and 1800. As you would expect, the houses start out sparsely furnished. There are few chairs—few of anything. In the first period, from 1639 to 1670, "the average inventory contained two beds, one or two chests, possibly a few stools, and a 'form' (that is, a backless bench) or some chairs. In some households people possibly sat on boxes and chests, and children may have stood while eating," Sweeney reports.

As Wethersfield prospered, the rich led the way, buying looking glasses, writing desks, "dressing tables," expensive cupboards, sets of china dishes, "presses" (tall cabinets to hang clothes) and a "somewhat newer furniture form," chests of drawers. When a cabinetmaker moved to town in 1730, the "case of drawers" (a "high chest" or "highboy") became more common. Inventories late in the century show that the average house had two chests and was more likely to have a table. The quantity of furniture had doubled, and even tripled in some homes, by the mid-eighteenth century. Houses had chairs in sets of six or even twelve, specialized tables like tea tables, and sometimes a looking glass. By end of the century, 150 years after the first probate inventory, the average house had three beds, some of them fully curtained, two sets of chairs (twelve in all), three or four chests, three or four tables, one or two looking glasses, stands and candlestands, and sometimes a clock. But still, by today's standards, these inventories are sparse. FlyLady's 27 Fling Boogie would empty out even the wealthiest house in Wethersfield in an hour or less.

Attics were empty; closets didn't exist. Late seventeenth-century inventories of Dedham, Massachusetts, find only grain, hops, Indian corn, wool, and some dried fruits and vegetables. Grain might also be stored in upstairs rooms, which if used for sleeping would have only a bed. There were no closets right through the nineteenth century. Wealthy homes sometimes had small built-in china cupboards, and the rare, shallow closet, fourteen to eighteen inches deep, to hang a few clothes on hooks.

There was no need for closets. Consider this shopping list kept by Harriet P. Bradley of Watertown, Connnecticut, as noted by Merritt Ireley in *Open House*:

Bought 1 Skein of yarn. . .
half a yard of Muslin. . .
1 Pair of Leather gloves. . .
1 skein of Hacks. . .
Pen knife. . .
1 Pr of Morocco Shoes. . . Strings
1 Pr of Leather Shoes. . .
Half a paper of pins. . . 1 Leno Ruffle.
That's what Harriet Bradley bought in 1819. It's her entire year's purchase.

∼

The America of houses with one clock, one mirror, a few tables and chairs, and no closets gave way after the Civil War to the making of the America we know, the consumer utopia. As huge industries turned out goods cheaply, the home was transformed. Proper Victorian parlors were crowded with plush furniture, drapes and swags of cloth, lamps, plants, art, figurines, souvenirs, china, dried flowers, and collections displayed on a newly popular kind of shelving called "étagères" or "whatnots." The parlor, reserved for special occasions, became a museum of the family's aspirations. Here they hoped to show themselves in the best light.

Dr. J. G. Bailey's parlor in Santa Ana, California, was typical. Photographed circa 1876, the Baileys' best room had all this: a large sculpture of two cavorting classical figures on a pedestal entwined in vines, a painting or a print on an easel, and above that, another painting or print with cloth tassels, and above that vines or flowers, a tiled fireplace with a mirror above and a mantel jammed with vases and other objects sitting on a floral-patterned lambrequin that draped over the edge, a painted fire screen, glass-front bookcases with a big bust above, a modest chandelier, a big basket carrying something decorative, a low side chair with an embroidered seat and back, a table in the center of the room with another tall sculpture of two figures, pottery, flowers, and other stuff, a carpet with a busy floral pattern, lace curtains on the windows, and more paintings or prints on the wall, hanging one above the other. And, oh yes, if you look closely, there behind the vine-covered sculpture is a mustached man we can presume is the doctor. His wife sits at distance in her chair, partially hidden by the sculptures on the central table.

"Provided there is space to move about, without knocking over the furniture, there is hardly likely to be too much in the room," advised the popular writer Harriet Spofford in 1877.

The overstuffed parlor, a hallmark of the Victorian era, became a convenient target. Critics would go apoplectic. They would start by listing a room's contents until they were ready to scream. It's a genre unto itself. The English poet and socialist Edward Carpenter, lecturing on "The Simplification of Life" in 1886, took one short tour around the parlor:

"It cannot be too often remembered that every additional object in a house requires additional dusting, cleaning, repairing; and lucky are you if its requirements stop there. When you abandon a wholesome tile or stone floor for a Turkey carpet, you are setting out on a voyage of which you cannot see the end. The Turkey carpet makes the old furniture look uncomfortable, and calls for stuffed couches and armchairs; the couches and armchairs demand a walnut-wood table; the walnut-wood table requires polishing, and the polish bottles require shelves; the couches and armchairs have casters and springs, which give way and want mending; they have damask seats, which fade and must be covered; the chintz covers require washing, and when washed they call for antimacassars to keep them clean. The antimacassars require wool, and the wool requires knitting-needles, and the knitting-needles require a box, the box demands a side-table to stand on, and the side-table involves more covers and castors-and so we go on."

Edith Wharton and architect Ogden Codman were more restrained in their 1902 classic, *The Decoration of Houses*:

"Who cannot call to mind the dreary drawing-room, in small town houses the only possible point of reunion for the family, but too often in consequence of its exquisite discomfort, no more use as a meeting place than the vestibule or the cellar? The windows in this kind of room are invariably supplied with two sets of muslin curtains, one hanging against the panes, the other fulfilling the supererogatory duty of hanging against the former; then come the heavy stiff curtains, so draped as to cut off the upper light of the windows by day, while it is impossible to drop them at night: curtains that have thus ceased to serve the purpose for which they exist."

The writing table is "banished . . . in some dark corner where it is little wonder that the ink dries unused." Where the table should be is a cabinet "surmounted by a picture made invisible by the dark shadow of the hangings." The hearth, "covered with inflammable draperies," sits cold, and "no one cares to sit about a fireless hearth." The family, bullied by its possessions, abandons the parlor and jams into a small room.

A reaction set in. "How much money has been wasted, how much capital let lie idle, in furnishing and keeping up these ceremonial deserts!" wrote Clarence Cook in *The House Beautiful*. The nation was in a mood to clean house. Between 1890 and 1910 there was an "abrupt and dramatic" move to simplify the Victorian home, writes historian Clifford Edward Clark Jr. Out went Queen Anne houses with their towers, turrets, tall, thin, decorated brick chimneys, recessed second-story porches, billowing ground-floor porches, roofs trimmed with finials and cresting, eyelid dormers, circular bay windows, wavy "fish scale" shingles and diamond-patterned shingles mixed with clapboards, board and batten, classical swags, and carved wooden panels sometimes in sunflower or sunburst patterns on the attic gables—a house that in profile was like a mountain village of houses.

The new preference was for a low-slung house, its broad roof often pressed down on the front porch like a man's hat pulled low. The compact bungalow had fewer rooms, halls, stairs, and finishes. A "living room" and often an adjoining dining area replaced the "ceremonial deserts" of the parlor and front hall. Bungalows were "natural," "organic," and "simple." Simplicity was in fashion. Charles Wagner's *The Simple Life* was a bestseller in 1901, impressing President Theodore Roosevelt, who invited the author, a French-born pastor, to dine at the White House. "I know of no other book . . . which contains so much that we of America ought to take to our hearts," said Roosevelt.

Rooms were emptied out. Magazines—some of the same ones that today offer tips on decluttering—urged readers to use fewer pieces of furniture. The bungalow interior was free of whatnots. Living rooms had exposed wooden beams, high wainscoting, built-in bookcases and seats, a band of windows, some with stained glass, a "big hospitable" rough stone or brick hearth, and, when possible, French doors opening out to a porch and garden.

Spaciousness was the ideal. This is evident in the bungalow magazines and catalogs, and in the rooms designed by Gustav Stickley, furniture maker and a leader of the Arts and Crafts movement. When I first saw these illustrations, I thought that the magazines had wanted to highlight one table and one chair. But no, this was the intended interior. It's sparse by Victorian, and even by contemporary, standards. (Arts and Crafts enthusiasts usually overlook this key tenant of the movement and jam in as much booty as they can, reverting to their inner Victorian.)

A photo of living room number 595 from the 1912 edition of *Practical Bungalows* shows what was possible if you built with the company's plans. The living room has exposed wooden beams, a brick fireplace, a few simple hanging lights, high wainscoting reaching halfway up the wall, wallpaper, some scattered carpets, and only three or four visible pieces of furniture: one rocker by the hearth, one small library table, one side chair, and the edge of what may be a cabinet. There is plenty of room by the rocking chair for another rocker or two and small tables, or a Morris chair or possibly a Mission settle.

Stickley, in his magazine, *The Craftsman*, printed examples of living rooms, such as this one in July 1906: a fireplace with a mantle that has two vases, a small candelabra, and a picture; a glass-front bookcase; a carpet; "a shadowy landscape frieze" above a plain wall; and one Morris chair and one side chair. The chairs are a little adrift in space, recalling a newlywed's first house. A photo of another larger Stickley living room, published the next year, has built-in bookcases flanking the fireplace, a library table with a lamp and a runner, and two arm chairs. The caption calls attention to "the sense of space which means so much to the beauty of the main room."

"We need to straighten out our standards and to get rid of a lot of rubbish that we have accumulated with our wealth and commercial supremacy," Stickley wrote. "We have wasted and misused our energy precisely as we have wasted and misused so many of our wonderful natural resources. All we really need is a change in our point of view toward life and a keener perception regarding the things that count and the things that merely burden us." The place to begin reordering our lives is at home, he said.

The start of the twentieth century was one of our national moments of decluttering, a moment when we ask, *What is a house?* It's a question that comes up each generation in America, whether it's Thomas Jefferson at Monticello, Henry David Thoreau at Walden, or Catherine Beecher preaching ethical homemaking.

This is the question that all those clutter books and websites are asking: Is your house a place for stuff or people? Are we living well? Are we living at all or just staring at different screens?

∾

The small ad for California Closets promises emptiness—a room with white walls, a clear desktop facing empty cubbyholes, and a plain gray rug is on the floor. Even the staircase is stripped of its banister.

"Make the Most of Your Home," the ad says, implying: hide your stuff in our closets.

Here's what California Closets is selling: nothing—the appearance of nothing. Make the *Least* of Your Home. Emptiness is the product. The Simple Life is a high-end purchase. In a culture of commerce, a society of material abundance, minimalism is showy. It implies clarity, order, a spiritual focus. It boldly says, "These things are just things."

We pledge allegiance to the simpler life, the uncluttered house, and go out and shop.

~

People are suffocating. They are drowning. That's what they say when the rescue squad arrives. "My clients say things like, 'I was buried under all that stuff,' 'I was drowning,' 'I feel like I'm suffocating,'" said Peter Walsh, a straight-talking Australian who has risen to stardom by telling Americans to pick up after themselves.

Walsh sees the advanced cases. He worked with one couple who had remodeled their garage into a family room in the early 1980s, but they had long ago buried the room. "The wife said, 'I know there's a piano in here. But I haven't seen it in 17 years.'"

He takes this talk of suffocation seriously. "We use those metaphors because clutter robs us of life," Walsh said. "The words 'organized' and 'organic' come from the same base word. Something is organic when it lives and breathes. So if something is not organized, it lacks life; it's suffocating."

Clutter is the stuffy air of our time. Our houses have grown stuffy with stuff. Just as the nineteenth-century air-tight stoves and tight houses suffocated the inhabitants, so it is with our stuff—actual and virtual. If Catherine Beecher were around, she would shame us into tidying up. Her books would have diagrams to organize closets and households. Decluttering is ventilation.

~

Emma Willard was a pioneering educator and women's rights advocate. She wanted to make the "whole world home-like." Today we would be grateful for making the home more homelike.

But what is homelike? The German word *heimlich*—at home, friendly, comfortable—offers an insight. *Heimlich* is private life, hidden from strangers. In this privacy is an opposite meaning. "On the one hand," wrote Freud, *heimlich* "means what is familiar and agreeable and on the other, what is concealed and kept out of sight." *Heimlich* turns into *unheimlich*, the unhomely, something that is secret that has come to light. The *unheimlich* is strange, frightening. An *unheimlich* house in the common phrase of Freud's time was a haunted house. Freud insisted that the horror isn't "new or alien, but something which is familiar and old—established in the mind" that has become alienated by repression. It was not supernatural, but rather superordinary. Gothic tales of haunted houses have given way to horror movies, and home is usually the horror. The dolls come to life at night, the killer is living in your attic, the stranger is calling the babysitter from inside the house. The ordinary comfortable home threatens to murder us.

Cluttered houses in their extreme are presented as modern horror stories. "*Stuff robbed Dee Wallace of love.*" Things take over and stalk the inhabitants of the house. Things suffocate them. Repressed emotions come to light: fear of being denied something, fear of death, fear that there is no love, and fear that *heimlich* has become *unheimlich* in what should be our refuge. Trying to smother the un-homeliness in the home, people keep adding more and more things, the equivalent of gorging on junk food. More things do not make for more of a home.

We are most at home when we're sheltered completely, body and soul. And when we're not, we feel the chill breeze of *unheimlich*. We are lonely; housed, but homeless.

～

I watched an online video about a "Spiritual Home Makeover." A Turkish house whisperer, as I call her, visits the troubled house. She begins by putting slippers on the homeowner and herself so they can keep their feet from the "negative energies" of the dirty floor. Together they put away toys and laundry, set out lemon-scented candles, sunflowers, a Buddha, and little mirrors. But what will happen when her children and husband return?

The housewife says that she loves her house but "the kids are running through and the dog's running through and the cat's running through and the husband's running through—"

The Turkish house whisperer cuts her off. She doesn't want to talk about the husband.

But hearing this, I think that the housewife may have a "Yellow Wallpaper" problem. Her family is driving her a little crazy. Being a housewife is driving her a little crazy.

"The Yellow Wallpaper" is a story of madness. A husband takes his wife away to the country to rest and recover from her "nervous weakness." She's kept in a "big, airy room," alone most of the time, with "repellent, almost revolting" yellow wallpaper. At first the wallpaper seems to be looking at her with a pattern of "unblinking eyes." She thinks that she sees a hidden, skulking figure. As the days go by, she's sure. "It's like a woman stooping down and creeping about." By moonlight, "the woman behind it is as plain as can be." She can feel the woman in the wallpaper moving. She starts rubbing the paper. There could be many women. When she looks out the window, she sees the wallpaper woman there, too, "on that long road under the trees, creeping along, and when a carriage comes she hides under the blackberry vines." All she can think of is tearing off the wallpaper. She works at it through the night. "As soon as it was moonlight and that poor thing began to crawl and shake the pattern, I got up and ran to help her. I pulled and she shook, I shook and she pulled, and before morning we had peeled off yards of that paper."

Charlotte Perkins Gilman said that she wrote the story after her own treatment for nervous breakdown and melancholy. The doctors prescribed the "rest cure" and sent her home to bed, telling her "never to touch pen, brush, or pencil again." She followed the advice for three months until she "came so near the borderline of utter mental ruin." With a friend's help, she rejoiced in returning to work.

Her story has been read as a haunted house tale and it's been read as an indictment of how women were once treated. But Gilman's story may have a wider application. In our cluttered houses we are suffering from a touch of the Yellow Wallpaper Syndrome. The walls are alive and they're eating us up. We're locked in our consumer utopia. Get us out of this room! We're suffocating.

～

"The goal at the end of the day is to live well," said one decluttering guru. The great interest in clutter books and TV shows and all the rest says that we are not living well. If we believe the gospel according to decluttering, an awakening awaits those who clean house. Somewhere under all this junk is what we think we've lost—ourselves, our home, our family, our sanity, our soul.

But the decluttering gurus seem to be looking for a material solution to a spiritual problem. They are confusing symptoms and causes. A cluttered house—a buried piano—is a symptom of materialism run amok. It's not the cause. Cleanliness is good, but is it really next to Godliness? You may be no more happy or wise in a cleaner house.

This mess is us. Forget the lists of seven simple steps that morph into hundreds of steps, forget the "in-home design consultation" with the California Closets organizer. The lesson that the lists seldom arrive at is this: our lives are finite. That's the lesson we never want to hear. So take FlyLady's advice: Grab twenty-seven things and remove them. Repeat. It's simple and it will leave you with time to dwell upon this statement by Thomas Merton:

"If you want to identify me, ask me not where I live, or what I like to eat, or how I comb my hair, but ask me what I think I am living for, in detail, and ask me what I think is keeping me from living fully for the thing I want to live for. Between these two answers you can determine the identity of any person. The better answer he has, the more of a person he is," Merton wrote at age twenty-six as he faced the biggest decision of his life, to enter the monastery.

What's keeping you from living? Throw it all away, step over it, push it into a corner, under a tarp, into the garage, barn, storage shed. Mice, rats, mold, mildew will have their way. Just go live your life.

❧ Finding Heaven in the Most Hated House on the Block ❧

The house on the corner is surprising. It's a low-slung arrow, as taut as an Army cot. When Frank Lloyd Wright designed this Usonian house for Isadore J. and Lucille Zimmerman in 1950, nine out of ten new houses built were ranches. The Zimmerman House was an upscale cousin to the ranch; now it is estranged. Today, new houses look like a collision at the corner of Queen Anne and Colonial. This house is not aging. It is getting more modern as the years pass.

Inside the air is a little musty, a little warm and close on the summer day I visit.

It is, after all, a closed-up house, a house without the comings and goings of its owners to stir things up. The Zimmermans, who died in the 1980s, left the house and an endowment to the Currier Museum of Art, just across the city from their house in Manchester, New Hampshire.

The house is peaceful and calming. The narrow front hall with its low ceiling creates suspense. Entering the house's one great space, the Garden Room, you have a sense of arrival. The street seems far, far away. The small backyard seems to be a part of the room and far larger than it is. Tight as a small boat inside, the house opens to the outside in a way that is spacious and liberating. You don't feel like you are looking out of a box to the outdoors. It is all of a piece. On this small three-quarter-acre corner lot, Wright performed a magic trick.

You are aware of each moment in the house, Hetty Startup tells me as she shows me around. Startup is a former site administrator for the house. She was at the Currier Museum of Art for twelve years. Only the Zimmermans may have spent more time at the house. "It is just the most amazing authentic space," Startup says. "You get that kind of *and now and now and now* feeling about nature and light and ephemeral aesthetic qualities. It's a very rich environment." She adds, "It's maybe too rich, maybe too full of things to look at."

This is a house museum, but without any hokum. Things are not arranged to look as if the Zimmermans have just left. The house is subdued and dignified. It is complete and grown-up in the way few houses or American spaces are.

This house is not that old, but it belongs to a different age. There is no television, no computer, no winking green and red LED lights on all the digital devices. And there's also no sprawling space, no walk-in closets, media room, or a kitchen with a granite island the size of an aircraft carrier.

It is a small house—that's what almost all the visitors say. But at seventeen hundred square feet, a "Usonian deluxe," it is actually more than two-thirds larger than the average new house of its day. And yet, the rooms and halls are small. Many Americans have walk-in closets in their "master suites" that are far larger then the Zimmerman's bedroom. The Garden Room is the one grand—six hundred square foot—space.

Visitors also find it too dark inside. But that's because we've lost an age-old sensitivity to shadows, says Startup. "We're overexposed. And we don't live with enough shadows," she says, referring to Junichiro Tanizaki's famous essay about spiritual repose, "In Praise of Shadows." "Look at the way light is modulated in this house by the texture of the materials. It's so much more restful and peaceful." In our houses everything is foreground—bright lights, computer lights. Shadows are mystery, depth; they used to be a part of shelter. They were places of the spirit.

In short, the Zimmerman House just seems alien to many people. The neighbors hated the new house, dubbing it the "chicken coop" for its low profile. Of the 2,650 visitors who don the blue laboratory booties for a tour each year, Startup says, half don't like it. They wouldn't move in if you paid them. My own entirely unscientific poll surprised me: People hated it. "That awful house! Those people were prisoners in their own home," one visitor told me. "He bullied them. Can you imagine?" They thought Frank Lloyd Wright's patrons were dopey pawns confined to little rooms with everything built in—everything Frank Lloyd Wright and no room for the hapless inhabitant, the homeowner. This is not dislike or indifference, but a kind of white-hot hatred. "It's a visceral response," says Startup. The Zimmerman house offended them. Why? Is Wright's democratic design totalitarian?

∿

House of Surveillance

This is not a house to have a fight in; it's not a house where you'd build a model airplane at the kitchen table (on a hobby board or wax paper). It's not a house for toddlers with all that plastic Playskool stuff. It's a house for a refined dinner party with polite talk here and over there. The Zimmerman House is quiet and cultured.

The Zimmermans hosted formal evenings of live music each Tuesday. Guests followed the music by reading the score. They sat in the Garden Room's high-backed banquettes, or tried to. Finding the banquettes as uncomfortable as a church pew, they would lie down. (The Taliesin apprentice who oversaw the construction had suggested a redesign for the banquette-pews.)

In the Zimmerman House all is out in the open as a New England town common, as a meetinghouse—all pews in daylight, all open to view. There is no retreat, no layers of privacy. This house will allow no secrets; we will be found out. People are unnerved by this taint of surveillance. This Usonian house might as well be a lab experiment with two-way mirrors to observe the test subjects.

I had regarded the house as an elegant object, neatly crafted; each item, each brick and art object united in one story. But are houses ever just one story? Isn't that when we get nervous, feel as if we're being edited? Is it this we don't like about new houses and big modern interiors? One idea. We are Play-Doh squeezed through the mold.

~

House of No Improvement
Visitors are put off by the totality of the house. It's complete. It's done. You've arrived. And if you can't be happy here and now, you will not be saved by the prospect of home improvement. But home improvement is our domestic Manifest Destiny. There's always a project awaiting—a new bathroom, a kitchen makeover, a new deck, new carpeting, a new addition—knock out the back wall, push up through the roof. Flip the house and start all over.

But what happens when your house is finished? And now you have to be happy. You have no excuses. A new floor, a new room, isn't going to save you. (This may be what an unfinished house preserves for people—the possibility of arrival, the last push through the mountain pass to paradise. If you stop before you're done, you can't be disappointed.)

No home improvement, no promise of expansion—it's un-American. Your house is defined. That means that your life is finite after all. Home improvement is the domestic outpost of our restlessness.

The Zimmermans never would have had a discussion about pushing out a wall to expand the bedroom or getting rid of the Wright furniture for something more modern. They had forsaken part of our Domestic Manifest Destiny—to sprawl across the land, across our lot, and in our house. The Zimmerman House is an arrow into the heart of the Do-It-Yourself Republic. The house is finished. You are freed to live your life.

∾

Happy House

The story of the Zimmerman House is not the usual Frank Lloyd Wright saga. The story is the Zimmermans. Some visitors mistake them as servants to Modernism.

The Zimmermans were happy here for thirty-six years. They gardened; they played music. Yes, they were Wright disciples—"Frank Lloyd Wright nuts," says one volunteer tour guide. They sought his approval for their furniture, dishes, and art. (And the letterhead for Dr. Zimmerman's stationery.) They even volunteered to work on the Usonian model house that was built on the future site of the Guggenheim. But this isn't a shrine. The Zimmerman House is a complete, carefully curated Wright house, but it is not the full-on Oak Park worship. It feels like the Zimmermans' house. It has a happy home vibe.

In a short book about the house published by the Currier Museum of Art, what comes across is how at home the Zimmermans were here. One photo shows the Zimmermans and friends on a Sunday, sitting around reading the Sunday newspapers. Dr. Zimmerman is dressed in a suit and tie. Mrs. Zimmerman is perched over the paper by the fireplace. (They seem European, even though she was raised as a Kentucky Baptist.) Two friends, sitting opposite, are also reading the paper. Two things dominate the scene—the sprawl of Sunday newsprint, a Niagara that overwhelms all homes—and their dog, a Dalmatian. It's surprising to see a dog here. (What would Wright say? And a Dalmatian? If asked, would he have prescribed a dog with earth tones—a chocolate lab? Dachshund?) The disorder domesticates the house.

Isadore and Lucille Zimmerman loved their house. This was home. (There is a memorial to them in the garden.) They weren't forever planning additions or thinking of moving. No. This was it. Their spot on earth. How many others can say that of where they live? "The Zimmerman house is Heaven," they wrote to their architect. "It is the most beautiful house in the world. . . No words can express our gratitude." Wright's architecture performed as promised—it liberated them to live a rich life.

Maybe that is what people can't accept: The Zimmermans were happy. Here lived two Americans who didn't want more. They were happy with what they had. Radical.

⌁ The Perilous Career of a Footpath ⌁

The pedestrian who walks through the planning manuals is a hunted beast. He or she is given seven seconds to cross the street in the *Manual on Uniform Traffic Control Devices*—or less. It is accepted practice to shorten the crossing time to four seconds. The manual assumes that you'll step out smartly at four feet a second. But if you're an older citizen crossing a six-lane road, you may find yourself stranded in the last lane as the light changes, a candidate to become a hood ornament. You have used up the "Available Green Time." You have gone overtime on the allotted "Pedestrian Clearance Time." You are in "conflict" with traffic. You are that worst thing, a "flow interruption."

The imperiled state of the walker is revealed in the approved standard signs: Pedestrians on the planet of Uniform Traffic Control have no feet. On Warning Sign W11-12 the pedestrian has no feet and no hands. But the farmer on his tractor on W11-5 gets a jaunty wide-brimmed hat and his tractor has big gnarly tires. Things are no better on the Recreational Signs, like RL-100 Trail (Hiking): walking stick, backpack, legs, but no feet. RS-010, Skater (Ice) is also problematic. Legs and blades. No feet! The horse depicted in RL-110, Trail (Horse), has hooves. Bikes and all-terrain vehicles have wheels. Why can't walkers have feet?

The signs are more truthful than intended. Walkers are quarantined. "Pedestrian control" is one of the objectives of the manual and other key texts like the *Highway Capacity Manual*. It's not out of malice, but concern. Traffic engineers want to keep pedestrians and cars apart.

The pedestrian is restricted to narrow corridors. Federal programs designed to encourage walking, like Safe Routes to School, are all about building safe corridors, an approach that is not unlike those wildlife crossing tunnels constructed for salamanders. The walker is treated as an endangered species. Traffic engineers design "pedestrian refuges"—median strips to shelter the stranded walker. Advocates of "walkability" plead that "we're all pedestrians." (We're born without cars.) These well-intended federal programs and advocates want to build what is in essence a highway system for pedestrians, paving to match paving. In the arms race of paving, pedestrians and bicyclists are playing catch-up. All of this is upside down. Cars should be limited, not people. But we have chosen otherwise.

∾

There is no hiding from the paving arms race, just as there is no place safe from the nuclear arms race. Paving is the prevailing ethos. I know this firsthand. For more years than I care to admit, I chaired a committee in our town—a planning committee. Those two dreary words when placed next to each other create a multiplier effect of dread. It's like placing the words "root" and "canal" next to each other.

Our committee was in charge of making changes and not making changes. We were supposed to fix everything and leave things just as they were. That's contradictory, of course, but so were the "facts on the ground," as the generals say. Our village, built in the late-eighteenth and early-nineteenth centuries, is a classic New England small town. The handsome Main Street leads to the town common, a perfectly paced procession that gives us our library, store, café, inn, meetinghouse, post office, and town offices. Our Main Street is a historic district on the National Register of Historic Places. But Main Street is also a state road, a two-lane major route. A state road running through a historic working landscape is a bad fit; it's like ice wedged into a granite boulder. Given enough winters, ice will conquer granite.

A modern road is a landscape with its own rules—the rules in the manuals to maximize traffic flow. Each detail is mandated by law, regulation, or the religion of traffic engineering. But the town has its own landscape, one shaped less by regulations than by foot and hoof, by once-common ways of building. We have meandering dirt "cow paths" instead of sidewalks. We have grassy edges and mud puddles instead of curbs and paved shoulders. We have an old "soft" landscape.

The hardscape of the road—all of us rushing everywhere—chafes against the soft, pre-automobile landscape, and once it does we call in the victors, the traffic engineers. Their solution is to harden the landscape. This, in sum, is what our plans and meetings were all about: how to fix the old townscape without "hardening" it. How could we keep it a place where, on a summer's day, children swimming in the pond across from the common could walk barefoot on the path under the trees to the village market to get a Popsicle?

How could we make sure that cars stop for people three and four feet tall, with towels draped like capes over their shoulders?

While that's not the language of planning, it should be the goal. Somewhere in the *Manual on Uniform Traffic Control Devices*, in the *Highway Capacity Manual*, in all the federal and state laws, it should say: a village, a neighborhood, is a place for people, not machines. People first. Otherwise, as Lewis Mumford warned in 1957, we are planning our life to fit the automobile, which shows "that we have no life that is worth living."

~

Streets were once public space. The streets of nineteenth-century downtowns were a tangle of people, horses, oxen, wagons, carts, carriages, and trolleys. All that has been cleared for the monoculture traffic jam of cars and buses. The pedestrian is banned from the street, except for those seven seconds at the corner. In many cities, if he steps anywhere else in the sacred precinct, he can be fined for jaywalking.

When the first motor car enthusiasts began to wedge into this mess, they cursed the pedestrian and the horse-drawn cart. Why can't they get out of the way? Pedestrians were blamed for accidents. This became the official line. "The pedestrian was a most serious hindrance," said a traffic engineer in the 1920s. "The pedestrian is the most difficult 'problem child' of the accident prevention movement," said one traffic safety consultant in 1950. He is his "own worst enemy" and "he must change his walking habits or become a casualty," the consultant said. (This attitude has persisted: in 2007 the secretary of transportation complained about having to devote 1.5 percent of her budget to pedestrians and bicycles, which "are really not transportation.")

Out in the countryside, people did not yield to the first cars. The first British law restricted the speed of electric cars to four miles an hour and required that someone run ahead with a red flag. In the United States, farmers treated the early motorists to frontier justice. In one Minnesota town the locals plowed up the roads. Near Sacramento, California, they dug ditches across the roads, trapping thirteen cars. In parts of Germany, Switzerland, and the Netherlands they threw rocks at passing cars. Woodrow Wilson shared the sentiment. He said that he understood those that shot hit-and-run drivers.

But we know how this story turns out. Historically, Americans have been obsessed with transportation. "If Americans agreed in any opinion, they were united in wishing for roads," Henry Adams wrote of the early republic. Americans were in a fever to build roads, bridges, canals, and railroads. Turnpikes were pushed over hills and through swamps. A mania for canals gave way to an even bigger mania for railroads. European visitors were astonished to find railroads everywhere, pushing up steeper hills and twisting around tighter turns than were allowed back home. In just fifteen years the Americans had built the largest network of railroads in the world. "This country is completely cut up with Railroad Tracks, Telegraphs, Canals," Andrew Carnegie wrote home to a cousin in Scotland. "Everything around us is in motion."

The first motorists banded together to mark routes and to lobby for good roads. State highway departments were established; the first traffic signs and signals were designed. The road as we know it began to take shape. The first *Manual on Uniform Traffic Code Devices* appeared in 1935 as a mimeographed booklet. (Today it's more than 750 pages.) The federal government tentatively entered the road-building business in the 1920s and took the lead with President Eisenhower's massive interstate highway program starting in 1956, the largest public works project in history. The "pursuit of happiness," as it turns out, requires a lot of driving.

We have a few programs now to build sidewalks, but we also need paths. We love soft surfaces, but the life of the "soft" in the era of legislation and liability is endangered. We love the fall and rise of the hoof-made, foot-made roads. When we lose the swoops and dips, we're a little farther from the earth. We lose that quality of intimate adjustment, step by step, foot to earth, year after year. We need a Good Paths movement.

∼

From the *Maryland State Highway Administration Bicycle and Pedestrian Design Guidelines*, Chapter 9, Section 9.2, Meandering Sidewalks: "Meandering sidewalks (sidewalks that weave back and forth within the right-of-way) are generally discouraged. While they may seem visually interesting, pedestrians prefer a direct, non-circuitous route."

～

The word "path" occurs about seventy-five times in the *Manual on Uniform Traffic Control Devices*, but never referring to a meandering dirt walk. It occurs in phrases such as "path of conflicting vehicles," and "road users' path." *The Highway Capacity Manual* is about a world far removed from the foot and hoof (though it does treat bicycles as their own category of traffic flow management). There are no prescriptions or rules for building or restoring or maintaining a "cow path."

Our planning committee looked around, visiting other small towns that were restoring their Main Streets. We saw green commons cut through with black rivers of asphalt. We saw wide cement sidewalks out of proportion to the old houses, as if the sidewalks had been airlifted in from a city. And we did see some hopeful signs, towns that used brick and granite pavers, and towns that had used crushed stone, but neither was appropriate for a country village in our part of New Hampshire. Laying down a brick walk in our village would be like playing dress up.

The traffic engineers we had hired knew their surveying and their designs for road drainage, but when we talked about how people in town wanted us to preserve the paths, they were at a loss. (When we showed our engineer our design to break up a small run of granite curbing with grass, he was upset. "Other engineers are going to see this," he said.) Their best practice told them to construct walks at least three feet wide to accommodate wheelchairs under the Americans with Disabilities Act (ADA) and five or six feet wide so two people can walk side by side. In most settings this was sensible advice. The ADA is an important law, if one that can be hard on historic buildings. I have sometimes heard it derided as something required for *them*. But it's for all of us. We're all TABs—temporarily able bodied, an expression I learned from two disabled friends who are activists for disability rights.

Not only did people in our town want to keep the old paths, they wanted one of them cleared in winter. In the past, the paths were left to slumber under the snow and we all walked in the street. There was getting to be too much traffic for that now. We needed a surface to stand up to a snowblower, and one that wouldn't puddle or ice over. We were left on our own to keep our antique, while satisfying the ADA and the demands of a New England winter.

As the months went by, we realized that we needed something that doesn't exist: preservation engineering. We needed designs and rules that respect the vitality of old landscapes. We needed engineers who could see the wisdom in the mismatching crockery of ordinary paths.

Fortunately our road agent, who is the director of the town's highway department and serves on our committee, is open to new ideas. He trolled the Web looking for solutions. He came up with two prospects. One used a system of support like plastic egg cartons to lock in the gravel, which made a grass lot strong enough to park a fire engine on. Or so the company's website claimed. It was almost too good to be true, but I wanted to believe. The other prospect was a polymer that had been used with some success by the National Park Service. The gravel is mixed with the polymer to harden the surface. The path looks old, but it is a fake, a new old path. The old soft path would be wearing a coat of armor. Better living through chemistry.

We took the idea to the town for a vote. At Town Meeting, the voters approved building a section of walk, one hundred feet long, to test out the two hybrid surfaces. We were now preservation engineers.

～

Is building a hard/soft, new/old path a good thing? I don't know. What we had engineered was better than paving the path into oblivion, and it does represent the conflicting wishes of my neighbors in town.

They loved the country spirit of the village, the "ragged edges" where the grass was worn into dirt. Don't make the town too cute, too pretty, they said. Don't tart it up like so many made-over towns that strut their stuff for tourists. But the facts on the ground were, once again, contradictory. We pledge allegiance to the softer qualities of a rural landscape, but we want speed and equality of access. We want to get in our cars and go like hell. We want to buy the same bag of chips anywhere. We want anything we desire shipped to us overnight. This opens the books of regulations and mandates, the approved, standardized designs. Our bag of chips comes attached to an ugly landscape of signs and signals, turn lanes, asphalt and cement.

Sprawl is planned. Calling it sprawl lets us off the hook, as if sprawl, like

a hurricane, was beyond our control. But it took thousands of hours of planning and public meetings to conjure these mistakes. Sprawl is us.

~

On a plan, a cow path isn't much. It's one line among many lines. Night after
night, we studied the plan of Main Street rolled out on the table before us. The
Sheldon house, built in 1781, the Whitcomb house, built in 1813, are rectangles,
the path is a line crowded into other lines, old maples are circles, and lilacs are
outlined like grounded clouds amid the survey numbers and property lines.
The plan excelled in marking the bounds of property, sorting out who owns
what, the town and state right-of-ways. Divisions and edges showed up much
better than unities.

A "40-Scale" plan, in which one inch equals forty feet, is a way of seeing
the world. It is a tool, and like all tools it transforms what it touches. A door
built with a hand plane is different than a door built with a machine planer. A
plan makes it easy to move around lines, sketch a change at the corner of the
common. But what you can't see is how plucking this line here affects all the
lines in the little flat-earth kingdom that you rule. Even two or three "little
changes" knock into each other like pool balls until *clack-clack-clack*—you
are someplace else. Unintended consequences. You are on your way to making one million mistakes. That's how many mistakes are possible, says architect Christopher Alexander.

Each line on a plan represents a choice. "Each element has the possibility of being wrong," says Alexander. Designing a house, an architect is faced
with about five thousand important decisions, he says. Siting the house presents another set of important decisions. In a planned community of just 150
houses he estimates that there are one thousand decisions to be made about
locating the houses. Multiply the five thousand possible mistakes per house
by 150 houses and add the site-plan mistakes and there are "one million total
possible mistakes." "Unfortunately this is not fanciful," says Alexander, "but
a fact about the way we design and build our houses today."

"A window sill may be just right to put things on—or it may be too small.
A window may look at a favorite tree, or it may be placed to look at a wall,"
he writes. "The light in a room may be placed to create a comfortable atmos-

phere at night, small pools of light in just the right places, or it may be merely a light fixture wherever the builder put it. . . . A stair post is either just in the place where your hand comes down as you walk down the stair or not." An inviting small front porch is a good example. "It is full of subtle adaptations: the seat up on the right, the railing on the left . . . the boards on the deck, the arched opening framing the trees beyond, and the special choice of paint color giving the trees their special luster." Each of these choices "makes life more worthwhile, more practical, without disturbing the harmonious character of the place."

The same is true for the path. It, too, is "full of subtle adaptations"; it is different at each point, shouldering close to the old houses, a few steps from the porch of the inn, accompanied by white-picket fences, narrowing to a follow-the-leader path, widening to a cement sidewalk in front of the café and market. Each spot is unique. If we take our eyes off the path and look around, we can begin see what a path really is. A path lives in its relationship to everything it passes. A path is not one thing, but a relationship among things. It is a pattern, says Alexander.

Patterns are key to understanding what is ailing our landscape. There is an order, a language, for the way a good street is created. There are recognizable parts that make up a good village townscape. Each part—a fence, a lilac, a walkway, a wall, a front door, a roof—each part works with the other parts to create a place that could only be that place in the whole world.

This is the brilliant insight of Alexander's amazing book, *A Pattern Language*. You may have seen it around—it's a yellow brick of a book that presents 253 patterns. There are large patterns for country towns, neighborhood boundaries, and ring roads. And smaller patterns for street cafés, pedestrian streets, porches, fruit trees, compost, alcoves, fireplaces, children's secret play-spaces, dancing in the street. This book can be read in any order—just as a walk across a city or town can take you many places. And it can be read as a long poem in praise of the delights of ordinary places. It's a stirring book, and like a first encounter with Bach, it opens a view to a better self, a better place. Alexander makes you feel like you can go out and build something beautiful.

A Pattern Language shows us that the relationships between things matter—and that there are no things, really, but relationships. There isn't a chair, but the relationship of the parts that make up a chair. There isn't a house, but a series of patterns—a pattern language that creates a house. And that house is a part of other patterns creating a yard, a street, a village.

We are misled by the English language's preference for nouns: chair, house, tree. Instead see these things as relationships, as patterns, Alexander says. Scientists will tell you that there is no such thing as an atom—an atom is the relationship of all of the protons, neutrons and electrons spinning around, a cloud of subatomic particles attracting and repulsing each other.

Think of a dinner party. When you invite your guests, you're thinking that they might like one another. The party—the talk and good spirit—arise from the relationships, from the way people interact. The party is created by the people there. The same goes for a congregation praying, for any group thinking or discussing. There is no Town Meeting—an unchanging object taken out of the closet each year. It is created anew, a tradition rekindled, by the people present, by what takes place as we all spin in our orbits around each other.

There is great power in understanding patterns. It was not just a path we were seeking to preserve, but the pattern that makes up the village. It's the language of the village.

In places that have yet to surrender to the automobile, village life is still vibrant. Alexander talks about a group of men he saw passing the time, happily talking, on a street in Guadeloupe. "The houses are rudimentary, the road is roughly paved, two of the men are barefoot." Yet for "all its poverty, which is certainly real," this small street is a beautiful, living space. "The road goes just where it is needed. It interferes little with the land. . . . The ordinary old porch, steps, windows, and doors—how pleasant the way they sit with the street. One man sits happily, half on his side, comfortable, looking at his friend, and leaning on the ground. The trees, the columns, the deck chair, the tree branches have all happened step by step. . . . Buildings and plants, even the people with them, have unfolded together, making something comfortable, ordinary, and profound." The Caribbean neighborhood had slowly evolved. It had "unfolded" as a flower unfolds—each pattern giving rise to the next.

We love places that have tenaciously held on to their identity. "When we visit traditional towns and villages, we love them very often, because each part is recognizable. Each house, door, curtain, garden gate, seems a unique being, specific to its place and time, unique in all the world."

But, Alexander says, the world we have built has laid siege to the special quali-ties of unique places. "I believe that, at root, this is one of the most profound reasons why people of the 20th Century began to feel alienated and despairing. Deep in our hearts, I suspect we know that every situation is unique, each person, each moment, and therefore each place, must be unique. To live in a world which denies this truth, by creating an appearance of sameness . . . is degrading and impossible to bear."

We don't build villages anymore. You can't follow the zoning code, the traffic code, and build villages. Our landscape is a direct report of our hyper-individualism. We build the trophy house on the big lot, the big box store on the bigger lot, the condo tower, office skyscraper by the Big Name architect on its own superblock, or build it so it shoulders aside and extinguishes the old neighborhood.

But great places—the places where we want to live, the places we visit—are built of relationships between small and large buildings, public and private, square and street, old and new. They are ensemble acts; they are dialogues—sometimes raucous arguments, sometimes a mix of comic and tragic, jesting and pathos, eros and piety, sometimes a chorus of well-trained voices. But always there is life there.

In his lament for a rapidly modernizing Japan in the 1930s, Junichiro Ta-nizaki wrote: "We find beauty not in the thing itself, but in the patterns of shadows, the light and darkness that one thing against another creates."

We're not putting one thing against another. Our landscape of isolated buildings in acres of parking is a physical manifestation of our civic lifeless-ness. We're not creating patterns. We're pattern dead. We build singularities.

"No pattern is an isolated entity," writes Alexander. "Each pattern can ex-ist in the world, only to the extent that is supported by other patterns: the larger patterns in which it is embedded, the patterns of the same size that sur-round it, and the smaller patterns which are embedded in it.

"This is a fundamental view of the world," he writes. "It says that when you build a thing you cannot merely build that thing in isolation, but must repair the world around it, and within it, so that the larger world at that one place becomes more coherent, and more whole."

~

Our test of the walkway surfaces worked. We selected one of the hybrid surfaces, went several more rounds with engineers fending off asphalt, and built
our path. With great care the construction crew followed the old crooked route.
It lacked the rude interruption of new construction; it looked wobbly, like it
had been there for years. And the first day people were walking on it. This is
just one small thing—one pattern that upholds other patterns, one small thing
that makes life better.

Our longing for the old "soft" landscape is more than nostalgia. We have
a hunger for the older values because they are closer to the earth. We bend
toward this as a plant to light. We want to live in houses and towns that are
"comfortable, ordinary and profound." An old worn path can be a lifeline
thrown to us in the shipwreck of planning manuals, zoning codes, traffic engineers, and planning committees. But this is the era of the seven-second pedestrian. We hurry along, not stopping to ask ourselves: Why do we engineer
our own exile, banishing the things we love?

DWELLING IN DESTRUCTION

In its buildings, pictures and stories, mankind is preparing to outlive culture, if it need be.

❧ Walter Benjamin, *Experience and Poverty*, 1933

❧ The Hut on Fire ❧

The first thing I ever built may have been a shelter in the woods. It was a bower of branches. There were several trees at the edge of a field. We played there often. Between the fields of corn and our neighborhood there was a line of trees and a path that ran through them. This may have been only a string of trees, a margin of land, but on a summer's day, growing up, it was the world.

At one place the path opened up into a room-sized space, sheltered by two or three old trees with sweeping branches that draped to the ground. It was a natural house. I wish I knew what those trees were. They may have been beech.

One day without discussion or planning, as I recall, my friends and I began to finish the room, complete the shelter. We added branches to the branches. Form suggested form. By laying up branches, we easily enclosed the room. We were building a bower, recapitulating early human history, perhaps. We knew none of that. We were boys, maybe nine, ten, eleven, I don't recall. We no doubt called it a fort.

It was fun building this place, our secret place, and of course we got in trouble. A neighbor made us take it down. He said that it was a fire hazard or a threat to national security or someone would lose an eye; again, I don't recall.

I had not thought of that bower in almost forty years, but reading of an architect's pleasure in building a hut where she found solace, there it was, the memory of that bower. Gaston Bachelard says that childhood memories are eternal, a primitive immensity that never leaves us. And somewhere with me, packed away, as I traveled and moved from house to house, was that first shelter.

We always have the primitive hut with us. It's where we began, says architectural historian Joseph Rykwert. For many architects, the hut is a "perfect house," a survivor from before recorded history. The first hut is the ideal; it measures an architect's sophisticated work and finds it lacking in truth and in "necessity." Rousseau and many others imagine the first hut as being of nature, having an elusive rightness. It just is. There is no groping after style, no ego, status, or fashion.

The founding ur-myth in architecture is that our shelters arose out of the meeting of four trees. The nineteenth-century French architect Eugene Viollet-le-Duc, in a popular work, thought that the first hut was built by bending down branches and tying them with rushes to make a roof. From the tree comes the column, the story goes, and from there, after a stop at wooden post-and-beam construction, the Greek temple.

This is just speculation. Elizabeth Marshall Thomas says she's seen the origins. Thomas and her family first lived among the Kalahari Bushmen, or San, in 1950. Over the next fifty years she would witness the sunset of an ancient life that she calls "the Old Way."

The first shelter may have been like the nests built by our next of kin, the great apes and the chimpanzees, says Thomas. In Africa, when our ancestors faced a changing landscape as the rain forest gave way to open woodlands and later the open savanna, the first shelters they set up were like these nests, a "half-dome shelter of grass and branches."

"The people we knew in the 1950s used such structures wherever they camped. A woman would break branches from a bush, set these in the ground, weave the tops together into a basket-like frame, a half dome, and cover it with handfuls of grass...."

"Could such a custom continue for so long?" asks Thomas. That's a question only we would ask, she says. We are accustomed to rapid change, but our rainforest relatives stuck to what they knew because it insured their survival.

We are a long way from living in huts, but we hold on to them. We still build huts at festivals, like Succoth, the Jewish harvest celebration. Huts survive in children's play as treehouses and dollhouses, and in adult play as small cabins at the lake or in the woods, or on the frozen lake as bob houses for ice fishing. "They incarnate some shadow or memory of that perfect building which was before time began; when man was quite at home in his house, and his house was as right as nature itself," says Rykwert.

When Thomas first met the Bushmen, their shelters were, to her eyes, invisible. "And I treasure the memory of not noticing the little nest shelter—the *tshu*, as it was called—but only the small bag hanging from it, as if suspended in the air. This is what the Old Way looked like. Bushes and grass."

~

I built other things as a kid. I was an avid Lincoln Log builder and usually had a house tucked behind the couch in a corner. I can still remember those few pieces that our dog had chewed and how the red plastic chimney in the newer of the Lincoln Log sets never seemed right atop the fading green flat roof pieces and the round logs.

I also built an entire world's fair in our basement. My father was "finishing" our basement, but work had stalled at the two-by-fours and never resumed. There was all sorts of lumber and scraps around. My world's fair had pavilions made out of scrap two-by-four blocks, roller skates, plastic bowling pins, and other cast-off items. It wasn't that removed from the real thing, which we had visited, the 1964-65 World's Fair with its Ferris wheel as an eight-story Uniroyal white-wall tire, and other toy-like buildings that were far from sober.

In the Ford pavilion I was at the wheel of the company's brand-new car, the Mustang, as we traveled through time on the "Magic Skyway," past dinosaurs and on to the golden future. At General Electric's "Carousel of Progress," we watched the years spin by as life got easier and easier for the "Audio-Animatronic" mannequins on stage. When they sang "It's a Great Big Beautiful Tomorrow," who could argue?

～

At the same time as we were building our little forest shelter, there were burning huts on television. The United States was burning down homes in another country. The specific report was filmed by Morley Safer in August 1965 for CBS news. It's one of the iconic images of that war: the Marine—your kid, the neighbor's kid, a good kid—lighting a hut's grass roof aflame with his Zippo cigarette lighter. And as their village burns around them, the women are crying, the children are crying.

Everyone knows this scene, even if they haven't seen this report. If you wanted to stage photos to show the brutality of war, you couldn't top the photos out of Vietnam: the man standing with a pistol held to his head, at the moment of his execution; the girl, naked, on fire, napalmed, running down the road; the murdered villagers lying in the road of My Lai; the soldier with the Zippo lighter torching a hut.

The report opens with a soldier holding his hand up to the grass roof of a hut. He has a cigarette lighter. The roof catches fire. In the next scene, Safer walks into the picture. "This is what the war in Vietnam is all about," he says.

Behind him, a thin old man in front of a burning hut is pleading. "The Marines burned this old couple's cottage because fire was coming from here," Safer says. It first appeared that snipers were shooting from this hamlet. (The Marines' only injury that day was from "friendly fire.") We see two women trying to save their hut, poking at the flames with a long pole.

Safer asks a prone Marine if he has burned any huts. No, he says respectfully. He was down the line. Was he taking fire? "Somewhat, not too much," he answers.

The Marines "had orders to go in and level the string of hamlets that surround Cam Ne village," says Safer. "And all around the common paddy fields a ring of fire." A flame thrower lights up a roof. "One hundred and fifty homes were leveled in retaliation for a burst of gunfire." Soldiers stand by, watching the houses burn.

"In Vietnam, like everywhere else in Asia, property, a home, is everything. A man lives with his family on ancestral land. His parents are buried nearby. These spirits are part of his holdings," says Safer. If there were Viet Cong in the hamlet, they were long gone, he says. We see women and children huddled together, sitting on the ground. We are looking down at them. They are crying. "The women and old men left here will never forget that August afternoon," Safer says.

He faces the camera to close his report:

"The day's operation burned down one hundred fifty houses, wounded three women, killed one baby, wounded one Marine, and netted these four prisoners. Four old men who couldn't answer questions put to them in English. Four old men who had no idea what an I.D. card was. Today's operation is the frustration of Vietnam in miniature. There is little doubt that American firepower can win a military victory here. But to a Vietnamese peasant whose home means a lifetime of backbreaking labor, it will take more than presidential promises to convince him that we are on his side. Morley Safer, CBS News, near the village of Cam Ne."

Three minutes of television, in black and white, that no one has ever forgotten.

$\sim$

Safer was thirty-five years old. He had reported other wars, and he had been in Vietnam seven months. He thought he had been chosen to open CBS's Saigon bureau because no one expected the Marines to be in Vietnam for long. The escalation of the war was just beginning—the Marines had been there only five months.

A young officer told him that they were going to "take out a complex of villages." "I'd never heard anything like that," said Safer. "I'd heard of search-and-destroy operations; I'd seen places ravaged by artillery or by air strikes. . . . He said to 'take out' this complex of villages. And I thought perhaps he's exaggerating.

"They moved into the village and they systematically began torching every house—every house as far as I could see, getting people out in some cases, using flame throwers in others," Safer recalled. "No Vietnamese speakers, by the way, were among the group with the flame thrower. The trooper with the flame thrower was ordered to zap a particular house, and our cameraman, who's Vietnamese—Ha Thuc Can, this wonderful man—put his camera down and said, 'Don't do it! Don't do it!' And he walked to the house and then I went with him, and a sergeant came on up. We heard people crying.

"Now, every Vietnamese house had a shelter of some kind. Often it was an underground dugout to store rice. There was a family down there, probably six people, including a practically newborn baby. They were frightened stiff. I coaxed; they didn't want to come out. Ha Thuc Can spoke softly to them, and he coaxed them out. The house was torched, as every house along the way was torched, either by flame throwers, matches, or cigarette lighters—Zippos. Those guys, by the way, called themselves 'the Zippo Brigade.' . . .

"Cam Ne was a shock, I think," Safer said. He was truly shocked by what he had witnessed, as were the CBS executives back in New York when they first reviewed the film. "This conjured up not America, but some brutal power—Germany, even, in World War II," said Safer. "To see young G.I.s, big guys in flak jackets, lighting up thatched roofs, and women holding babies running away, wailing—this was a new sight to everyone, including the military, I suspect. Which is perhaps one reason why there was such immediate denial." "Cam Ne" has become shorthand for why the U.S. military distrusts the media and restricts war coverage.

"It was the end of a certain kind of innocence among the public, really,"

Safer said. "So it had a really profound effect." Here's your war, America, here's your tax dollars at work.

When Safer's report appeared on the evening news, in each time zone a new wave of angry viewers called CBS, many of them swearing. *How dare CBS show our boys doing things like that? Our boys don't do that.* If you had missed the evening news, the next morning's newspapers ran an AP photo of a Marine lighting a hut afire with a Zippo lighter. That morning, President Lyndon Johnson called his friend Frank Stanton, the president of CBS. David Halberstam reported what happened in *The Powers That Be*:

"'Frank,' said the early-morning wake-up call, 'are you trying to fuck me?'

"'Who is this?' said the still sleepy Stanton.

"'Frank, this is your president, and yesterday your boys shat on the American flag.'" Johnson had Safer investigated; he was sure that he was a Communist. When Johnson was told that, no, Safer wasn't a Communist, he was a Canadian, the president said, "Well, I knew he wasn't an American." Johnson was also convinced that Safer had bribed a Marine to burn down the hut. The Marine Corps Washington headquarters said that Safer had faked the whole thing, but then backed away from that story. The Pentagon public relations office tried to ruin Safer's reputation, get him recalled, and get the Vietnamese cameraman, who had saved a half-dozen lives, fired. Around CBS it was known that Stanton wanted to fire Safer. In Vietnam, Safer carried a pistol because he had been told that there might be "a little accident."

∾

A burning hut is war reduced to its essential brutality. Burning down a house is a transgression. It's an obvious sin, even if few ministers had the courage to call it that on any given Sunday in the 1960s. This grim scene is one we know is wrong—no argument, no statistics are needed. Even at this distance, more than forty years later, to read this letter home from a soldier is to be kicked in the gut:

> Dear Mom and Dad:
> Today we went on a mission and I am not very proud of myself, my friends, or my country. We burned every hut in sight!

It was a small rural network of villages and the people were incredibly poor. My unit burned and plundered their meager possessions. Let me try to explain the situation to you.

The huts here are thatched palm leaves. Each one has a dried mud bunker inside. These bunkers are to protect the families. Kind of like air raid shelters. My unit commanders, however, chose to think that these bunkers are offensive. So every hut we find that has a bunker we are ordered to burn to the ground.

When the ten helicopters landed this morning, in the midst of these huts, and six men jumped out of each "chopper," we were firing the moment we hit the ground. We fired into all the huts we could. . . .

It is then that we burned these huts. . . . Everyone is crying, begging and praying that we don't separate them and take their husbands and fathers, sons and grandfathers. The women wail and moan.

Then they watch in terror as we burn their homes, personal possessions and food. Yes, we burn all rice and shoot all livestock.

~

The burning hut was nowhere in mind at the World's Fair. The World's Fair was a festival of technology worship. This attitude wasn't much questioned. Some critics thought that Ferris-wheel tire was notably crass, and that the fair lacked the magic of the previous landmark in technology worship, the 1939 World's Fair. At GM's Futurama II, six scenes showed how the "machines of tomorrow" would "clear the way for man to enter, exist within and develop lands which lie unused today."

One scene showed a monster road-building machine that devoured the jungle and spat out a road, a Frankenstein born of the American love of roads. The road-builder would be eighty feet tall, as long as three football fields, and powered by an on-board nuclear reactor. It would be "capable of producing from within itself one mile of four-lane, elevated superhighway every hour," said a GM press release. "The road builder is indeed a factory on wheels. Fully-automated, it levels the ground, sets stanchions, casts and places the road-surface slabs and links each unit into the highway which emerges in its wake." To prepare the way, laser beams would "saw off the age-old trees at their base" and chemical defoliants would finish the job.

"The roadway goes where it can serve most effectively. It also provides an outlet for the jungle's products—its lumber, its minerals and chemicals. . . . The road-builder brings more than a highway to the jungle; it brings progress and prosperity as well." This proved to be an eerie forecast of the war against the earth in Vietnam, the jungle we poisoned with Agent Orange, burned, and bulldozed. As the soldiers said, "Only you can prevent forests." Futurama reveals the American capacity for vast destruction delivered by pragmatically engineered overkill.

~

The hut is still on fire. The power of the report from Cam Ne is proved by the intense debate that is still going on more than forty years later.

The vehement denials of that one image are all over the Internet: It didn't happen. It was staged. It did happen, but that's not the whole story—it was necessary. We had to burn down the villages to save the villages. But all over the Internet are the veterans' letters and recollections: We burned the huts; that's why everyone had Zippos. The soldiers were haunted by what they were doing. The country was haunted by the image of the burning hut.

In particular, there are three lines of dismissal. One: It was all made up. Safer gave those boys the Zippo lighters. He staged the whole thing.

Since the war, these "Zippo Raids" have been widely reported. Army criminal investigators have documented seven massacres of Vietnamese and Cambodian civilians by U.S. soldiers, in addition to the 1968 My Lai massacre. "My Lai was a shock to everyone except people in Vietnam," says Kevin Buckley, who covered the war for *Newsweek* from 1968 to 1972. He reported on operation "Speedy Express," in which nearly eleven thousand were killed but only 748 weapons were recovered.

In 2003 *The Toledo Blade* uncovered "the longest series of atrocities in the Vietnam War." "For seven months, the elite Tiger Force soldiers moved across the Central Highlands, killing scores of unarmed civilians—in some cases torturing and mutilating them—in a spate of violence never revealed to the American public," the *Blade* said. In one valley, Tiger Force spent two months burning down villages. "If you wanted to burn a village down, you burned it down. . . . Who's going to say anything to you?" said William Doyle, a soldier. Army investigators had urged him not to report war crimes.

The Blade won a Pulitzer Prize for its report, which was otherwise almost universally ignored. Historian Nick Turse, who has studied the nine thousand-page declassified (and now closed to the public) archives of Pentagon investigators, says, "Unfortunately, this seven month atrocity-spree is not nearly the longest on record. Nor is it even the longest string of atrocities by one unit within its service branch."

The second line of dismissal: This *image* lost the war. It was treason to show Americans their boys burning people out of their homes. This view asserts that CBS showed this report over and over. It didn't. Television wasn't a twenty-four-hour loop back then. The image lingers because it was powerful. People saw it and they knew that it was wrong. It spoke directly to their conscience. Scholars who have watched every frame of the network TV reporting from 1965 to 1967 say that the report from Cam Ne was the exception. Reports questioning what the authorities said were rare. TV and the press held to the official story that we were fighting the Reds there so we didn't have to fight them in San Francisco. (It was always San Francisco and never Los Angeles, Portland, or Seattle.) The media wanted to support the war and this is what they did most of the war, says media scholar Daniel C. Hallin. The myth is that the war was lost on the nightly news.

And finally, there is the view that says this is just war-as-usual. It isn't good manners, but it's no big deal. During the 2004 presidential election, John Kerry's famous 1971 Senate testimony about burning villages was much debated. One conservative commentator, Mona Charen, said, "Still, burning down someone's straw hut, while not exactly polite, is far from the sort of war crime Kerry had conjured in his Senate testimony." I'm sure she'd have a different view if it were her hut—or even her garden shed—on fire.

And note: It *is* a war crime. The Fourth Geneva Convention, enacted in 1949, prohibits the destruction of personal property by an occupying power. The Convention also forbids the use of collective punishment. However, international law hedges, allowing destruction that is required by "military necessity."

～

But all this talk takes us away from the hut on fire. Look at it again. One film archive summarizes a few minutes of film: "Soldiers walk past burning hut.

Soldier throws grenade into tunnel in village. Soldiers enter damaged village; pass burning hut. Vietnamese woman and children in foreground. Burning hut. Soldiers stand in foreground. Close-up hot, sweating soldiers walking in the sand. Soldiers setting fire to huts. Long shot huts burning. Soldiers resting before moving out. Officer speaks on radio. Long shot UH-1B copter attacking enemy positions. Hut burning as soldiers and a tank move past."

It is painful to turn and face the evidence, to stand close to the burning hut. That's our past on fire; it's paradise or the promise of paradise. What's on fire is the Old Way. Huts represent the lost sense of being at home in the world, says Rykwert. "Paradise," he says, "is a promise as well as a memory." So put a Zippo to that, burn down a hut as women and children and old men cry and plead.

In Vietnam we waged a war against the earth. The villagers were dwellers; they were of the earth. We were on the side of technology, of helicopters and Agent Orange and flame throwers. It's as if you were watching humanity extinguishing its older self.

∾

The hut continues to burn. The war against dwellers, which two scholars call "domicide," continues. In 2005, Dr. Annie Sparrow worked for Human Rights Watch in the camps for the refugees from Darfur. When she interviewed parents, she gave crayons and paper to their children.

Leila, age 9, a child of Darfur, made a drawing of her home.

"What is going on here?" she was asked.

Leila replied: "My hut burning after being hit by a bomb."

She had drawn a scene from her village, showing helicopters bombing huts.

❧ Keep The Home Fires Burning ❧

How Houses Were Targeted in War and Resurrected in Peace

I: Bombing Dwelling Thinking

The twentieth century was the century of the burning house. More houses were set afire in war than at any other time in history. Great advances were made in bombing and burning houses. A house could be smashed by high-explosive bombs. It could be set ablaze by various mixes of gasoline, napalm, magnesium, thermite. It could be vaporized by the splitting of an atom, or it could be torched, up close and personal, by one soldier with a Zippo lighter.

In World War II, millions of workers were employed, and billions were spent, to burn down houses.

One raid can stand for many. On the night of June 28 to 29, 1943, Cologne was bombed by the Royal Air Force (RAF). Five hundred forty airplanes dropped 1,614 tons of bombs. It was not the worst attack of the war, nor would it rank high in a listing of that war's horrors: 3,460 people were killed and 400,000 lost their homes. It was just one of the many air raids of the war—on Cologne, on more than fifty other German cities, on a dozen English cities, on more than sixty Japanese cities. On this night it was Cologne, but it was a scene repeated thousands of times, a scene suffered by millions.

Waiting in the cellar as the bombs fell, Cologne's residents listened carefully. "Every bomb had its own peculiar sound. If there was a rustle like a flock of doves flying up, it was a bundle of small stick bombs breaking apart, with each stick finding its own target," wrote Josef Fischer. "If there was a short, sharp explosion, it was a 12-kilogram firebomb, which could spread fire eighty meters in all directions. If it was like a bucket of water splashing in the street, it was a 14-kilogram liquid firebomb, which could spread liquid rubber and benzine fifty meters around the impact area. If it plumped down like a wet sack, it was a fire canister holding twenty liters of benzol, somewhat cruder but as effective as benzine. If it cracked like an explosive bomb as it hit, it was either a 106-kilogram bomb that threw out rags soaked with benzine or heavy oil or a 112-kilogram firebomb, which covered nearby houses with a thousand 'cowcakes' of benzol and rubber. And there were still, of course, the explosive bombs and mines, which tore out the doors and windows to provide air to feed the flames and surpassed the effects of an earthquake, so that those in the cellar thought of themselves as perched in the heart of a volcano."

And after the all-clear sounded, in Cologne, in Coventry and London, in Tokyo and Nagoya, the citizens of the city emerged and did the only thing they could do. They returned to their homes at any cost. "We repair because we must repair, because we couldn't live another day longer if one forbade us the repairing," wrote Ruth Andreas-Friedrich, who worked in the Berlin resistance. "If they destroy our living room, we move into the kitchen. If they knock the kitchen apart, we move over into the hallway. If only we can stay 'at home.' The smallest corner of 'at home' is better than any palace in some strange place. For this reason all who have been driven out of the city by bombs return home someday. They work with shovel and broom, with hammer, pliers and pick-axes. Until one day over the bombed-out foundations a new 'at home' exists. A Robinson-Crusoe lodge perhaps. But it is still 'at home.' The last thing one saves from a burning house is a pillow because it is the last piece of 'at home.'"

Dehousing

The official policy of wartime England in the spring of 1942 was to "dehouse" Germans. Dehousing was the sum of a cost-benefit analysis, the way to achieve the most death for your investment. "The following seems a simple method of estimating what we could do by bombing Germany," said Lord Cherwell, the British government's chief scientific adviser, in a memo to Prime Minister Winston Churchill. His "Dehousing paper" was based on the observations of the damage to English cities. "Careful analysis of the effects of raids on Birmingham, Hull and elsewhere have shown that, on the average, one ton of bombs dropped on a built-up area demolishes 20-40 dwellings and turns 100-200 people out of house and home.

"We know from our experience that we can count on nearly fourteen operational sorties per bomber produced. The average lift of the bombers we are going to produce over the next fifteen months will be about three tons. It follows that each of these bombers will in its life-time drop about 40 tons of bombs. If these are dropped on built-up areas they will make 4000-8000 people homeless."

More than twenty-two million Germans were good candidates for dehousing. They lived in densely populated towns and cities, which made them easier targets. There were fifty-eight cities with more than one hundred thousand people "which, with modern equipment, should be easy to find and hit." The British were building ten thousand heavy bombers. "If even half the total load of 10,000 bombers were dropped on the built-up areas of these fifty-eight German towns the great majority of their inhabitants (about one-third of the German population) would be turned out of house and home. Investigation seems to show that having one's home demolished is most damaging to morale. People seem to mind it more than having their friends or even relatives killed. . . . On the above figures we should be able to do ten times as much harm to each of the fifty-eight principal German towns. There seems little doubt that this would break the spirit of the people."

The math was disputed, the policy debated and finally adopted by the cabinet. The RAF had failed at "precision bombing." The RAF was having trouble hitting factories. Only 10 percent of the bombers raiding the industrial Ruhr region were able to drop bombs within five miles of the target. An entire city made for a larger target; the working-class neighborhoods would be at the bull's-eye. The RAF adopted a new policy of "area bombing."

In speeches, officials always emphasized the military targets in the cities, maintaining a window dressing of waging a just war justly. Bombing civilians had been taboo. The "ruthless bombing" of "defenseless men, women and children has sickened the hearts of every civilized man and woman, and has profoundly shocked the conscience of humanity," President Franklin Delano Roosevelt said in 1939. When the Americans entered the war, they were committed to a policy of bombing only factories and military targets, but that would change. At the war's start, the English had limited their air raids; a weak RAF was under orders not to attack targets on mainland Europe. The Germans struck first, bombing Warsaw, Rotterdam, and then, accidentally, London in 1940. The next night, the RAF was sent to bomb Berlin.

Dehousing was a euphemism, says one historian. Dehousing is a policy of targeting civilians, of bombing cities and laying waste to houses, churches, museums, schools—the entire culture of a place—until the place itself is erased. Destroying your neighbor's dwelling is at the center of war.

Building Better Fires

The firebomb was the weapon of dehousing. The small four- and six-pound incendiary bombs were the most devastating weapon of the war. Four-fifths of the damage in English and German cities was from fires. In Japan the toll from fire was more than 90 percent. The incendiary bomb, more than the high-explosive bomb or the atomic bomb, put people out of their houses. It was designed to fall into the roof or top floor and start a fire that would burn downward. Even masonry buildings had timber roof supports and floors. Incendiaries were particularly effective for burning down churches, lodging in the large attics to burn undetected. The English public was encouraged to move the small bombs. During the London Blitz volunteers had shoveled incendiaries off the wooden dome of St. Paul's Cathedral. Explosive incendiaries were also in the mix, but this was little publicized.

It was a small bomb, dropped by the ton, and it played an unexpected role in the war.

$\sim$

Wars bring surprising reversals. In World War II, fire protection engineers—professionals dedicated to the science of fire prevention—became partisans of fire from the air. They became advocates of spreading fires. They studied bombing reports from the Army Air Force and the Royal Air Force, worked with chemists to design new bombs, and tested them on sections of buildings and later on "doom towns"—towns built to burn.

The early incendiary air raids were "haphazard," the engineers said. To make big fires, they said, the American and British air forces needed the experts who had studied fires. The fire engineers should be planning the targets, they said, calling to mind the reoccurring figure of the fireman turned arsonist.

The fire engineers were propagandists for fire. They eagerly sold their wartime product—death by fire—to the military. Firebombs were "humdingers," the chief engineer of the National Fire Protection Association told one Army Air Force colonel. At the war's start, the military, here and in Britain, was developing high-explosive bombs. In the U.S., the Chemical Warfare Service was in charge of incendiary bombs, but had assigned only two soldiers and six civilians, part-time, to the task. The Chemical Warfare Service was "preoccupied" with the dangers of a gas attack, as was anyone who remembered the mustard gas of World War I. A gas attack on London or Paris was one of the nightmare scenarios that haunted the public in the years between the wars.

Fire as a weapon had been set aside with the introduction of gunpowder in the fourteenth century. The ancient Assyrians had used pitch, probably petroleum seepages from what are now Iraq's oil fields. The Byzantines had defended Constantinople for centuries with "Greek Fire," a secret composition (which was eventually revealed to be pitch, sulfur, quicklime, and naphtha). A few oil bombs were tried in World War I, but they produced disappointing smoldering fires that could be extinguished. At the end of that war, the German air force was preparing to firebomb London and Paris, but the kaiser forbade the attack, knowing that the war was lost and Germany would have to sue for peace. At the start of World War II, Japan dropped phosphorous bombs on Chungking. Phosphorous burns with enough heat to ignite straw, paper, and dry grass—and thus much of Chungking—but it cannot burn wood or other combustibles.

Phosphorus could also be dropped from airplanes as wet sheets of guncotton or nitrocellulose, a flutter of papers floating down from the sky. Once the sheets dried out, they caught fire. The phosphorus sheets were sometimes disguised as ordinary printed material. "These 'letters' or 'visiting cards' are exceedingly dangerous, since they may be picked up and carried about innocently by persons—especially children, who may be attracted by the color or printing on them—and taken into buildings where they may start serious fires," said Columbia chemistry professor J. Enrique Zanetti in a lecture to "fire specialists" early in the war, before the U.S. was involved. "Since they weigh much less than an ounce, tens of thousands may be carried by a plane and widely distributed over forests, farm lands, and factory districts with practical certainty that at least some will fall on combustible material."

Zanetti's main task was to review the chemistry of starting fires and to advocate for the revival of this forgotten weapon. He was working for the Chemical Warfare Service. The chemists wanted a hot fire that spread, a fire arising from stable, light materials, with a low flash point—the temperature at which vapors catch fire. Magnesium was "a very effective incendiary." It was light and strong and burned "fiercely," but it was in short supply in America. Thermite, a mix of metallic aluminum and oxide of iron, produced "a white-hot fluid that flows like water, setting fire to all combustible matter which it comes in contact with and melting brick and cement." It was hard to extinguish once started, but needed various binders to keep it stable. Germany burned London with magnesium-thermite incendiaries and Britain used similar incendiaries to desolate German cities. "Not the least of the dangers of the magnesium-thermite bomb is the silence with which it works. It is impossible to locate until the fire has been set," said Zanetti. In an air raid, with five hundred-pound bombs exploding, and anti-aircraft artillery, the noise of a four-pound bomb "crashing into an attic will hardly be noticeable." As it ignites, it makes only a "hissing sound, audible only a few yards away."

Even without surrounding explosions to mask the sound, the small bombs had a way of arriving unannounced. "One minute a street would be quiet, the next incendiary bombs would be heard plop-plopping all around and seen bursting into flame," said the commander of Britain's wartime fire service, recalling what it was like to fight fires in the midst of an air raid. (The firemen got used to the bombs falling, he said. "There was quite a lot of space where bombs *did not* fall.")

The London Blitz in September 1940 changed the way World War II would be fought. Ton for ton, incendiaries did five times the damage of high-explosive bombs. Watching London burn around the dome of St. Paul's Cathedral, Arthur Harris, who would take command of the RAF's Bomber Command, vowed revenge. "They sowed the wind, and now they are going to reap the whirlwind," Harris said. Out of the ashes rose not the Phoenix, but more ashes. Out of the ashes rose the fury to destroy. "I do not personally regard the whole of the remaining cities of Germany as worth the bones of one British Grenadier," Harris wrote in his journal five years later. By that time he was known to the public as Bomber Harris and to some of his men as Butcher Harris.

The American fire protection engineers were first called to work with the British. The fire engineers studied aerial photos of cities the RAF had bombed. Squinting through a stereo viewer, they mapped what had burned and what had not. They drew red lines around the fires, creating "fire susceptibility maps." The goal was to create a firestorm, a raging hurricane of fire that would consume a city. The "one great dread of the city," said Zanetti, is "the merging of separate fires into a conflagration."

The American military was not interested at first, but as more of Europe burned, serious research began. The Army Air Force set up committees to study how to start a firestorm. How many tons of incendiaries would it take? Should there be explosives in the mix to keep firefighters away or would the explosives blow out the flames? What's the optimal weather for a firestorm? (These were known as "good fire days.") What's the most effective bombing pattern to wipe out a city?

Chemists experimented with mixes of gasoline, magnesium, thermite, phosphorous, and napalm, looking for the right amount of heat and "splatter" to do the most "good," as one said. They worked at Harvard, Brown, University of Chicago, Stanford, and at Kodak, Dupont, Monsanto, Standard Oil, and other companies.

At Harvard, chemist Louis F. Fieser developed a jellied-gasoline bomb "that would scatter large burning globs of sticky gel." The firebomb used rubber to thicken gasoline, but after Pearl Harbor, Japan had control of the rubber plantations. Fieser created a substitute thickener made, in part, with an aluminum soap from coconut oil. (U.S. Patent 2,606,107, Incendiary Gels.) He named this jellied gasoline "napalm."

∼

The fire engineers took aim at the attic, starting fires at various distances from the eaves with six-pound napalm bombs. Once a bomb hit—lying on its side or stuck nose down in the floorboards—it was designed to throw the fuel out over the widest area. A small explosive charge, they found, would throw a sock of flaming fuel about fifty yards until it "struck an obstruction"—a beam, rafter, joist, floorboard, or wall.

The Standard Oil Development Company tested more than twenty thousand bombs to get the most effective design. Using a mortar the company launched the bombs into small mock-ups of "typical enemy domestic and industrial structures." The testing moved on to abandoned farm buildings in Indiana. But since the Germans and Japanese did not live in Indiana farmhouses, Standard Oil built German and Japanese houses in the Utah desert.

The German village was designed with close attention to the details and materials by two noted German architects, the modernist Eric Mendelsohn and Konrad Wachsmann, who had designed a prefabricated wooden summer house for Albert Einstein. The architects re-created six German row houses ("rent barracks"), each two-and-a-half stories, like those found in Berlin's crowded slums. They researched the roof construction, producing three houses with central German clay tile-on-batten roofs and three with the slate-on-sheathing found in the Rhineland. The wooden framing was built with Douglas fir from British Columbia to match the pine and spruce used in Germany. The fir was selected after extensive laboratory testing by the Forest Service, which measured the burn rate of different pine specimens. The wood's moisture content was critical for the firebomb tests. Thirty years of weather data in the *Handbuch der Klimatololgy* was studied to determine the humidity in the average German apartment.

The RKO movie studio's "Authenticity Division" and German-trained craftsmen built the furniture. The correct German linen was used for drapes and bedding. Since incendiaries either lodged in the attic or broke through to the top floor, only the second-floor apartments were furnished. The placement of the furniture was an important factor for testing how the fire would spread from the sofa and easy chair to the side table or the radio cabinet, or in the bedrooms, from the single beds to the baby crib.

The Japanese town was designed by a Czech-born architect, Antonin Raymond. He had spent twenty years in Japan, arriving with Frank Lloyd Wright's crew to build the Imperial Hotel before opening his own office in Tokyo. Raymond was one of the few people in America who knew how Japanese houses were constructed. He overcame his reservations about this commission. "In spite of my love for Japan, I came to the conclusion that the quickest way to terminate this war was to defeat Germany and Japan as quickly and as effectively as possible," he said.

The Japanese houses, twelve double apartments, were built with Sitka spruce as a match for "hinoki," and with Southwest adobe as a match for Japanese mud and plaster. They were roofed with tile over plaster-and-wood sheathing, or with sheet metal on wood sheathing. The houses were furnished with futons, zabutons (sitting mats), and tatami (straw mats). A Standard Oil employee searched the West Coast and the Hawaiian Islands to find tatami and the Navy got the shipment home.

The two villages were built in forty-four days by prisoners from the Utah State Prison. From May to September 1943, the villages were bombed from as high as twenty thousand feet. They were rebuilt many times. The Allies were desperately trying to figure out why Berlin wasn't burning. The RAF would try sixteen times to start a firestorm in the capital of the Reich. The rowhouses from the German village still stand in the desert at the Dugway Proving Ground. After the war they were used in tests of chemical weapons. The Japanese houses were bombed with the amado (sliding shutters) open and closed. They were bombed at day and at night. They burned more readily than the German housing; they no longer survive. The village cost $1 million to build and to rebuild during the tests.

The fires were graded. A: any fire that was beyond control of a good fire brigade within six minutes. B: a fire left to itself that proved destructive. C: a fire that failed to destroy a house. A six-pound napalm bomb, designated the M-69, won out over other bombs, producing A-grade fires in the German village 37 percent of the time, and in the Japanese houses 68 percent of the time. Several times during the tests the little town was almost lost to a small firestorm.

The British had also built doomtowns but their results differed from the Americans'. Eventually it was found that the buildings in the dry desert burned too readily (even though the moisture had been closely monitored), and that conditions at the British doomtowns were too damp. The British edition of a Japanese house was in error, said the architect Raymond. They had been built like temples with large timbers. He could tell that the designer had never been to Japan.

The test bomb, the M-69, was the bomb that would lay waste to Japan. The 6.2-pound bomb had 2.6 pounds of napalm. The M-69 could penetrate three inches of concrete. It was dropped in clusters of thirty-eight bombs.

Ten tons of M-69 bombs, it was estimated, could start two thousand fires in a city, half of them too large to put out without firefighters. And no city is equipped to fight a thousand fires at once. The M-69, said one fire engineer, was "almost in the class of the oft-mentioned 'secret weapon.'"

The doomtowns were voodoo dolls. That's also part of the reversals of war.

Our government builds houses to burn them down, builds them as a school for destruction. It's like sticking needles into your enemy's hearth. It's a reversal that gives new meaning to that sentimental song from World War I, "Keep the Home Fires Burning":

> Keep the home fires burning,
> While your hearts are yearning,
> Though your lads are far away
> They dream of home.

≈

All these committees of scientists and soldiers were about one thing: burning down houses. They would say that they were about winning the war. The usual statement is: if we can end the war one day sooner, it is worth it. ("It" meaning the killing and destruction of a particular mission.)

We don't think of the living room as a military target, but it took the concentrated effort of an international war machine to smash the front parlor, to bring the roof down on the bedrooms. Three thousand miles away from the targeted houses, in rooms the size of football fields, civilians built the bombers—assembling rows of shiny wings and fuselages. The vast scale and repetition of the scene was meant to comfort the "home front." This was the start of the long production line to deliver the bombs, which included the ferrying of the airplanes and oil, supplies, and spare parts across the Atlantic, the thirty or so personnel to prep the airplane, the brave pilot and crew of ten at sixteen thousand feet taking aim at family keepsakes, food in the cupboard, rugs on the floor, linens in the closet. Lord Cherwell's "Dehousing paper" had moved the front line to where the Germans lay their heads down to sleep. It was truly a living-room war.

Imagine the fire protection engineers, the university and corporate chemists, the bomb makers, the colonels and generals on the research and targeting committees discussing your home. Yes, they would say, it's a one-story balloon-framed ranch built in the 1960s. It has a roof of plywood sheets and asphalt shingles. A cluster of six-pound incendiary bombs dropped from five thousand feet should be able to punch through the roof and drop in the attic. It likely has fiberglass insulation, six inches thick, circa 1973, that might hinder our fire, but once started the rest should burn well—hardwood floors, drywall, nylon carpets, much paper, many appliances. The entire dwelling should slump into the cement basement within a half hour to an hour after our attack, depending on the humidity and the wind. It's thirty feet to the houses on each side. Catching the next-door house on fire will depend on the wind...

Yes, you do think of the family in that house, said U.S. Army Air Force General Curtis LeMay, who developed the flying formation to bomb Germany and led the air force against Japan. But you're a soldier; you get on with your business, he said in his autobiography.

"You drop a load of bombs and, if you're cursed with an imagination at all, you have at least one quick horrid glimpse of a child lying in bed with a whole ton of masonry tumbling down on top of him; or a three-year-old girl wailing for *Mutter* ... *Mutter* ... because she has been burned. Then you have to turn away from the picture if you intend to retain your sanity. And also if you intend to keep on doing the work your nation expects of you," said LeMay, who speaks with love about his own daughter in the same autobiography. "But to worry about the *morality* of what we were doing—Nuts. A soldier has to fight.

"And so we in the Eighth Air Force had put down twenty-six thousand tons of high explosives on the city of Berlin," said LeMay. "We had knocked the place down; had battered it, burned it, slain or mutilated many of the inhabitants."

~

In the summer of 1942 the RAF dropped a pamphlet on Germany. It was reportedly the text of a broadcast in German by Arthur Harris, the head of the RAF Bomber Command:

"We are bombing Germany, city by city, and ever more terribly, in order to make it impossible for you to go on with the war. That is our object. We shall pursue it remorselessly. City by city; Lubeck, Rostock, Cologne, Emden, Bremen, Wilhelmshaven, Duisberg, Hamburg—and the list will grow longer and longer. Let the Nazis drag you down to disaster with them if you will. That's for you to decide. . . . We are coming by day and by night. No part of the Reich is safe ... people who work in [factories] live close to them. Therefore we hit your houses, and you."

Hamburg

On the night of July 27, 1943, Air Chief Marshall Harris sent more than seven hundred bombers to attack Hamburg, Germany's second largest city and its largest port. This was the second air raid in a week on that city, but this time it was "a good fire day," hot and dry. In twenty minutes, two out of three buildings were on fire in a four-and-a-half square mile area. Sixteen thousand buildings were burning at one time. Hamburg was consumed in a hurricane of fire— a firestorm. Fresh air raced in to replace the superheated rising air. Winds reached one hundred miles an hour, pushing clouds of sparks, "a blizzard of red snowflakes." The fiery whirlwinds made "a shrill howling in the street," said one survivor. Trees three feet in diameter were uprooted. The flames shot up two-and-a-half miles in the air. As they flew home, the bomber crews could see the fire 120 miles away.

A series of air raids over the next week and a half destroyed half the city. In four raids the RAF dropped more than nine thousand tons of bombs, most of them incendiaries. (There were some high explosives for the terror it produced, and some time-delayed explosives and incendiaries to interfere with firefighters and rescue efforts.) Thirty square miles were damaged and 12.5 square miles were completely burned out. The destruction was equal to two of the atomic bombs dropped on Hiroshima. About three hundred thousand "dwelling units" were lost and 1.25 million people became refugees. Two-thirds of Hamburg's population had been "dehoused." The total number killed is unknown; forty-five thousand corpses were found in the rubble.

Harris took the code name for the attack from one of the biblical cities destroyed by a rain of brimstone and fire—Operation Gomorrah.

≈

This was the first firestorm in history raised by bombing. The Germans and the Allies studied the deaths at Hamburg. How did people die? Did they burn, explode, suffocate? Applying the scientific method to the dead city is also horrific, as if the civilians had died for an experiment, for the advancement of the knowledge of killing. German pathologists conducted twenty thousand to thirty thousand autopsies on the air-raid victims in many cities and, after the war, the Allies studied their reports.

About 70 percent of the dead had been killed by carbon monoxide poisoning. This was unexpected. They were the fortunate ones. In the bomb shelters they were often found in "peaceful positions." There were no signs of struggle. In the streets, people dropped as they ran, desiccated by the great heat, or they burst into flame. They jumped into the city's canals or into bomb craters filling with water from burst pipes and drowned. The heat of some burning city blocks exceeded 1,400 degrees Fahrenheit.

The dead were found in the streets as naked and desiccated mummies, many shrunken to the size of an infant with hard brownish-black skin. This was common enough that the German studies termed these corpses *Bombenbrandschrumpfleichen* ("incendiary-bomb-shrunken bodies"). In shelters these shrunken bodies were "frequently found lying in a thick, greasy black mass," said one post-war report.

In the months after the raids, the smell of rot, of charred household effects and the dead hung over the wasteland. "And this smell was as visible as a dry plaster dust that was blown everywhere," wrote Hans Erich Nossack, a native of Hamburg. Cellars thick with maggots had to be cleared with flamethrowers to retrieve the dead. Fat rats and flies ruled the city. The flies "were large and of a shimmering green; no one had ever seen flies like this. They wallowed in clumps on the pavement," wrote Nossack. "When they could no longer fly, they would crawl after us through the narrowest crevices, soiling everything, and their rustling and buzzing was the first thing one heard in the morning."

~

The language of bombing is official. It's expressed in policy, in cabinet papers, in pronouncements about tonnage, shortening the war, taking the war to the enemy. It's brutal in its abstraction. But the language of loss is intimate—the deaths of children, of friends, the loss of household treasures, the loss of the past.

Three months after the firestorm, Hans Erich Nossack wrote a psychological portrait of mass trauma. He describes a feeling of weightlessness, of incoherence. He talks of not wanting to own much anymore, but missing each domestic object, painfully. It's an interior report in a city that no longer has interiors, in which the private life—the life lived in private rooms—has been extinguished.

It's possible to mourn for "a single house torn from the midst of the living," but how can one mourn the loss of an entire city? Nothing was left, "not the corpse of the city, not something known," Nossack wrote in *The End: Hamburg 1943*. "What surrounded us did not remind us in any way of what was lost. It had nothing to do with it. It was something else, it was strangeness itself, it was essentially not possible."

On the night of the firestorm, Nossack and his wife were staying in a small cottage just outside the city. They watched Hamburg burn and met the first refugees streaming out of the city, some in their nightshirts and barefoot, all of them silent. "It was a river for which there was no bed; almost soundless, but inexorable it flooded everything. . . . None of these people knew they were carrying their restlessness with them like a disease, and everything that was touched by it lost its stability."

Days later he was able to make his way into the city by hitching rides on cars and trucks. When the trains resumed later, they were jammed. "People climbed in through windows and hung on to the sides of trains like grapes. When you finally arrived you were completely exhausted.

"Countless numbers of people traveled like this every day. I have the impression that, by and large, these trips were by no means necessary, be it to salvage something or to go on a search for relatives, or for business reasons. But neither would I claim that it was mere curiosity. People were simply without a center; the roots were torn out and swayed back and forth in search of some soil. . . "

Was this rubble Hamburg? That's what people wanted to know. As long as they stayed and wandered, they might meet up with a vanished piece of their city and their home—a surviving friend, a piece of the good china. If they left, home was lost. They would be refugees. They would belong nowhere, have no claim; they would be strangers in their own country. "The pain of tearing oneself loose can hardly be described," he wrote.

On an another journey into Hamburg, this time on an overcrowded bus, Nossack saw everyone straining to recognize something of the vanished city in the "silent plain . . . stretched to infinity. . . . Only during the brief crossing of the Elbe bridge was the spell lifted for a moment, while everyone began to count the towers of the city. Oh, and with what affectionate nicknames they were summoned, one by one! And where was the most beautiful of them all, the tower of Saint Catherine's Church?" (It had caved in.) But they were quickly over the bridge and into the strange "cemetery" that had replaced Hamburg.

Nossack couldn't recognize places that he once knew. He couldn't tell where streets and buildings had stood. "Each time one emerged again from the haze of the city, it was like coming to after having fainted."

"It must have looked as if we had a lot of time," he wrote, but "we no longer had any time at all, we were outside of time. Everything we did immediately lost its meaning." They had no past, he said. They felt this loss "painfully" when they came across people who still had a past, an ordinary present, and plans for the future. Walking through the ruins with his wife, "we saw inside a house that stood alone and intact in the midst of a vast expanse of rubble a woman cleaning her windows. We nudged each other. We stood as if spellbound. We thought this was a mad-woman. . . . And one afternoon we arrived at a completely undestroyed suburb. People were sitting on their balconies drinking coffee." Didn't they know that the world had ended?

He and his wife had lost everything. He was "crushed" by the weight of what was missing. Three or four times they stood before their wrecked apartment house. On the first visit they could see the dining room radiator dangling on the top floor. Then that wall collapsed and the rest was dynamited. "Just a small, much too small, heap of stones remained. We kept saying: But that's just not possible. Where is the heavy old table with the lindenwood top? And the chest? There should be a lot more lying there."

He missed the trivial—an old deck chair they had re-covered the Sunday before the firestorm—and he missed the irreplaceable, like family photos, childhood dolls, works of art. They were only things, but they were also signposts of the private life of a household. They, too, were landmarks, just as St. Catherine's Church was a landmark. "These things have their life from us, because at some time we bestowed our affection on them; they absorbed our warmth and harbored it gratefully in order to enrich us with it again in meager hours. We were responsible for them; they could only die with us. And now they stood on the other side of the abyss in the fire and cried after us, begging: Don't leave us!" The torment of this loss grew from week to week.

Nossack mourned for all of Hamburg. He even missed the worst of Hamburg, as he saw it, the poor neighborhoods he had once scorned. "Didn't we say: This is an ugly district, unfit for human habitation, ripe for demolition; these streets, so narrow, and everyone's yelling; these backyards without light, without color, without air; these houses, all stunted and dirty? How could millions of people live in this narrowness and not explode it with their breath? And the staircases smelled of food and of ordinary people; we turned our noses up at the thought.

"Who would still dare to make fun of these things? Why are there no smells on these stairs any longer? Why is there no laundry drying on the rack outside the window? Didn't people sometimes bake a cake on Sunday? Wasn't there in every one of these numberless apartments, whose contours were now discernible only in what was left of the walls, a housewife who polished the floors and dusted the furniture day in, day out; who was afraid of her neighbors yet wanted to be envied by them?"

In their absence he could finally see them. Where were these people now?

Though the authorities forbade it, people flooded back into Hamburg. It was "better to live in a cellar in a ruin" than to be a refugee. People built small fireplaces in the paths amid the rubble to cook or boil clothes. "At least it was life. In other parts of the city there wasn't even that."

The Arithmetic of Devastation

Lord Cherwell had claimed that one ton of bombs could destroy twenty to forty houses. That was his dehousing equation. Talking about the war's destruction, it is difficult to keep both sides of the equation in view: bomb tonnage, aircraft, big maps, big battles; and the sitting room ablaze, books and plates and lamps tumbling into a heap with the bricks and the bodies.

Fifty-four principal German cities were bombed. On average 40 percent of a city was destroyed. Twenty-two percent of housing in Germany was destroyed. Another 23 percent had some damage. This is an extraordinary figure and yet Germany's war production increased throughout the war until the closing months, and with each bombing, civilians clung tighter to home and resolved to fight on. Dehousing did not bring victory. The proof of its failure could be deduced at home: One of five English dwellings had been "affected by bombings." Others lost windows, roofs, tiles. And no one in England ever spoke of surrendering.

The British got in the house-wrecking business out of faith and fear. They put their faith in the airplane to transform war, as they feared that transformation. Since the 1890s the public had been fed science fiction that forecast sudden annihilation from the sky. Popular French and German pre-WWI novels of adventure showed civilization bombed from on high. One of the products of Western civilization became the imagined scenarios of its own destruction.

The stories and predictions by experts tended to lead to three conclusions: The next war will be so terrible we can't think about it; it will be so terrible it won't be fought; or if it will, it will be over in two hours. Promoters of air-power claimed that bombing key industries or just the city itself would cause panic and break morale and stop a war, perhaps after the first air raid. Only H. G. Wells foresaw the bombing of cities as devastating yet inconclusive.

The bombing of England by German zeppelin and Gotha bomber in World War I confirmed forecasts, even if there was no widespread panic or calls for immediate surrender. The British military studied the lesson; bombing cities was added to the nation's war plans.

To build their air forces, promoters in all countries oversold their product. The war in the air, it was argued, would obsolete fighting on the ground. Armies would not be tied down in trench warfare for years as they had been in the Great War. But in its first World War II missions, the Luftwaffe accidentally bombed a German city. The RAF's first attempt to bomb the Ruhr Valley industries was so ineffectual that the German intelligence services couldn't discern the intended target. And the Americans had boasted that with their secret bomb-sight they could put a bomb in a pickle barrel from eighteen thousand feet. They weren't even close.

Bombing policies were improvised throughout World War II, shaped by what the airplanes and their crews could accomplish. So much preceded by guess—about how much the bombs were destroying, how much industry was hindered, and how civilians would react. The "fog of war" obscured the "just war." One of the troubling aspects of the air war is how similar it is to other human endeavors. It's marked by office politics, by not knowing and not wanting to know. It proceeds as if all its directors and executioners were blindfolded. To stumble along killing hundreds of thousands seems especially wrong, even though the dead are as dead as if they were killed by men and bombs guided by a hardened doctrine.

What may surprise us today is how much the generals of the U.S. Army

Air Force debated the morality of bombing civilians. They were faced with an impossible task, to float a colloquium on justly fighting a just war while they were pushed and pulled toward the all-out firestorms of Dresden and Tokyo. The moral issue was ever present and elusive. The morality of bombing was debated, abandoned, picked up again. G-en. George C. McDonald, director of intelligence for U.S. Strategic Air Force in Europe, said that if leveling cities is the best way of fighting the war, then tell the ground forces "to kill all civilians and demolish all buildings in the Reich, instead of restricting their energies to the armed enemy." Restraint was applied differently—with some care, it seems, in Italy, not at all in Bulgaria, Germany, or Japan.

In the years since the war, the morality of the policy has not often been questioned. But we have to ask if bombing civilians was a crime against humanity. To ask this question does not diminish the bravery of the bomber crews, nor does it equate one evil with another, somehow reducing or pardoning the Japanese and Nazi war crimes, says the English philosopher A. C. Grayling. "It is unquestionably true that if Allied bombing . . . was in whole or part morally wrong, it is nowhere near equivalent in scale of moral atrocity to the Holocaust of European Jewry, or the death and destruction all over the world for which Nazi and Japanese aggression was collectively responsible; a total of some 25 million dead," writes Grayling in *Among the Dead Cities*.

Other historians have wrestled with the dilemma of the air war. "When democracies go to war and they find themselves in total wars, they have to work through a set of moral choices that are sometimes extremely difficult and extremely painful," says historian Tami Davis Biddle. "Fighting Nazi Germany, in the end, meant fighting all out; meant utilizing every resource that we had. But in order to defeat this enemy we had to make some choices that were in some ways regrettable." And historian Conrad Crane says, "I see this idea of just killing civilians and targeting civilians as being unethical—though the most unethical act in World War II for the Allies would have been allowing themselves to lose."

Grayling is at pains to show that the bombing was ineffective, that it was carried out in vengeance, in the need to do something—anything—and at last because the presence of bombers forced their use. (Lord Cherwell had promised to destroy twenty to forty homes with one ton of bombs. In practice, say some historians, it took one ton of bombs to destroy just one home.)

Once the bomb-dropping machinery is in place, it's hard to stop. These things develop their own momentum. The Allies learn how to build better planes, more accurate ways to drop bombs, more lethal bomb mixes. It's a learning curve, like any industry. The product changes, improves. Here the product was destruction. The Western Allies dropped 60 percent of the total tonnage of bombs on Germany in the last eight months of the war. When all else fails, bomb a whole city with incendiaries. The final months of bombing German cities "contributed little to the defeat of the Nazis, and cast a moral shadow over the Allied victory which has never been lifted," says historian Max Hastings.

A small city such as Wurzburg was bombed in the last weeks of the war because it could be bombed. It was an act of reflexive vengeance. Wurzburg was destroyed because the bombs had been made, the bombers and the crews were there. And it was destroyed because advocates of the air war had claimed that they could win the war from the air. They didn't, but still the mind-set was to show themselves essential.

Wurzburg's destruction was a matter of a bland corporate decision. There's more passion and concern around the advertising for a new cracker.

II: Dehousing on the American Plan

The American policy of dehousing was improvised. There was no formal doctrine, no cabinet debate. This policy was created by one general in the field. He had the tools at hand, a new airplane the air force was still learning to use, and the firebombs that had been tested in the Utah desert.

Tokyo

A childhood memory of a toy village guided General Curtis LeMay's destruction of Japan. "It was one of those villages that you set up . . . the houses come all flat, but they're hinged at the corners; and then you spread 'em out and shove the roof down, with the eaves going up through the slots and so on; and thus your house sits like a strawberry box. Well I remember they had the village all set up in the backyard and some mean kid says, 'Let's see if we can burn it down.' So he set fire to the first house. And, brother, they all went."

Tokyo was built of wood and paper. Tokyo was a strawberry box awaiting the torch.

LeMay reflected a growing consensus. The fire protection engineers were lobbying the Army Air Force for incendiary raids; various civilian and military research groups argued that firebombing could inflict "a national catastrophe . . . entirely unprecedented in history." Winston Churchill addressing Congress in May 1943 had called for "the process, so necessary and desirable, of laying the cities and other munitions centers of Japan in ashes, for in ashes they must surely lie before peace comes back to the world."

Japan's wooden cities were densely populated. In the Tokyo ward at the center of the target zone, 135,000 people lived per square mile. Even though the city had burned in the great earthquake of 1923, Tokyo relied largely on volunteers to put out fires with hand-pumped water, straw brooms, and sand. The city of 6.7 million had only three modern hook-and-ladder trucks, of which only one was working. The government had destroyed swaths of housing to create twenty miles of firebreaks, but on the eve of Tokyo's destruction, some of that wood sat in heaps. The firebreaks would prove too narrow to stop most of the fires.

Before the war an American visitor in Osaka had asked a fireman what he would do if three fires broke out simultaneously in that congested city. "I don't know," said the fireman. "They only teach us how to deal with two fires."

~

The U.S. Army Air Force would fight differently in Japan. It had a new bomber and new challenges. The B-29 long-range bomber was the most expensive weapon of the war, costing $3 billion to develop (about $34 billion today; it cost even more than Manhattan Project's $2 billion, or $23 billion today). But two thousand missions had not inflicted what the military calls "decisive damage." Curtis LeMay was called in.

LeMay changed the way the Army Air Force was attacking Japan. He abandoned the daytime, high-altitude bombing of factories and ports. The jet stream above thirty thousand feet was pushing the B-29s off course. The airplane's engines, straining to gain altitude, were overheating. He would fly in as low as five thousand feet at night in bombers stripped of guns and firebomb cities. By flying low and without armament, he was able to double the bomb load. It was a radical notion. His men cursed the "Big Cigar's" suicide mission. The Pentagon didn't know of his plan until the day before he took off. "My decision and my order," said LeMay.

On the night of March 9 to 10, 1945, LeMay attacked Tokyo. Sixteen square miles, 250,000 buildings, burned to the ground in six hours. It was a larger area than LeMay had targeted. "The destruction was complete; not a single building escaped damage in the area affected," said a post-war damage assessment. Forty percent of the capital city was gone. It was as if two-thirds of Manhattan were wiped out.

Drafts from the fires bounced the airplanes into the sky "like ping-pong balls," said LeMay. The large bombers were pushed up thousands of feet in seconds; some flipped over. The crews could smell burning flesh; they fought off choking or vomiting. The bombers returned to base blackened with soot.

Once again there were scenes of hell as the fires merged and the winds increased to the hurricane force of a firestorm. Fifteen hundred tons of small incendiary bombs "scattered a kind of flaming dew that skittered along the roofs, setting fire to everything it splashed and spreading a wash of dancing flames everywhere," said one witness. There was so much smoke that even the firefighters got lost. Fast-moving walls of flames blocked escape; thousands jumped into the city's canals, but in some districts the shallow canals were boiling; in other canals people were crushed under foot by panicked crowds and drowned. Those in the canals who survived were burnt on the head and neck from the rain of sparks. Disfiguring burns went untreated; many hospitals were destroyed and those that were left had little medicine. Corpses burnt beyond recognition were piled in the streets and canals. It was so horrible that Japanese investigators couldn't bring themselves to report what they had seen.

The rapidly spreading fire was more furious than the Hamburg firestorm. In one night eighty-seven thousand people died, maybe one hundred thousand. More than forty thousand were injured and more than one million were dehoused.

The Tokyo raid was the deadliest single attack in the history of war. "We scorched and boiled and baked to death more people in Tokyo on that night of March 9-10 than went up in vapor at Hiroshima and Nagasaki combined," said LeMay with his usual frankness. "I suppose if I had lost the war, I would have been tried as a war criminal."

$$\sim$$

The Tokyo raid was a "dream come true," said *Time*. "Properly kindled, Japanese cities will burn like autumn leaves." LeMay's superior, Chief of Staff Lauris Norstad, said the fire raids were "nothing short of wonderful." There was no U.S. press on the ground, of course, to record the agony. They had filed their reports before the bombers took off. The air raids were presented in the press as "pin-point incendiary bombing." Following the Tokyo raid, LeMay bombed Japan's next largest cities. In ten nights LeMay destroyed thirty square miles of Japan's four largest cities, killing at least 150,000 people. And then he ran out of bombs. A month later, resupplied with firebombs, and with increasing numbers of airplanes, he resumed. LeMay was determined to "bomb and burn them until they quit."

In city after city, the devastation was beyond anything previously seen in the war. In one raid, as part of "psychological warfare," the Army Air Force warned the city of Hachioji that it would be attacked. The Japanese rushed extra firemen and trucks to the city, to no avail. Eighty percent of the city was destroyed. Tokyo was bombed four more times, destroying an additional forty square miles, including the grounds of the Imperial Palace, which was said not to be a target.

LeMay led the Twenty-First Bomber Command to firebomb sixty-three Japanese cities. One hundred seventy-five square miles—mostly city centers—lay in ruins. These raids, on average, destroyed 45 percent of a city. He was ordered to save several cities so the effects of a secret weapon could be clearly seen. After Hiroshima and Nagaski, the fire raids continued; Yawata (21 percent destroyed), Fukuyuma (73 percent), Kumagaya (45 percent), Isezaki (17 percent). Kyoto, the capital of ancient Japan, was the only large city that was not bombed. Secretary of War Henry Stimson was adamant that its cultural heritage deserved special protection.

By the time Japan surrendered in August, there were no more big cities left to burn.

LeMay was moving down the list to target 180 towns with a population of thirty thousand or more. Had the war continued, those towns would have been wiped out by November. The Army Air Force was drafting plans for chemical warfare to poison the rice crop. They were looking at building twelve thousand modified V-1 rockets. This was a war of extermination. The Japanese had fought to the last man on the Pacific islands. They had not surrendered. Miles of their capital city had been reduced to charred desert and they had not surrendered.

"It was not necessary for us to burn every city, to destroy every factory, to shoot down every airplane or sink every ship, and starve the people," said the post-war U.S. Strategic Bombing Survey. "It was enough to demonstrate that we were capable of this."

⌇

Japan became a laboratory for starting firestorms. After the war, the fire protection engineers and the U.S. Strategic Bombing Survey tabulated the damage and plotted the "Probability of Fire Spread Across Various Exposure Distances." They checked their recipe for firestorms and found that dropping two hundred tons of incendiaries per square mile got good results—dropping more didn't usually destroy more.

There were many firestorms to be studied, a typology of hell: in still conditions the pillar of fire rose almost vertically, but, initially, the heat was insufficient to ignite the vapors as they ascended in the dense smoke. "As the fire gained headway, these vapors or gases would ignite and burn in orange and blue colored flames.

"Under conditions of high humidity, the establishment of the pillar was often retarded and smoke began to spread out like a horizontal blanket. In a few cases the pillar would hit a stream of cold air, causing the moisture to condense and fall back in large black drops directly to leeward."

If the pillar of fire "slanted appreciably to the leeward," the hot burning gases helped to ignite combustible materials on the ground. This type of firestorm was marked by "an extended wall of fire . . . preceded by a turbid mass of pre-heated vapors." The "inrushing fire wind," which whipped fires into a storm, usually developed fifteen minutes to one hour after the first fires.

Some 93,000 tons of incendiaries and just 650 tons of high explosives and fragmentation bombs were dropped on Japan, less than 1 percent of the total. (In Germany high explosives were about half the total dropped.) Most of the firebombs were the six-pound M-69 napalm bomb, which had been tested on the Japanese doomtown in the Utah desert. Less than 3 percent of the destruction visited upon Japan was from the two atomic bombs.

One-quarter of the urban population, 8.5 million, fled the cities. Some 2.3 million homes were damaged or destroyed. An estimated 330,000 to 900,000 civilians were killed, and anywhere from a half million to 1.3 million were injured. In the last six months of the war, Japanese civilian casualties were nearly double that suffered by their military in forty-five months of fighting.

～

No one ordered the Tokyo firestorm that killed eighty-seven thousand or perhaps one hundred thousand people. The bombing of Japan was ad hoc, lacking in direction from Washington or guidance by an over-arching theory. With the generals pressing LeMay for results, he devised a new way to use the B-29s. "LeMay's bombing proceeded largely unmonitored and unnoticed by diplomats and statesmen in London and Washington," says historian Michael S. Sherry.

By the time the war reached the Japanese home islands, there were no restraints. The Japanese were viewed differently than the Germans. They were routinely portrayed in the wartime publications as vermin. The Army Air Force leadership wanted revenge for the cruel treatment of POWs. The Allies roamed the skies of Japan after April 1945, firebombing cities and strafing passenger trains. A B-29 was safer over Japan than in training back in the States, said LeMay.

～

Long after the war, LeMay told his story with the help of author McKinlay Kantor. *Mission with LeMay*, published in 1965, is infamous for one quote, in which the general proposed to bomb Vietnam "back to the Stone Age." LeMay disowned the statement, but it is of a piece with his thinking. "Don't strike at flies, hit the manure pile" was his prescription for fighting North Vietnam. He refused to renounce the first use of nuclear weapons and pushed for bombing the Cuban missile sites during the crisis.

Mission with LeMay is a war yarn, a Boys' Own Adventure Story. It's told in LeMay's voice—as he told it to Kantor; cleaned up a bit no doubt. It's a rough grumble tale of men and their machines that reads as if it were dictated while he had a cigar in his teeth, as was his habit. At times it's a romp, as when he visits France not long after D-Day. He drives around with his buddies to see the war on the ground and is "liberating" a new car when the Germans bomb them. At first he thought someone had thrown dirt on him. He'd never been bombed on the ground. War is hell, but war is fun.

One reads *Mission with LeMay* to see if this airborne General Sherman is a moral animal. The evidence is inconclusive. He checks in at all the appropriate moments to talk of death and how hard it is to lose men, but he quickly hits the next beat, saying this is war. If he sees any of his lost men again in some unspecified heaven or hell, he wants them to know that they were lost in a good, well-run operation.

The "bunk flying," jocular, plain-spoken, man-and-his-bombers tone of *LeMay* is broken by his vehement insistence that he's got no moral qualms about bombing. It would be worse to use less force and let the war drag on, killing yet more people. "Killing Japanese didn't bother me at that time. It was getting the war over that bothered me," he said. "All war is immoral, and if you let it bother you, you're not a good soldier." He's so strident about even considering the moral questions that either this is his true voice, which has been candied-up in the rest of the book, or he is shouting down his critics and his own conscience. "There was no transgression, no venturing forth into a field illicit and immoral, as has so often been charged," he said.

Today we can quote LeMay and penalize him for his honesty. Unlike Churchill or Roosevelt, he didn't talk in public of bombing only military targets and then order the destruction of cities. The prime minister and the president are not going to stand before the House of Commons or in some "Fireside Chat" and proclaim that we are daily boiling and baking thousands to win the war.

When LeMay says that children die in their beds and thousands are boiled and baked in fires, he's being honest. All war is immoral, as he says. But that doesn't excuse him from making moral judgments. In modern war, men of limited imagination are given weapons of unlimited means.

We wanted him to torch Japan, but we don't want to hear about it in such frank terms. Give us the oatmeal talk of politicians, give us duplicity, please, to shelter our hypocrisy. In peacetime we can forget what we asked of him. We can indulge a little indignation. But as historian Richard Overy notes, in World War II, civilians directed the military to bomb civilians.

LeMay was a necessary monster. The monster we send out to slay the monster at our city gate. But we don't know whether to greet him as a hero, or feel ashamed for his transgressions on our behalf. "Our entire nation howled like a pack of wolves for an attack on the Japanese homeland," said LeMay. He was a monster created by the war. He was our monster.

Flash Blindness

Flash blindness: The temporary or permanent impairment of vision resulting from an intense flash of light. —The Oxford Essential Dictionary of the U.S. Military

One night, after dinner at our friends' house, we take our dogs for a walk in the moonlight. Full moon. Quiet village. Behind their house, and the neighboring meetinghouse, the land opens up and curves like a bowl around a pond. On the Fourth of July this natural amphitheater is packed with families on blankets, little kids waving glow sticks. In the winter, it makes a good run for sledding. The rest of the time it is blissfully empty, the elegant curve of the horse sheds for the meetinghouse echoing the bowl of the land and the shore of the pond. We walk the dirt lane to the graveyard. The meetinghouse spire is a sentinel in the moonlight. It's a blessed, peaceful place.

Our friends live in an old house built around 1810. It lists a little to the right, as houses may do on a voyage across the centuries. These older houses in the landscape are astonishing in their grace, creating an ache if you acknowledge that we only fleetingly partake of their beauty.

We fight this feeling of impermanence. Our heritage of destruction has overwhelmed evanescence. A glowing sense of the temporary, the holiness of the passing moment, has been subsumed by a dread of possible sudden destruction.

Desperate to deny the bombs in the backyard, we exaggerate our permanence and, too often, exterminate the softer, evanescent qualities of our homes— the lean and bend of the years, the sag in the threshold, the shadows pooling in the corners. We are determined to arrest the house in an armor of vinyl and laminates, in a wrap of faux surfaces and digital images and broadcast noise. Where the qualities of softness and quiet should be, where peace itself should be, there are instead defenses and fear. A peaceful day can be revoked within seconds.

After the bombing of Berlin in December 1943, the *New Yorker* agreed that it was a "necessary action" and that it "serves the bastards right." But the writer added: "One implication, however, is still, as far as we know, fluttering around untrapped. Nobody has pointed out that the destruction of Berlin established the fact that it is now possible to destroy a city and that every city, but for the hairline distinction between potential and actual, is afire, its landmarks gone and its population homeless. From where we sit, the flames are clearly visible."

III: Learning to Dwell Again

War is about destroying your neighbors' home. Mostly that. When General William Tecumseh Sherman marched through Georgia, when General Curtis LeMay's bombers flew in low to burn Tokyo, when GIs in Vietnam destroyed villages to save villages, they were pushing their neighbors off the earth. That's what we do in war. We destroy dwellings.

"Destroyed" was the most frequently used adjective in Europe just after the war, said historian Mario Praz. "Wherever you looked, you could see only shattered, ruined buildings, the hollow orbits of windows, and fragments of walls, houses split in two, with the pathetic sight of some still furnished corner, dangling above the rubble, surrounded by ruin: pictures hanging on broken walls, a kitchen with the pots still on the stove. . . ." The ruins are our "reality," said Hans Werner Richter in 1947. "They are the outer symbol of the inner insecurity of the people of our age. The ruins live in us as we in them."

The war turned the inside outside, made the private public: The old patterns were broken and exposed for examination. In each city block smashed bits of the private life were torn open to daylight. The ruins prompted questions. We had made the earth into hell. How could we go on living here? In a century of "domicide," of war carried right to the hearth, when everyone is on the front lines, how do we rehouse ourselves? Can we dwell again?

Dwellings are sacred, writes the scholar Mircea Eliade. They contain the world. Hence our anguish about bombing houses and burning huts. We feel it in the gut. When we destroy a house, we destroy the world. We destroy a sacred space. The sacred re-creates creation and stands at the center of the world, says Eliade. The sacred is real. "Where the sacred manifests itself in space, *the real unveils itself*, the world comes into existence." The burned-out desert of Hamburg was unreal, said Nossack. It was the sacred cosmos reduced to chaos.

Modern dwellings do reflect our world: secular, in a hurry, and built without belief, or trust. They are transitory without being transcendent. Today's houses are often derided as ugly, ticky-tacky, sprawl, all words that measure a lack of grace, presence, and "the real." We can't build the real without the sacred. "If a 'construction' is to endure," says Eliade, "it must receive life and a soul. . . . The house is not an object, a 'machine to live in'; *it is the universe that man constructs for himself by imitating the paradigmatic creation of the gods. . . .*" Or as J. B. Jackson wrote, "The dwelling is the primary effort of man to create heaven on earth."

∼

After the war, new cities were built in the places where the old ones had stood— a new Tokyo, a new Osaka, a new Lubeck, a new Berlin, a new Coventry. The survivors clung to the rubble. The city planners wanted to complete the work of the bombers. They saw opportunities in a brutally cleaned slate.

The architects and planners on both sides of the Channel no longer believed in the ensemble act of the city. They didn't believe in the street and the thousands of details that make a place. Long before the war, the Modernists had turned against the city. They wanted to design free-standing towers in parks. They wanted to free the city from the old streets. They had put the city on trial and found it guilty, an ugly mess that was in the way of the coming Machine Age. The air raids confirmed their view. In their eyes the city was part of the old order that had brought the world to war. In the ravaged cities, they tore down more buildings—sometimes as much as a third of what had survived intense bombing. They wanted to free the city from history.

The "fire blitzes have shown us how shoddy, how inconvenient, how unhealthy, how unworthy are the centers of large towns," said British architect Eric L. Bird, a year after the war. Bird was editor of the *Journal of Royal Institute of British Architects.* "If we have learned this lesson and profit by it, future generations may even look back on this time and talk of the benefits conferred on civilization by the bombing aircraft!" Protecting against fire attack, said Bird, "accords very well with the aims of providing light, air, traffic, space, and amenity."

Each city debated how to rebuild, and each debate came down to the question of making copies—complete copies—of pulverized buildings. The citizens wanted the old twisting lanes, narrow buildings, the skyline of church spire and dome. The city's leaders, architects, and planners usually took a colder view, seeing a chance to modernize, widen streets for traffic, make bigger building lots to allow for the scale of contemporary commerce. Widening streets and carving out new streets was more important than some impractical notion of saving medieval Lubeck, said that city's planner. "That would produce a false romanticism, the atmosphere of a bratwurst stand." German city planners avoided the word "reconstruction." They wanted to build new cities.

The cities were rebuilt with token islands of the old city pattern and with new, wide streets. They were rebuilt with a simplified, stripped-down edition of the old buildings—"half modern," said one critic. The roof pitch is the same, as is the building's size. The materials are traditional, but what's lost is that feeling of particularity, of odd buildings wedged in, of an endless wealth of small, handmade details.

Compare two photos of a Nuremberg city square, before and after; the before photo is full of visual delight—dormer windows, oriel windows, a sundial on the wall, the geometry aslant and askew just a bit. The eye hunts out treasures, surprises. There's variation in the order. There's theme and counter theme. The place has grown and been altered over time. The post-war square is like something that has come off a machine lathe—the buildings are at the right scale, but they are too rational for their own good. They have been scrubbed clean of "bratwurst-stand" sentimentality. They are sober, the grudging work of architects who'd rather be designing crisp new modern buildings than doing an impression of the old city, a pastiche, as they saw it. Their heart isn't in the work and the buildings lack heart.

Each city rebuilt a few curios—an old city wall, the palaces and churches, a few narrow lanes—as a nod to saving the city's "historic character" and the "heimatgefuhl"—the feeling of being at home. This feeling is what had perished in the bombing and in the modern architecture that rose up on the ruins. Germans often reported feeling alienated from their rebuilt cities. The new cities are ugly; they don't look like Germany, they said. One critic appraised the rebuilding of Munich as the "second destruction of Munich." Another said, "Urban planning somehow completed the destruction of the urban centers." The new cities lacked conviction. They just didn't feel like home.

∼

After the war three philosophers asked: *What is a house?* Can it still matter? Or to rephrase it as Eliade might: Can we give it a spiritual place? If the house is diminished, then we are diminished.

The philosophers examined this world that had been pulled inside-outside. Martin Heidegger, in a famous lecture, "Building Dwelling Thinking," defined the essence of dwelling. Max Picard, a Catholic philosopher, made an eloquent case for silence—not as the absence of noise, but as the wellspring of the soul. And Gaston Bachelard, a Sorbonne professor who had risen from a humble start, mapped the intimate dreamscape of home as it had never been done before and has never been done since.

These three managed to talk of home in ways that usually escape architects and polemicists. In their writings are the qualities of dwelling, the way we really live in the world. These three philosophers are usually read separately. I make no claims to be a scholar of the demanding Heidegger, the elusive Picard, and the charming Bachelard, but significant parts of their post-war work tell the story of what was lost in the flames, and what we have yet to recover. Only one, as far as I know, makes a passing reference to the ruins and refugees all around them, but they are writing in response to the fire protection engineers' experiments in burning bed and baby crib. The philosophers are conducting their own experiment, a project to undo "dehousing" and to ask if we can recover the security of dwelling in a new age of instant death from the sky.

They are looking for a way home. It is an act of restoration, an attempt to return dwelling, silence, and dreams to the world after the largest war in history. These three philosophers are all the king's men putting Humpty Dumpty back together again.

Dwelling

With Germany in ruins—nearly half of its housing was destroyed or damaged—one of that country's most famous philosophers, Martin Heidegger, gave a surprising lecture in 1951:

"On all sides we hear talk about the housing shortage, and with good reason. Nor is there just talk; there is action too. We try to fill the need by providing houses, by promoting the building of houses, planning the whole architectural enterprise. However hard and bitter, however hampering and threatening the lack of houses remains, the real plight of dwelling does not lie merely in a lack of houses. The real plight of dwelling is indeed older than the world wars with their destruction, older also than the increase of the earth's population and the condition of the industrial workers. The real dwelling plight lies in this, that mortals ever search anew for the nature of dwelling, that they must ever learn to dwell," said Heidegger in his lecture "Building Dwelling Thinking" (*Bauen Wohnen Denken*), a title lacking commas to emphasize the unity of the concepts.

We are not homeless only because we lack housing, Heidegger told a conference of architects, engineers, and philosophers. We are homeless because we have forgotten how to dwell.

In his lecture he defined dwelling. Heidegger packed a manifesto and a faith into that one word, "dwelling." We have many buildings that provide shelter, he said. "Today's houses may even be well planned, easy to keep, attractively cheap, open to air, light, and sun," but they are not dwellings.

The reason could be found in the language. "What, then, does *Bauen*, building, mean?" he asked. "The Old English and High German word for building, *buan*, means to dwell. This signifies: to remain, to stay in a place. The real meaning of the verb *bauen*, namely, to dwell, has been lost to us." A "covert trace" remained in the origins of the word "neighbor." In Old English, *neahgehur* is a near dweller. Another trace of *bauen* remained in the common phrases *ich bin*—I am—and *du bist*—you are. They meant: "*I dwell, you dwell.*"

The "true meaning" had fallen into "oblivion," he said. "Dwelling is never thought of as the basic character of human being. . . . The way in which you are and I am, the manner in which we humans are on the earth, is *Buan*, dwelling. . . . The old word *bauen* . . . however also means at the same time to cherish and protect, to preserve and care for, specifically to till the soil, to cultivate the vine."

"Let us listen once more to what language says to us. The Old Saxon *wuon*, the Gothic *wunian* like the old word *bauen*, mean to remain, to stay in a place. But the Gothic *wunian* says more distinctly how this remaining is experienced. *Wunian* means: to be at peace, to be brought to peace, to remain in peace. The word for peace, *Friede*, means the free, *das Frye*, and *fry* means: preserved from harm and danger, preserved from something, safeguarded. To free really means to spare. . . . We 'free' it in the real sense of the word into a preserve of peace."

"The fundamental character of dwelling is this sparing and preserving."

Heidegger's description of dwelling sounds, more than a half century later, like a forecast of the environmental movement. When we dwell, we are stewards of the earth, he said. We are caretakers; we "cultivate" and "nourish" a place. We do not dominate and control nature. We are homeless when we lose the poetry of the "fourfold" world—"earth, sky, mortals, and gods." We are homeless when we lose touch with the soul of a place and thus our essential "Being."

The mystery that sits at the center of our lives is our "Being"—the basic, powerful, strange starting principle that we exist. People ignore this daily, said Heidegger. We are "forgetful" of " Being"; we are cut off from the essence of existence. "All of Heidegger's thought can be construed as an attempt to articulate this place of being," explains philosopher Jeff Malpas.

A "genuine building" brings us nearer to "Being." It opens the world to us, Heidegger said. It "gathers to itself in its own way earth and sky, gods and mortals." We recognize this in the exceptional—the Golden Gate bridge, the Parthenon, or Falling Water, for example. These works are like a lens, focusing and defining the spirit of that place. In their presence we have a heightened sense of what is eternal and what is fleeting. They honor the ordinary as sacred. A peasant dwelling also does this, said Heidegger.

"Let us think for a while of a farmhouse in the Black Forest, which was built some two hundred years ago by the dwelling of peasants," he wrote. "Here the self-sufficiency of the power to let earth and heaven, gods and mortals enter in simple oneness into things, ordered the house. It placed the farm on the wind-sheltered mountain slope looking south, among the meadows close to the spring. It gave it the wide overhanging shingle roof whose proper slope bears up under the burden of snow, and which, reaching deep down, shields the chambers against the storms of the long winter nights. It did not forget the altar corner behind the community table; it made room in its chamber for the hallowed places of childbed and the 'tree of the dead'—for that is what they call a coffin there: the *Totenbaum*—and in this way it designed for the different generations under one roof the character of their journey through time. A craft which, itself sprung from dwelling, still uses its tools and frames as things, built the farmhouse."

"Only if we are capable of dwelling, only then can we build."

~

In his short lecture, the Black Forest farmhouse was the only example he offered of an authentic dwelling. He did not mean that "we should or could go
back to building such houses," he said. But it led some critics to dismiss his
lecture as provincial nostalgia, a stew of Black Forest romanticism, Hellenic
pantheism, and a sour Sunday sermon that scolds us to behave better, to get
right with the universe. This is nostalgia, they said, and worse: It is fascist. This
is the old Nazi talk of Homeland (*Heimat*) and "Blood and Soil" repackaged for
post-war consumption.

Heidegger gave his lecture in the "Age of Rubble" (*Trummerzeit*), when
the ruins of German cities were the playground for a generation of children,
Trümmerkinder as they were called. West Germany needed to build 5.8 million "units" of housing. Millions of refugees had crowded in from the east;
anything available was converted for housing: air-raid shelters, factories, stables, as well as refugee camps. The housing crisis was not an abstract problem
to him; the Heideggers were ordered to share their house with other families.
And yet here he was saying the production of housing was not the chief problem. Even the term "housing units" was symptomatic of what was wrong.

What does a Black Forest farmhouse, a *Schwarzwaldhofe*, have to do with
a nation of refugees? This agrarian ideal is of little use to refugees awaiting
housing, who may be sharing a flat with strangers. They want a room of their
own, a job, a routine. They are desperate for the mundane. What is Heidegger
saying? Go home—you'll never dwell here—you can't know the rhythms of
this soil? Divorced forever from their native land, he seems to say, they will
never dwell.

"Building Dwelling Thinking" was one of the first lectures he gave when he
was permitted to teach again after the war. Heidegger had eagerly served Hitler at his university. As rector of the University in Freiburg, he exhorted, "Do
not let doctrines and ideas be the rules of your Being. The Führer himself,
and he alone, is the present and future reality, and its law." At his insistence,
he was recast as "Fuhrer-Rector" with broad powers. He applied the new
Nazi "cleansing" laws to the student body and faculty and promoted a book
of pro-Hitler speeches by professors. He urged students to join the party and
serve Hitler; on national radio he called for ratification of Hitler's withdrawal of

Germany from the League of Nations. The next year he resigned the rectorship.

For years Heidegger has been portrayed as an accidental Nazi, his rectorship a foolish adventure, but the opening of East German archives has revealed that he was an anti-Semite who informed on his colleagues to the Gestapo and paid his Nazi party membership dues until the war's end (card number 312589). When the National Socialists seized power, he thought that they would put his philosophy of "Being" into action; he thought that he could lead Hitler. He was caught up in the hero worship of Hitler and his officers. He believed in the "inner truth and greatness of National Socialism" and that there was a "dangerous international alliance of Jews." (He admired a biography of Hermann Goering, in which Goering spoke of exterminating the "subhumans." He gave it as a present to a friend.)

After the war he misrepresented his actions, going so far as to tamper with already published speeches. He never once spoke about the Holocaust. He claimed that he knew nothing of the fate of the Jews, though the 20,600 Jews of Baden, where he lived, had vanished. He never examined the war. He looked right past the destruction and dislocation of World War II. Though severe, it was just more of the same, a symptom of a rootless technological society. In an alarming comment, he equated modern agriculture with the death camps. He said, "Agriculture is now a motorized food-industry—in essence, the same as the manufacturing of corpses in gas chambers and extermination camps."

Heidegger was another twentieth-century monster who failed to see what was around him. He has left a dilemma for his readers, a raging debate. Two things are true: Heidegger was a Nazi; Heidegger recast modern philosophy. His character and his work are still on trial.

∽

The rector who had made furious Nazi speeches in 1933 left his rectorship and repositioned himself as the rustic "shepherd of being." Part of the year he lived in a hut on the slope of a wide mountain valley in the Black Forest. The small hut had no electricity or running water in its first years. He took pride in dressing like a peasant workman, chopping his own wood, and speaking with the local dialect. He made a show of his simplicity. He liked it to be known that he loved his hut. He was photographed there as some kind of *über* provincial. He had few visitors, but they got the full *Heimat* maneuver: a walk, some wood chopping, listening to the great man talk for two hours as the room faded into darkness.

Heidegger felt most at home here. He had shunned a big appointment, the chair of philosophy in Berlin. He found universities "stuffy" and "stifling." He loved being by the small stream, looking out on the groomed Alpine valley. He loved walking through the countryside. At his hut he wasn't just sightseeing or visiting, he took care to say. The rhythms of the place itself were part of him, of his thought.

"On a deep winter's night when a wild, pounding snowstorm rages around the cabin and covers everything, that is the perfect time for philosophy," he said in a 1934 radio address, "Why Do We Stay in the Provinces?" "Then its questions become simple and essential. Working through each thought can only be tough and rigorous. The struggle to mould something into language is like the resistance of the towering firs against the storm. And this philosophical work does not take its course like the aloof studies of some eccentric. It belongs right in the middle of the peasants' work. When the young farmboy drags his heavy sled up the slope and guides it, piled high with beech logs, down the dangerous descent to his house, when the herdsman, lost in thought and slow of step, drives his cattle up the slope, when the farmer in his shed gets the countless shingles ready for his roof, my work is of the same sort. It is intimately rooted in and related to the life of the peasants. . . . The inner relationship of my own work to the Black Forest and its people comes from a centuries-long and irreplaceable rootedness in the Alemannian-Swabian soil."

If his hut is the dwelling he has in mind in "Building Dwelling Thinking," it would be available to very few. And very few Germans lived in an eighteenth-century Black Forest farmhouse, but this one example explains Heidegger's philosophy of dwelling.

∾

Heidegger walks us through the farmhouse, showing how the house has been shaped by generations of life—by the family's work and rites. The family, with its animals under this one roof, is self-sufficient. They work here, eat together, pray, and die here—a place awaits their *Totenbaum*, their coffin. Life, work, and death are condensed in this one house—a house they have built and altered over time. It was not a product, a finished thing the family moved into. A dwelling is not a "turnkey" operation: sign the papers, unpack a few boxes, and set the thermostat. A house isn't a "machine for living" or a product. It's how we experience the earth, in our activities, our imaginations, life, and work. When we are cut off from that experience, we are cut off from life, cut off from the earth itself in many contemporary houses.

Housing is built. Dwelling unfolds. The life in the Black Forest house unfolds day by day, generation by generation. This is how "we dwell poetically," said Heidegger in a lecture on a poem by his favorite poet, Friedrich Hölderlin. Again, he went to the root of the word: *poetry* is from the Greek *poeisis*, making. When we dwell, we are poetically making our place. All creative acts are making, he said. But poeisis is more subtle than that. To the Greeks, poiesis meant to bring forth "out of concealment," as a bud brings forth a bloom, as a sculptor brings forth a figure out of marble. To live well is to bring forth, unfold, the spirit of a place. When we dwell, we are cultivating the earth.

"Building Dwelling Thinking" can be read as an orientation lecture—you are here—and this is how you know you are here. Heidegger is building a compass for moderns, marking the points as earth, sky, mortals, and gods. "Building Dwelling Thinking" is a call to experience ourselves experiencing the earth. It's an argument for the here and now.

"Heidegger's work provides us with perhaps the most important and sustained inquiry into place to be found in the history of Western thought," said philosopher Jeff Malpas. Heidiegger's philosophy is about returning to home, but not in a provincial way, said Malpas. By home, Heidegger means the place we are near to the earth, at peace, relaxed in "Being."

"The 'homecoming' of which Heidegger speaks is a return to the *nearness* of being," Malpas writes. "Such nearness is a matter of allowing things to be what they are." This is a return "not to what is familiar, in the ordinary sense, but to that which is essentially 'uncanny,' inexplicable, wondrous."

To dwell is to live fully in our Being. Building and dwelling have become separated because we've lost our connection with our essence, with Being.

∼

Dwelling is our basic character, and it is imperiled, Heidegger said. Modern technology destroys "nearness," destroys our sense of being here.

Saying that technology annihilates space and time was a commonplace of the Industrial Revolution. The railroad broke with animal strength, took the hoof and foot away from the earth and disoriented many riders. Even at a dozen miles an hour, places became a blur.

But it was Heidegger's insight to show that this new technology destroys all distances, far and near. Technology robs us of "here." It sets us spinning and it never stops. "What is happening here when, as a result of the abolition of great distances, everything is equally far and equally near?" he asked. "Despite all conquest of distances the nearness of things remains absent."

Technology became the "framework," the one world view. It claims to be neutral, but it sets all questions and all values. There are no longer "beings," Heidegger said, "there are now only resources that are held in readiness for being consumed." "Everywhere everything is ordered to stand by, to be immediately on hand, indeed to just stand there just so that it may be on call for a further ordering." Our inmost selves are changed, as are our encounters with others.

We have lost our essence and the essence of all life around us. We have lost "nearness." Even at home, we are far away from our being, our selves. We are disenchanted.

Modern technology reduces places to space—a uniform, measurable, tradable commodity—and leaves us nowhere. It's a great, improving way of knowledge, but it shuts out all other ways of knowing. It leaves us fed but hungry, sheltered but without dwelling. It starves us in the modern way, alienating us from the old ways. The dominance of technology is causing an "oblivion of being," said Heidegger, making ours a "desolate time," a time, as the poet Hölderlin wrote, of the "world's night."

∼

The longest description of something physical in "Building Dwelling Thinking" is of a bridge. The bridge makes a place—it gathers meaning. By crossing the bridge daily, walking under the bridge, we experience the river, the river banks, and sky. The bridge means something to us; the earth at that spot means something to us.

Places gather meaning, said Heidegger. The idea of a place "gathering" is also suggested by the German word for place, *Ort*. The *Ort* is the point of a spear, where all the energy of the weapon comes into focus. (Bombing obliterated places—it turned the point of the spear back on itself: the energy of the weapon came into focus on the dwelling and destroyed it. In war, place gathers death.)

In a later essay, Heidegger offered another definition of dwelling. "*Ethos* means abode, dwelling place," he said. We dwell "in the nearness of God." Here is another insight into the sin of destruction. To destroy a dwelling is to destroy ethos—the root of ethics. Bombing dwellings severs our "nearness to God."

〜

Heidegger turned to another rustic example of "dwelling poetically" in "Hebel—Friend of the House," his tribute to a regional poet and maker of an almanac, Johann Peter Hebel. He saw Hebel as a standard-bearer of dwelling.

Hebel, who lived from 1760 to 1826, was what literary historians call a "minor poet." But for Heidegger this minor poet's language was alive. His poetry and his almanac—his "house friend" as Hebel called it—"countrifies the universe," said Goethe.

The landscape and the peasant become one. "We are plants which— whether we care to admit to ourselves or not—must ascend with our roots in the earth, in order to bloom in the ether and bear fruit," wrote Hebel.

The almanac of 1811 carries forth the wisdom of a genial Enlightenment in which the moon watches over us, "watches how boys kiss girls." "The house friend sees to it that lovers are provided with soft radiance," said Heidegger.

Critics who believe that Heidegger was playing Black Forest peasant dress-up will find more proof for their argument in this one example. But Heidegger said Hebel was alive in ways that are dismissed today. Hebel was at home with the earth, moon, and stars. He loved his native Black Forest valley. "The house friend . . . is attached to the whole wide dwelling of humankind," said

Heidegger. "The house friend, like the highest-ranking official night watchman . . . watches over the right kind of rest for the dwellers; he watches out for what threatens and disturbs."

This house friend is what we lack. Technology and dwelling are "two alien realms and with a constant acceleration are racing even further apart," said Heidegger. The "mystery of the world" has been reduced to that which is "calculable."

Our world, said Heidegger, "is a house without a friend."

~

It's the simple that abides and will save us, Heidegger wrote in a short hymn to a path across a field by an oak tree. "The Simple preserves the riddle of the abiding and the great. Spontaneously it takes abode in men, yet needs a long time for growth," he wrote in 1949. "In the unpretentiousness of the Ever-Same it conceals its blessing. The expanse of all grown things which dwell around the Fieldpath bestows the world." But to a "fragmented and pathless" people, "the Simple seems monotonous. . . . The Simple has fled. Its quiet power is exhausted." Those "who still recognize the Simple" are "quickly diminishing," he said. But with "the gentle might of the Fieldpath," they will persevere.

The truth lies hidden to us because we are "forgetful" of Being, Heidegger wrote in a long letter to a student. "Homelessness is becoming the fate of the world." "Perhaps then language calls far less for an overhasty speaking out . . . than for the proper silence. Yet who among us today might fancy themselves at home on the path of silence in his attempt to think?"

The World Without Silence

Max Picard lived a quiet life by Lake Lugano in Switzerland. He had moved there for his wife's failing health, and after her untimely death he lived alone. Picard, said one admiring visitor, lived like a man in the eighteenth century. He rose at 4 a.m. and walked for two hours by the lake, spent his days writing, and retired by 8 p.m. He cultivated quiet. "Nothing has changed the nature of man so much as the loss of silence," wrote Picard.

Picard had studied medicine in Germany and practiced at a hospital where he was considered to be a good diagnostician, but he renounced medicine because he didn't like the "mechanistic" approach. He converted to Catholicism from Judaism. His great-grandfather was a rabbi. "He was more than either Christian or Jew; he was both, and, above all, a complete person," said his American publisher, Henry Regnery, after he visited Picard. "He was a wise man, had a deeply felt faith, and understood and appreciated, as few others do, the great works of the past."

He was little known—then or now—but he had strong advocates. Rainer Maria Rilke said he was "the simplest man, the most ingenuous man I know." An early Picard book, *The Last Man*, which said that people were taking on the character of their machines, haunted Rilke "like a nightmare." He's "a man who suffers and through suffering gains the advantage of a terrible precision," Rilke wrote to Andre Gide. "It is the holy timidity of those who derive all their courage from being forever engaged in a grand interior combat."

Gabriel Marcel, a pioneering existential philosopher, agreed with Rilke. "Never, I think, have I met a person who seemed to me so true and also so hungry for truth," said Marcel. He is simple, dignified, bound to God, spontaneous, and at times vehement. He's a sage, a poet, a visionary. Marcel struggled to portray him, finally settling on describing him as if he were a natural formation in his adopted home. "It is difficult to think of him apart from the surroundings in which he lives and has taken root.... He has been adopted by this good land in which grandeur and intimacy are united."

"A small man, he is yet informed with a certain majesty," said Marcel. "Majesty in him is allied to a complete simplicity" and "a horror of pretentiousness." "His dignity is that of one who knows himself to be a creature of God and who also knows himself as unalterably bound to his Creator."

Marcel thought his opinions were "often severe." He could be "pitiless" when speaking of some German writers because "with an almost infallible intuition, he senses in them something hollow—the presence of a lie."

"With him, intuition is everything," said Marcel. Picard was not a systematic thinker. He circled a topic, "surveying the whole of it from every successive viewpoint."

Marcel championed Picard's books. "Picard is amongst the few who can resist the universal vertigo and who appear capable of redirecting the remnants of the thinking elite."

~

Continuity is the central tenet of Picard's thought. Continuity between self and God, self and the world. The modern world is broken, adrift. People are adrift in a world adrift. Anything genuine is subsumed; all our relations, to each other, to the earth, are subsumed. In the time of faith it was exceptional to be cut off, just as now it is exceptional not to be in flight. Flight is the force and the field, just as faith once was.

The atom was smashed and split, and so it is with us and God, Picard said. What was once a strong force holding us in God's love is now a force that destroys us. "It is no coincidence that the atom bomb is an invention of our time, a time which lives and dies by splitting everything into pieces," he said. For Picard, Christ is unity. He healed the "abysmal discontinuity" between man and God.

Everything is swept up in a world in flight. It's a torrent, a flood, a monsoon, Picard said in *The Flight from God* (1934), the book he was best known for in his day. Everything is temporary, unstable, incomplete. Our lives are improvised. We have no roots. We "dwell" within the flight, which of course is not dwelling. It's a state of never being home. The soul flees; it no longer knows where to go. We live in flux—not on earth, not in marriage, not in love, not in faith.

There is no truth; there are no lies. There is no inner certainty, no inner faith. Anything is possible; horrible cruelties, war crimes seem only to be an experiment without consequences. Everything is emptied of value, of distinction. So the "I" fights for distinction, gathers at the feet of exaggerated personalities, slogans, and theories. Emptiness is being created, said Picard.

Perhaps the most terrifying aspect of Picard's portrait of modern times is God's non-absence. God isn't dead; God isn't silent. He's right behind us; He is waiting when the desperate arrive. "Wherever they find themselves, once more they flee away, for God is everywhere," he said.

"The originality of Picard's intuition, I would almost say his genius," said Marcel, "lies in having discovered that the Flight has assumed volume, structure and quantity." Picard's friend Karl Pfleger said that the Flight isn't "a mere idea," it's a "kind of living being, an uncanny, daemonic collective being . . . a relentless, omnipresent monster."

~

The Flight from God is a harsh, scolding book. It is tinged with a prophet's despair. His argument condemns the reader. Picard could have nailed this book to the church door, putting all on notice as sinners: Your lives are dross. You live in a world of no truth, no courage. It's fragmented, diffuse. Your language, your art, your relationships, all of them are fragments. Whether you understand it or not, you will still be imprisoned in "the flight." He offers no soggy hope. God is there; He pursues us. Only love resists; only love can save us, and this, too, is imperiled. But these are only moments in the torrent of his condemnation. *The Flight from God* has the aridity of angry books that speak of love with a clenched fist. It's pulpit talk; it's Jeremiad. It's thou shall *not*.

"One simply cannot believe that this is a world," said Picard. "One cannot believe that trees, meadows, rivers, clouds, can tolerate the sight of so much lack of being without being themselves dissolved into its haze."

It's hell-on-earth. It's a world of monsters—huge factories, huge wars. Quantity drowns out quality, serious thoughts are reduced to slogans. It's chaos. A person exists not as a single being, said Picard, "but only as a chaos of feelings, impulses, acts. None knows where his own chaos finishes and where that of another begins." People are in chaos and they meet each other in chaos.

The mechanization of the world was chasing away the "magic of the strange" in life, said Picard. The world was accessible, but empty. Nothing was left but speed and "mechanical correctness." Machines were taking over warfare and fighting as if no one was in control—a critique that forecasts what went wrong with the "precision bombing" campaign. It couldn't be done. The bombs fell off target, so the target was broadened. "How terrible it would be if things can make war without even the assistance of man," he presciently said in 1920, long before the Nazi's missiles.

After the war, Picard singles out the rocket bomb. It falls out of the sky to disrupt life, to bust up context. It seeks out continuity and smashes it. And what it doesn't hit, it leaves in uncertainty. There's no military target, no reason for this, just the terror that your mundane day will be smashed open in an instant. Commonly called a terror weapon, the rocket bomb is, more precisely, a *terroir* weapon—a weapon against a cultivated locality.

Picard found hope only in marriage. Marriage was the one organic thing that survives. In marriage, he said, life begins again. Life attains continuity. Marriage is a continuation of God's love. And when marriage fails, it's because of the loss of God's presence at the center of the family.

If family is the last redoubt in a broken world, a campaign of "Dehousing," a living-room war, is especially cruel—firebombs were family bombs. Young men, fresh from their families, were trained to bomb other families.

To talk of God and faith, love and family in a discussion of bombing may seem to be beside the point, but that is a measure of how much we have to deny within ourselves in order to target civilians asleep. "Dehousing" targets families; it targets love. It burns down churches. Where is God in all that?

Some philosophers contort themselves to bend mass killings into the form of a "just war." But it comes out as a math problem from a perverted textbook looking to equate death by firebombs to death by starvation, or death on the battlefield.

They end up as mathematicians of mass death, charnel house accountants.

These dry recitals of millions of deaths excuse us from the horror, from the most basic formula in the war: two sides worship one God who commanded *Thou shall not kill*, and then go out and kill.

~

How had the world come to war? Discontinuity is Picard's diagnosis. He wrote about World War II in *Hitler in Our Selves*, which was published at the war's end in 1945. *Hitler in Our Selves* isn't a political study or an examination of Hitler. It is, as the title says, about how Hitler got into people's heads. It's a kind of society-wide psychoanalysis. For Picard, Hitler is a symptom of our discontinuity. He arose out of unreality, out of the disconnection of soul and self, of God and the world. Hitler is a "nullity" that fills the void.

Picard's war began in the rot of the soul, in the loss of God and silence. This is monstrous—a word he uses often—and the Germans prepared the way by the broken nature of their lives. Picard damns his readers. Hitler is in *us*. That was how he ruled: he occupied the interior. When we don't live with God, we get Hitler, said Picard. A world of sick souls produced the dictator. In short, we are sick, soul sick, and Hitler is our symptom.

Hitler turned the world upside down, inverting the true order, said Picard, making evil permanent and banishing good. The Nazis excelled in the mechanical, ethos-numbing production of evil. Other regimes have been brutal, but this was different. It was a killing machine in a disjointed time. Mozart or the gas chambers are interchangeable products of this factory. There was no context.

The Nazi was a man without a memory, said Picard. After killing and gassing, he can return to his job as a clerk or a hotel manager. He'll chase you for blocks to give your correct change, give candy to a crying child. There's no remorse, no repenting, because there's no inner life. "The horrible thing is that such a man knows nothing any longer of his murders—just as when he murdered and gassed, he no longer was conscious of the fact that but a few weeks before he had sold stamps or cigars or had greeted hotel guests." And tomorrow, he can kill and gas once again.

"Mozart before or after the gassing of human beings, the poems of Hölderlin in the knapsack of an SS man, Goethe in the library of the guards in a concentration camp—all these are possible only in a world wherein things no longer exist in their essence but solely in *piecemeal*. . . . It does not matter at all what fills the moment and whether it be murder or Bach, gassing or Hölderlin. Himmler's hand, as in one moment it caresses the arm of a child, caresses in the next moment the valve which releases the poison gas into the death chamber. . . . Helter-skelter one thing stands by another, and helter-skelter one thing after another is done."

~

Since Hitler is but a symptom, Picard spends little time looking at him. Picard's quarrel is with modern life. His measure of the society that he said created Hitler sounds eerily familiar: he's describing the rise of mass culture—the world we know, with its emphasis on youth and sexuality, the replacement of the "Greco-Christian" ideals of a classical education with a "disjointed heap" of "subjects" taught by servile teachers, and the spreading gospel of psychoanalysis, which Picard sees as an invasion of the spirit, a reduction of a person to symptoms.

Part of what Picard objects to is the rise of the mass communications juggernaut of the 1920s—the incessant march of topics on the radio and in newspapers and magazines, each presenting the facts in fashion as a total explanation, with each reigning fact-fragment falling quickly to the next. He doesn't use the word "fad"—that comes later, or "news cycle"—much later—but he's describing a world becoming addicted to the caffeine buzz of the newsreel. *News on the March!* Faster and faster it would go. The cinema, the gramophone, all of it was "rubbish produced by the discontinuity machine, overstuffed with disjointed fragments of all kinds."

In particular, Picard hated radio. Radio talks and talks, it makes reality unreal. "The content hardly matters." Radio—"a constantly firing automatic pistol shooting at silence"—is part of the mechanical destruction of the world. "The whole world has become radio noise," he said. "God, the eternally Continuous, has been deposed and Continuous radio-noise has been installed in His place." One can imagine Picard in Switzerland listening to "the screaming of Hitler" on the radio, the voice like a dagger; the rallies like a storm surge. All of it ugly and painful. The radio is a termite, an infestation, a common road built right through your dream space.

"Radio noise fills up the space within man where the word used to be and man *does not notice* that the word has been taken away from him . . . and it makes him restless and nervous. It seems to me that this is the cause of many modern psychoses."

The demagogues of the 1930s, European dictators and American fearmongers, were the first to make devastating use of the new medium. We tend to fuzzy nostalgia when talking of the "golden age" of radio in the Great Depression—Franklin Roosevelt's Fireside Chats, "The Shadow knows," Little Orphan Annie decoder rings—but ask anyone who grew up listening to Father Coughlin attacking Jews and you can begin to understand the velocity of hatred hunting you out in your own home, the voice stabbing into you. The radio was another violation of Dwelling.

~

Picard rides his argument right past the Führer. He shows his noted vehemence attacking modern art. Its forced disjointedness is an error, another attack on the spirit. When everything is broken, it doesn't take "revolutionaries" to break it some more, he said. He quarrels with James Joyce and John Dos Passos, but he hates Jean Paul Sartre. Sartre, he said, out Hitlers Hitler. These artists degrade man to "the role of warden of an insane asylum of schizophrenics."

~

After Hitler, silence. But not silence of the kind that might be expected, a muteness in the face of evil. Three years after the war, in 1948, Picard published his astonishing, strange book, *The World of Silence*. Take the broken world of *Flight from God* and *Hitler in Our Selves* and invert it until you have the opposite, a world made whole. In silence we are with God. Silence restores reality, said Picard. *The World of Silence* is, as befitting its topic, quieter, more hushed and hopeful. It's a spiritual book.

The World of Silence was his *summa*, said Picard. It's the book that his few readers know him by today. *The World of Silence* is a book that people stumble across; it's each reader's private discovery. They find it in the library catalog or at a used bookstore, or in a footnote or bibliography. Books like this earn their readers. The reader is not driven to the book by a big reputation or a list of books one ought to read. It's as if they were called to the book.

Max Picard is little known, below the horizon of even a cultish following. I've asked tenured and retired philosophy professors about him and gotten blank stares. His work seems to exist on an island. His book emerges from silence, contains mystery, and returns to silence. The book has come to resemble the qualities of silence as Picard discusses them.

Part of the book's strangeness is the shift of background and foreground. Silence isn't only the absence of speech and noise. Silence is true time, true love. It's solid and speech is carved from it. Without silence, speech is corrupted. It is only noise; it races forth as noise to match noise. Without silence, speech can't be true. "Real speech is in fact nothing but the resonance of silence," said Picard. "There is . . . more silence in one person than can be used in a single human life. That is why every human utterance is surrounded by mystery. . . . There is something silent in every word, as an abiding token of the origin of speech. . . . When two people are conversing with one another, however, a third is always present: silence is listening. That is what gives breadth to a conversation. . . . "Words that merely come from other words are hard and aggressive. Such words are also lonely, and a great part of the melancholy in the world today is due to the fact that man has made words lonely by separating them from silence. . . . Language is surrounded by the dark rim of melancholy, no longer by the rim of silence."

Picard is an explorer mapping the world of silence. He shows us silence and its loss in contemporary and ancient language, the ego, the demonic, knowledge, history, myth, images, love, the face, gestures, animals, time, childhood, old age, peasants, nature, poetry, architecture and sculpture, radio, illness, death, hope, and faith.

The World of Silence has a bookshelf companion, Thomas Merton's *Thoughts in Solitude*. Merton credits Picard's "inspiration," but he doesn't range beyond the challenges of living a contemplative life.

Silence draws Merton nearer to God. It's a journey to God and away from the self. It's a risk, forsaking human company and the pleasures of this earth, hoping that you won't go mad, hoping that God will save you from yourself. Above all, said Merton, solitude is prayer. It's not negation, not just sitting without. It's activity; it's seeking. Silence doesn't change, he said, but each moment one goes deeper. Silence deepens, it's a view to eternity. "The further I advance into solitude the more clearly I see the goodness of all things," said Merton. "The great work of the solitary life is gratitude."

Merton is arguing for the dignity of solitude. He's making the case to shed the self, to sacrifice, be poor, to enter the large spaces of God's presence that can be felt in silence. He's marking the playing field and saying this is holy ground. Everything can't be secular.

~

It is difficult to speak of an elusive spirit, a quality without a name, but Picard is able to summon the lost world of silence as he said it was. In the old world of continuity, invisible qualities surrounded people: that was reality. The visible, mundane life was but a continuation of the unseen. Poetry contained eternal poetry, marriage was a visible proof of God's love, and in silence was the presence of the eternal.

Peasant life had this characteristic, a hidden well of a deeper reality, as did great paintings, said Picard, whose first books were about art:

"In the pictures of the old masters, people seem as though they had just come out of the opening in a wall; as if they had wriggled their way out with difficulty. They seem unsafe and hesitant because they have come out too far and still belong more to silence than to themselves. They stop and wait for another opening to appear in front of them through which they can get back again to the silence. It seems that in the silence the movements of these people meet before the people themselves meet. If you look at a group of these people together in a picture by one of the old masters—people who have each as it were just stepped out of the wall of silence—it is as though they were all gathered together in a waiting room, waiting for the great opening of silence to appear before them through which they can all disappear again."

In the old way, people were of their place and community. Their faces reflected each other, their home place, and "God's goodness." But our relationship to space and time is broken. Everyone is on the move. We are neither here nor there but everywhere, a "specter" imitating "God's ubiquity," he said.

Where silence dwells, people can dwell, they can inhabit the earth, let things be as they are, as Heidegger said. Picard, the solitary walker, pauses before a wall:

"Sometimes, when the wall of a house stands in the light of noon, it as though the light were taking possession of the wall on behalf of silence. One can feel the approach of the silence of the noonday heat. The light lies firmly on the wall as a sign that the wall belongs to silence.

"The gate in the wall is shut; the windows are covered with curtains; the people inside the house are very quiet, as though they were lowering their heads at the approach of the silence.

"The inside wall seems to expand through the silence pressing in on it.

"Then suddenly a song lights up on the wall from inside. The notes are like bright balls thrown at the wall. And now it is as though the silence rises from the wall and climbs upward towards the sky, and the windows in the wall are like the steps of a ladder leading the silence and also the song into the sky above."

Silence brought Picard closer to heaven. In silence he found renewal and hope. Silence is the "original beginning of all things: everything can begin again, everything can be recreated," he said.

"The earth was once no less occupied than it is today, but it was occupied by silence, and man was unable to seize everything in it as it was all held fast by silence. Man did not need to know everything: the silence knew it all for him. And as man was connected with the silence, he knew many things through the silence. The heaven of silence no longer covers the world of ideas and things, restraining them with its weight and pressure. . . . Man is not even aware of the loss of silence: so much is the space formerly occupied by the silence so full of things that nothing seems to be missing."

Picard closes his *summa* with a plea, by quoting Søren Kierkegaard: "The present state of the world and the whole of life is diseased. If I were a doctor and were asked for my advice, I should reply: Create silence!"

After the murder of millions, in a Europe of ruins, the man who walked for hours in silence each morning was calling for quiet. God is "sleeping behind the wall of noise," Picard said. Silence.

The Right to Dream

The word "reverie" is from Old French for revelry and rejoicing. This meaning—joy, delight, wantonness, wildness—is "obsolete" says the *New Shorter Oxford English Dictionary*. A "delirious" scene has given way to today's quieter daydreaming, musing, and meditation. Reverie is, in any case, not a word much in use, but for one unlikely thinker, it was a way into the interior.

"We are created by our reverie," said Gaston Bachelard, a popular professor of philosophy at the Sorbonne, "for it is reverie which delineates the furthest limits of our mind. Imagination works at the summit of the mind like a flame." He courted reverie. He was a daydream catcher.

Reverie is not *rêve*, dreams. In night dreams, the passions of the daytime are in the saddle and ride the dreamer. Night dreams are the province of psychoanalysis, said Bachelard. In his view, *rêve*—masculine in French usage—belongs to *animus*, the male soul, while *reverie*—feminine in French—is the "simplest and purest state of *Anima*," the feminine soul. "*Anima* is always the refuge of the simple, tranquil, continuous life," Bachelard wrote in *The Poetics of Reverie*. "It is *Anima* who dreams and sings."

For Bachelard, childhood is the well of reverie, the living core of a person. He is rapturous about childhood. It may be his favorite subject. Bachelard writes of childhood the way others write of love affairs. There is no end to the allegory and praise he heaps upon it. Childhood is our connection to the moments when we realized "the *astonishment of being*." It's when we enjoyed the great happiness of boredom. "In those times when nothing was happening, the world was so beautiful! We were in the universe of calm, the universe of reverie." Childhood is our love affair with the earth—with water, fire, and trees. We can't love the earth without it. "Childhood remains within us a principle of deep life, of life always in harmony with the possibilities of new beginnings." Childhood is, in short, the soul in its ship. It's not-commerce, not-war. It's the peace within us. It's the deepest well of our true being.

"Our childhood solitudes have given us the primitive immensities. By dreaming on childhood, we return to the lair of reveries, to the reveries which have opened up the world to us," he wrote. "The child sees everything big and beautiful. The reverie toward childhood returns us to the beauty of the first images." Just as "primitive societies" preserve the origins of the world in their stories, childhood preserves that for us, said Bachelard. If we lose touch with our reveries, we lose touch with ourselves. We are uncreated. We are dehoused.

He was methodical in his pursuit of origins, disciplined about daydreaming. Well aware of the paradox of an orderly intuition, he studied reverie as a phenomenologist—a systematic attempt to analyze the essence of phenomena.

The phenomenologist's goal is to make fresh contact with an image to understand its primitive meaning. Bachelard wanted to witness the "heart, soul and being" apprehending the world. Phenomenology is about the "call and response" of the self and the world, said the philosopher Gabriel Marcel. It tries to explain how we see the world with mind and body, with reason and sense, with deep memory and expectations of the future. It makes great claims to be "both a descriptive science and a mystical search" that, like all such searches, recognizes the "unsayable." Phenomenologists seek to get at origins, to return us to first things, to remind us that the world is new and strange and we are, deep inside, always, the child who went forth.

∽

Gaston Bachelard was a philosopher of science on a poet's mission. His career unfolded slowly over his long life. He was a late bloomer. He grew up in rural Champagne, in a small village on the river Aube surrounded by hillside vineyards and small mountains. His parents were shopkeepers and his grandparents were shoemakers. After completing high school he worked for the post office as a clerk and later a telegrapher, a skill he used for a year of peacetime military service. He returned to work in the post office in Paris until World War I. For three years he studied at night school, obtaining his first diploma at age twenty-eight, a *licence* in mathematics. He was studying for an entrance exam for an engineering program, and married only three months, when he was called up at the start of World War I. He fought in the trenches for more than three years, coming home without injury and with the Croix de Guerre. He gave up his plans to be an engineer and returned to his native village to teach physics and chemistry at his old secondary school. His wife died the next year, leaving a daughter. Bachelard never remarried.

At age thirty-six, following his wife's death, he began to study philosophy. With the *licence* he received, and the *agregation* two years later, the expected course would have been for him to abandon his science classes and teach philosophy at his secondary school, but he went further. He taught science and philosophy while working on two doctoral dissertations at the Sorbonne. He was awarded his doctorate in 1927; his dissertations were published. At age forty-four he began his career in philosophy.

He taught at the secondary school for three more years while also teaching at the University of Dijon. He went on to teach at Dijon full time for ten years, and then on to the Sorbonne, where he held the chair of the history and philosophy of science from 1940 to 1954.

Bachelard was "one of the great minds of the Sorbonne" and a beloved professor. "He had a rare talent for illustrating his lectures without diluting them, for charming his listeners into understanding his often difficult material, and for introducing those students too easily dazzled by abstractions to the wonders of an imagination inspired by matter," said one of his biographers, Roch C. Smith. "He was, as one student put it, 'Gaston the magician.'"

Outside the lecture hall "he was always approachable," said Colette Gaudin. "A white-haired patriarch, with the slow gait of a farmer at home on his native plot of ground, he would stroll along the Boulevard St. Michel talking familiarly with any student or friend. During such moments the essentially paradoxical nature of his mind coincided most perfectly with his charm: speaking in earthy accents, he tended toward ethereal thoughts; what might begin with casual references to the weather or polite inquiries concerning one's health would end with reflections on the need to dream well." At home he welcomed many visitors and his daughter made tea.

Bachelard became something of a national treasure. He was pictured with a long white beard, reading by candlelight, the very model of the scholar as a high priest or rabbi. "Give us this day our daily hunger," he said. He was a devoted reader. He "literally lost track of time" when he removed the pendulum from his clock to make more room for books.

He was seen as a rural sage in touch with the wisdom of the countryside. "He spends his childhood in the most rural province, where the man has neither lost contact with the first elements, nor broken with the religion of great events, with the hearth's fire or the riverside meadows," said one admirer. He was eulogized as a "teacher of happiness." Said one appreciation, "Thank you, Monsieur Bachelard, thanks to you I have been a little happier."

~

Bachelard was in pursuit of the rational when he found poetic reverie. As a philosopher of science, he studied how scientists think. Old discoveries could impede scientists, limiting the questions they ask. They should be free from established practices. "For a scientific mind, all knowledge is an answer to a question," he said. "If there has been no question, there cannot be any scientific knowledge."

Scientists must free themselves from the myths and misapprehensions of the past, he said. They shouldn't be seduced by images and words. They should examine their objectivity. If they did, they would find a primitive "naive realist" who harbors ancient beliefs about the earth. "Even in a clear mind, there are zones of darkness, caves in which shadows continue to live," he said. "Everyone should seek to destroy within himself these blindly accepted convictions." Bachelard wanted to free the scientific mind from "obstacles," just as psychoanalysis frees a suppressed person from subconscious worries.

"A rationalist?" he asked rhetorically. "We are attempting to *become* one." This does not come naturally. In the union of thought and dreams, he said, "it is always the thought that is twisted and defeated." To get inside the fallacies of the past, Bachelard searched out the old beliefs about fire, water, air, and earth. This was a surprising interest for a philosopher of science.

We are temperamentally attuned to respond to one element above all others, he believed. "He who listens to the stream cannot be expected to understand the one who hears the singing of the flame," he wrote in *The Psychoanalysis of Fire*, the first of a series of books on the imagination. *Fire* was followed by *Water and Dreams*—"murmuring waters teach birds and men to sing, speak, recount . . . there is, in short, a continuity between the speech of water and the speech of man."—*Air and Dreams, Earth and Reveries of Will, Earth and Reveries of Repose, The Poetics of Space, The Poetics of Reverie, The Flame of the Candle,* and *The Right to Dream.*

The first book in this line, *The Psychoanalysis of Fire*, which he wrote before his arrival at the Sorbonne, was seen as an oddity among his works on science. When a colleague read the title, before he had read the book, he thought that it was a typographical error, said biographer Smith. He "was convinced that there had been a misprint in the title of *La Pyschanalyse du feu* and that it was really meant to be a much less disconcerting *Pyschanalyse du fou. (Psychoanalysis of the Madman).*" After all, do flames dream?

The Psychoanalysis of Fire could be called *The Book of Fire Superstitions.* Fire dazzles us beyond reason, Bachelard said. Fire is a lesson in essence, leaping from wood. It's the sign of the seed and of the funeral pyre. Fire is good and evil, heaven and hell. "It's gentleness and torture. It's cookery and apocalypse," he wrote, recognizing the paradox of the fire of the hearth turned against the home in a rain of firebombs. "The primitive seduction is so definitive that it is still distorting views of the steadiest minds," he warned. Too many old fears and beliefs are repeated without question, even by scientists.

In a chapter on alcohol and punch, Bachelard delights in the contradictions of the "fire-water" brandy. "It is a water which burns the tongue and flames up at the slightest spark." He shows us the fireside scientists we all recognize from evenings around campfires and fireplaces:

"In my youth, at the time of the great winter festivals, they used to prepare a *brulot* (brandy burnt with sugar). My father would pour into a wide dish some marc-brandy produced from our own vineyard. In the center he would place pieces of broken sugar, the biggest ones in the sugar bowl. As soon as the match touched the tip of the sugar, a blue flame would run down to the surface of the alcohol with a little hiss. My mother would extinguish the hanging lamp. It was the hour of mystery, a time when a note of serious-ness was introduced into the festivity. Familiar faces, which suddenly seemed strange in the ghastly paleness, were grouped around the table. From time to time the sugar would sputter before its pyramid collapsed; a few yellow flames would sparkle at the edges of long pale flames. If the flames wavered and flickered, father would stir at the *brulot* with an iron spoon. The spoon would come out sheathed in fire like an instrument of the devil. Then we would 'theorize': to blow out the flames too late would make the *brulot* too sweet; to put them out too soon would mean concentrating less fire and con-sequently diminishing the beneficent action of the *brulot* against influenza. One of the watchers would tell of a *brulot* that burned down to the last drop. Another would tell about the fire at the distillery when the barrels of rum 'exploded like barrels of gunpowder,' an explosion at which no one was ever present. At all costs we were bent on finding an objective and a general mean-ing for this phenomenon. . . . Finally, the *brulot* would be in my glass: hot and sticky, truly an essence. . . . Yes, this is the true mobile fire, the fire which plays over the surface of being, which plays with its own substance, liberated from itself. It is the will-o'-the-wisp domesticated, the devil's fire displayed in the center of the family circle."

His aim here is not nostalgia, but to place a wake-up call. "We must show in the scientific experiment traces of the experience of the child." He cautioned his readers, and perhaps himself, not to be taken in by such appealing images. He is restrained, a spectator before the exhibits. He is a tour guide to folly. In later books, like *Water and Dreams* and his reverie on reverie, *The Poetics of Reverie,* he is lyrical. He enjoys revisiting the old beliefs.

Despite his warnings, the old ways win him over. As his description of the flaming punch bowl shows, he didn't have far to fall. The old alchemy works on him, converting a philosopher of science who is trying to clear the thicket for rational study to a man who is charmed by the old beliefs. He had set out to erect a *cordon sanitaire* around the fantasies of the past, but he ends up on the side of the poets. Bachelard conceded that "poetry might not be an acci-dent." We "may be on earth to sing its joys and sorrows."

He wrote his books of the elements during the war years, from 1940 to 1948, before returning to his works on science. He wrote about refuge, com-fort, warmth, sex. These studies may have been a refuge for him. With France occupied by the Nazis, these books can be read as a guide to a different kind of bomb shelter. During war he builds his firewall of reverie. He takes care to "dream well."

Bachelard wants to recover "the language of enchantment." He's looking for a way to maintain our connection to the power of simple things—water, fire, air, earth—in a scientific age. The village boy is making a trip home, returning from Paris to the Champagne countryside.

Had he written of these places directly, it might have been another nostalgic homecoming, another country boy in the city trying to conjure a lost world. But Bachelard makes his rounds through daydreams and by reading—a kind of slow daydreaming reading is what he advises. His analytical skills never waver, but his method has changed. He says that it takes images to understand images. He dreams his way into other dreams. He does not attack the old superstitions, but sees their truth. He wants to witness the soul perceiving the world. He wants to plunge deep and come back up with the powerful images of a lake or a flame that will reach us and "give us back the truth of our being."

Book by book, Bachelard constructs a vision of an earth that may be like his native Champagne village—it's quiet, private. It's a place of running streams and of still water, and of the mysteries of fire brought to the table with brandy. It's an earth where each element sings to us. Each element of the earth will give us lifelong riches if we allow ourselves to dream.

∼

"Now my aim is clear: I must show that the house is one of the greatest powers of integration for the thoughts, memories and dreams of mankind. The binding principle is the integration of the daydream," wrote Bachelard in *The Poetics of Space*. "In the life of a man, the house thrusts aside contingencies, its councils of continuity are unceasing. Without it, man would be a dispersed being. It maintains him through the storms of the heavens and through those of life. It is body and soul. It is the human being's first world. Before he is 'cast into the world'. . . man is laid in the cradle of the house. And always, in our daydreams, the house is a large cradle. . . . Life begins well, it begins enclosed, protected, all warm in the bosom of the house."

Gaston Bachelard is known in this country primarily for this one book, *The Poetics of Space*. In it he zeros in on the true nature of houses. For Bachelard, the house is a stage for reverie. It's the shell that protects our softer side, our *anima*. It's where we can float on our inmost dreams. "If I were asked to name the chief benefit of the house, I should say: the house shelters daydreaming, the house protects the dreamer, the house allows one to dream in peace," he wrote. A happy home is a home for reverie. This what dwelling means for Bachelard.

The Poetics of Space is not a pattern book or a manifesto. You can't plan a kitchen or pace off a porch from its pages. You learn nothing about designing a good living room or about buying and selling houses. This book is about, to steal a turn on a tired New Age phrase, your inner house. It's about the dream house within.

The Poetics is a daydreamy, daydream-inducing book. It's a dream-by-the-numbers book. He encourages you to daydream and so you drift along with him. He restores the luminous being to objects and thoughts. He finds the cradle in the house, the eye in the light in the window, the shelter in shelter. Houses live through us, for us, live eternally. The blueprint of childhood rooms never leaves us; we walk the floor plan in our daydreams. "We comfort ourselves by reliving memories of protection." This is a book that reads you. It walks you back to your childhood home.

In Bachelard's childhood memories of the house, things are animate. There's little or no distance between the childhood self and the walls and doors. In our earliest days, we are sorting out the animate from the inanimate, that which lives from that we consider inert. A child's house is like the shape-shifting world of fairy tales.

"In the cosmic reverie, nothing is inert, neither the world nor the dreamer; everything lives with a secret life, so everything speaks sincerely," he wrote in *The Poetics of Reverie*. "The poet listens and repeats. The voice of the poet is the voice of the world."

Each poet can be known by his or her metaphors, as a flower is known by its petals, he said. Applying a scientific approach, Bachelard studies the "poetic diagram," the "meaning and symmetry" of a poem's metaphors. The "poetic diagram" of *The Poetics of Space* is shelter within shelter, a series of nested boxes, shell on shell, between the daydreamer and the world so that the dreamer can dream the world.

The house of reverie is a utopia of small spaces. It's a realm of private realms. *The Poetics* goes from cellar to attic, from larger to smaller space, with chapters on House and Universe; Drawers, Chests and Wardrobes; Nests; Shells; Corners; Miniature; and Intimate Immensity. He concludes by contrasting large and small, outside and inside, and looking at "roundness." Each space is a report of a psychological truth. Each a possible way of living, a possible way of hiding out. Bachelard is seeking the smallest space, the furthest remove from the daily world. Shelter as armor; the self expanding into solitude.

He has an expansive view of tight spaces. Writing about bird nests, for example, Bachelard calls upon his wide-ranging lineup of writers, artists, and naturalists, among them Victor Hugo, Henry David Thoreau, Vincent Van Gogh, and Jules Michelet, a nineteenth-century historian and occasional naturalist who has charmed Bachelard with his description of nest building. A nest is built by a bird from the inside, pressing her breast round and round. The nest is the bird, said Michelet. The nest is precarious, swinging in the wind, open to predators, but we see the confidence the bird had, said Bachelard. We want to return to that confidence, that trust in building a safe place in a dangerous world. We want that intimate connection with home, heart, and self, he said. Nests are places of refuge. (Part of the hardship of refugee camps and homeless shelters is that they offer little or no sense of refuge.)

The "teacher of happiness" chose to examine only *"felicitous space."* He said right up front that he would not discuss hostile, evil spaces. He could have explored bomb shelters, hospital wards, morgues, orphanages, insane asylums, army barracks, trenches, or battlefield medical tents—many of which he likely saw in his three years of fighting on the Western Front. "Repression," he said, "is a joyful activity. . . . Every coherent thought is constructed on a system of sound, clear inhibitions."

Bachelard's dream house is a place that carries us away from reality, that liberates us to dream. The house dreams and we dream with it, he said. In the Bachelard house of daydreamers there is no family and there are no visitors. The radio is never on and there is no newspaper. Home is solitude, where we can "travel to the land of Motionless Childhood, motionless the way all Immemorial things are. We live fixations, fixations of happiness."

One gets the sense that Bachelard has told us a great deal about all the miles and miles of streets we have walked down in our life—past New York brownstones, and Parisian apartments, and Georgian terraces in London, and Victorian "Painted Ladies" in San Francisco, and miles and miles of serpentine suburbs—lawn-shrub-house, lawn-shrub-house. What's going on behind all these facades, folded primly like dinner napkins? Architecture books are all about the style of the facades and a little bit about the floor plan inside, the house laid out like a table for a dinner party. That's what architecture books usually tell us—how fork and knife and spoon are set up. But of course we know little of a dinner party from the location of the fork.

∼

"On the night of May 10, 1941, with one of the last bombs of the last serious raid, our House of Commons was destroyed by the violence of the enemy, and we have now to consider whether we should build it up again, and how, and when," Winston Churchill said during a discussion about rebuilding the historic chamber. Arguing for restoring the House in "its old form, convenience and dignity," Churchill famously said: "We shape our buildings, and afterwards our buildings shape us."

But Bachelard implies that it's circular, a chicken-and-egg riddle: our houses shape our daydreams—or our daydreams shape our houses. We daydream; we build what we can imagine. There is no separation between house and dreamer, subject and object. We are not shaped by our houses; we are our houses.

The housing we are building today is starving our imagination, and without a well-fed imagination, it may be impossible to build a better world. Bachelard quotes the writer and dramatist Jacques Bousquet: "A new image costs humanity as much labor as a new characteristic costs a plant."

If we take Bachelard at his word, we should not judge houses by style, location, or real estate value. We should not count closets and bathrooms. We should ask: Is this a good space for daydreams? Or, to use the language of the real estate agent—*location, location, location*. Is this a good location for the soul to dream? Will we be free to "dream well"?

House-hunting may be a project for *animus*—it's male—it is hunting, haggling, analyzing. It's about sniffing out deception and dry rot. But in the end—if we are to be happy—it comes down to *anima*. Sunlight and views, old trees and a hearth, prospect and refuge, speak to *anima*.

All houses are houses of dreams, said Bachelard. We live in houses and so we dream houses. We daydream there and daydream about them. We dwell in the idea of dwelling. They give us the shelter to enlarge ourselves. They are the vessel in which we go forth into the universe. A good house is a good daydreaming space. It is the universe.

Peace, Silence, Dreams

After the war, in the century of the burning house, three philosophers tried to find their way home through the rubble. Theirs was a rehousing project that differed from the one facing the governments of Europe. Housing could be re-built, but that wouldn't be enough. We need to be at home. We need to dwell.

Each philosopher expressed the lost essence of what it is to be at home: for Heidegger it was to dwell in the presence of the "fourfold" gathering of earth and sky, mortals and gods; for Picard to cultivate silence to be nearer to God; and for Bachelard to create ourselves through reverie, to be the child who goes forth, astonished at the earth's beauty.

Each searched for continuity. Each found home by "letting be," as Heidegger said. Each courted the invisible, whether it was God's love or the dream-life essence of how we encounter the world. Each searched for peace.

The convalescent collects himself to return home, said Heidegger. Each of these philosophers was a convalescent, each living in a Europe that was a convalescent. It's our world still.

∼

To dwell we need peace, silence, and dreams. This is obvious when stated, but who puts that on their list when buying or building a house?—a quiet street, a "good" school district, an updated kitchen, a short commute are important or nice to have. But what we need, what we crave, is not fine woodwork and old walls. We crave peace, silence, and dreams.

A world at war destroyed all three. Cities were rebuilt, but each went forward with shadow cities—the city that was destroyed and the city that can be de-stroyed again. The knowledge of terrible, swift annihilation is our inheritance.

⊷ The Storm After the Storm ⊷

A Few Days in April, a Year and a Half After Hurricane Katrina

When Hurricane Katrina hit Pascagoula, Mississippi, three waves raced in. The first was a twenty-foot storm surge—a wall of water two stories tall driven by winds of 145 mph. The waves washed thirteen miles inland, flooding more than 90 percent of the city. Along Beach Boulevard, when the waves receded they took with them houses that had stood through Audrey, through Camille, through all the hurricanes by which people here mark time. Hurricanes by which children mark birthdays. I was born after Frederic, a child will tell you.

Along the beachfront are steps and pillars, cement slabs. No houses. They weren't leveled by big wrecking cranes and carted off. They were just here and gone.

I am visiting Annie Card, a professional photographer from New Hampshire who dropped everything to volunteer with the Red Cross right after the hurricane. When she saw that more needed to be done, she and a friend set up a relief agency, Mississippi Home Again. They handed out appliances, hot water heaters, beds—swift and direct help. And now, a year and a half after the storm, Miss Annie, as she's called, is still here, working to build "100 Homes in 100 Days" in a poor Pascagoula neighborhood. She is showing me Beach Boulevard, where the town's grandest houses had stood.

We get out of the car and walk up a rise to some front steps; that is all that is visible at first—the steps and the old trees. A closer view reveals a small field of wreckage, a brick pile that had been a chimney, stubby brick piers that had married the house to the earth, and the back steps.

And there underfoot are bits of the former life—a corner of a marble table top; smashed pieces of good china—a delicate pattern of gold and pink and white; a rusted flashlight; a boot scraper for the doorstep made of horseshoes for good luck; shards of colored glass; a garden hose still wound up on its plastic dolly, standing next to a spigot from the remaining tangle of water pipes; and an intact cookie jar that says: After School Cookies. The cookie jar is in the shape of a house. Only the roof/lid is missing.

I take in the intimate scale of this destruction. A storm that is hundreds of miles across may smash one teacup and leave another behind. This was personal.

All morning I had driven past ruins along the Gulf Coast, but I had seen them only at a huge scale—hundreds of crushed motel rooms, concrete and mattresses spilling out like a waterfall; the footprints of vanished stores, houses, gas stations with their telltale pipes marking the end of now-gone gas pump islands; and Waffle House remains. For some reason it seemed that the tall signs—each letter in its own yellow waffle—had survived. (Or the Waffle House people had rushed out and fixed these signs long before they were to rebuild.) I was inadvertently compiling a field guide of the lost.

But this is the most poignant Katrina monument I have seen. On the back steps is a display, a broken flea market—pieces of cut glass bowls and dishes, an elegant glass, possibly for some kind of after-dinner drink, little bits of blue glass, a rusted and twisted coping saw. This is an altar to the vanished domestic life.

After Katrina, Annie tells me, she would see people picking through the ruins of their houses, setting pieces aside. Whatever little they found, they left. They were living in a FEMA trailer or living with their relatives. They had no room for any of it, they said. Maybe it wasn't what they had hoped to find. They had hoped to find a way back to the day before the wind and waves hit. Taking a piece of china or a soaked photo back to your trailer could be a bitter souvenir.

It's what we all fear: the forces of the earth—wind and water and fire and the ground itself busting open—coming down upon our family, our doorstep. A house is a small boat. A wall is the thinnest of envelopes, no matter how well built. We know that we will vanish, that everything we have and hold will turn to dust—but we don't want to believe that, and we certainly don't want to see it all go in one shake of the earth or one wave.

I look out to the Gulf, just for relief at first. The view from under the old trees to the silver-toned water is bewitching. I look down again around the foundation. Someone has mowed this lawn. Someone is tending this ruin.

Oh yes, says Annie. She came by here once, a few foundations down, and there was a man trimming the weeds away from his foundation slab. His house is now about three inches tall.

When I first got here, she says, if I had seen that, I would have thought that he was crazy. With all that needs doing, why do that? But she understands now: you do what you can to restart your life.

In another neighborhood, she was cruising with other Red Cross workers to see who needed help. Among the vacant, storm-wracked houses, one was in pretty good shape. A man stood outside watering his lawn.

No need to talk to that man, said her fellow workers.

No. Wait, she said. Annie went over and talked with the man. He was impeccably dressed. But the inside of his house was gutted—it was down to the studs. Each night he slept on a reclining chair. It was about all that he had. He needed help.

You can't tell from the outside, she says. The houses may be empty, the people suffering, but the roses are in bloom. She tells me about a police officer, dressed in his uniform every day for work, while at home his family slept on the floor of their gutted house. He was too proud to ask for help. And she tells me about a minister, dressed in a neat shirt and pants, working to help his congregation. He would never let on that these were his only decent clothes, or that his house was destroyed. As in life, as in the aftermath of the storm: we can't tell from the outside.

This is the storm after the storm. After all those photos of trees bending in the wind, of houses adrift, of people stranded on roofs or escaping in canoes and boats in the street; after the evacuation and the Red Cross rolling around handing out hot meals; after the storm itself has passed and the sun comes out, there are other storms, but these may be invisible. There are private torments as people struggle to hold on to jobs and marriages, as they struggle with the feeling that they have failed their family. The storm after the storm requires its own kind of relief effort. It takes a different approach. It takes someone like Miss Annie.

∾

The phone rings all day for Miss Annie: someone looking for help, someone volunteering, someone needing supplies at one of the houses that are being repaired. She takes these calls on her cell phone as she drives up and down the streets where work is now proceeding on twenty-one different houses. This being the South, these calls follow the protocols of a proper visit:

"Hi, Miss Annie," her caller says.

"Hi, Hon," she answers. Annie calls everyone "Hon" like a waitress in a good diner. She does this back home up north, and for some reason it works for her.

Often her callers don't identify themselves. (You don't reintroduce yourself when you visit friends or family.) "Who's this?" she asks.

"It's Sabrina!" the caller answers, as if Miss Annie were kidding her. She's still unsure. She thinks: Is this the Pascagoula Sabrina, the Ocean Springs Sabrina, or the Gautier Sabrina?

It's like traveling with the mayor of a small city. It seems as if everyone in Pascagoula and the county will call her eventually: A woman calls who had applied to receive a bed three months ago. She is finally moving back into her house. A man calls out of the blue to volunteer. He's a snowbird driving his motor home back from Florida to Massachusetts. He thought he'd stop and volunteer—does she still need help? "Do you have two good hands? One good hand?" she asks. "I've got two good hands and half a brain," he replies. "That's half more than I have," Annie says. She gives him directions. An Amish teen from Lancaster County calls. He's trying to charter a bus to come down to help. She encourages him; the Amish are hard workers. A volunteer working on a house calls looking for more yellow siding. One of the paid project managers calls to find something that another project manager should have given him. Like many construction sites, clarity is sometimes the first casualty.

Annie and her friend Tammy Agard have set up a volunteer center in an old high school gym that they had to repair. The gym had flooded with three feet of water, ruining the wiring and the flooring. The wind had broken windows, allowing the rooftop gravel to pour in. With volunteer help, Annie and Tammy shoveled out the gym, snaked mud out of the bathroom drains and created a friendly place that feels like a youth hostel. A hand-painted sign at the homemade reception desk says: "We Are Here For You—595—Days After Katrina." The numbers are like an odometer, with room to run into the thousands.

The gym is occupied by 150 colorful hand-built bunk beds. They were donated by a church that was closing its volunteer center and then painted and reinforced by AmeriCorps volunteers. They get a new crop from AmeriCorps

NCCC (National Civilian Community Corps) about every six weeks. High school graduates and college students earn money toward their tuition in this federal community service program. For many students, this is their first job. She has to teach them to improvise. "You've all got to be MacGvyers. We have no budget." The first AmeriCorps crew made shower curtains out of blue FEMA tarps and hung them with plastic quick ties. They made blue tarp tablecloths and banners. A large blue FEMA tarp divides the gym. The blue of the tarps is a common color: blue roofs, walls, houses, wrapped piles of stuff. When the last of the FEMA blue tarps disappear, Mississippi will have recovered.

The organization she cofounded with Tammy, Mississippi Home Again, is working with two other small relief groups, Jackson County Community Services Coalition and Hope Has a Face, to build or repair one hundred houses in one hundred days. The Red Cross and the Salvation Army have also contributed. They have a budget of $2.75 million to buy construction materials, reduce mortgages, and pay a team of professional contractors to direct the volunteers. At the end of the one hundred days, they hope that they will have also created a model for other relief efforts to follow.

One of Mississippi Home Again's big breakthroughs was to get two warehouses donated. The larger warehouse was a mess, a 150,000-square-foot derelict. They use about a quarter of that space. The floor was covered with dried sewage. The police had parked cars there seized in drug raids, cars with all sorts of syringes and needles.

Volunteers helped Annie clean the warehouse, but on many days she was alone raking the mess onto a big tarp and pulling it across the warehouse with her car to a Dumpster. Later, Northrop Grumman, which runs a shipyard in Pascagoula and is the state's largest private employer, donated a forklift and the gas to run it. They used to send over a driver in just ten minutes, until she had them teach her how to drive it.

With the warehouse, Mississippi Home Again was able to continue handing out beds, appliances, and building materials. People line up for "Warehouse Wednesdays." It's an operation so direct that national charities with large budgets send their clients to Mississippi Home Again. "All people want," says Annie, "is to have clean clothes to go to work, to send their kids to school, to sit down to dinner as a family. Just the basic things we all want.

It gets pretty simple once you've lost everything." After they had handed out $20,000 of appliances in the first months after the hurricane, they decided to go further. "Their gratitude shook us to the core," says Annie.

～

There are sixty-five volunteers working today. Miss Annie could use another 150 each day. In this small, poor neighborhood are volunteers from New England, the Midwest, and California. They are like birds blown off course by a storm.

We travel up and down the grid of streets: Testament, School, Bilbo, Skip, Dupont, and Robertson. Annie must see these streets in her dreams. The houses are small, about nine hundred square feet, or less than half the size of the average American house. Before the storm they were in rough shape, some houses sagging from termites and neglect. About 60 percent of these houses are rentals. One house—not one slated for repair—has recently burned, probably set on fire by drug addicts making crack. Some of these houses needed more work than was first thought: floors jacked up, roofs rebuilt, walls replaced. In these few blocks is a small encyclopedia of what years of heat and humidity can do to wood. It's like having a boat in the water.

At Mr. Randolph Johnson's house on School Avenue, nine young men from Detroit are nailing on siding. They are part of a program called YouthBuild, which is meant to teach them skills and help them earn a high-school equivalency diploma. A week before, the Amish women were up on the roof in their dresses. (No pictures allowed.) The Amish shingled five roofs in a week or less. They were fast workers. They also worked with a YouthBuild group from Chicago. The Amish loved meeting new people. A few doors down, at Miss Frozine Culberson's house, two high school students from Andover, Massachusetts, are finishing up her front steps. Farther down School Avenue, two retired schoolteachers from California are putting in windows at Mr. Melvin Patton's house. In another house, a family of four from Wellesley, Massachusetts, have become champion sheetrockers. Their daughter, age fourteen, is covered in white dust. "This is her spring break," her mother says. "All her friends went to Cancun." "How boring," Annie says. The daughter smiles, shy and proud, as Annie takes her picture. In an empty lot, some kids from a Brattleboro, Vermont, church are cleaning up where a new house will be built, throwing the last debris into a big blue Dumpster. At the corner of School and Bilbo, Miss Willie Mae Armstrong's house is open on all sides, as if it were a park pavilion or a bandstand. Parts of the house are draped in blue tarp. It's a rare old house (1930) for the neighborhood, with tall rooms and proportions that are graceful even in this state of undress. Miss Armstrong, age eighty-seven, lives around the corner in a FEMA trailer. She comes by every day to tend her flower beds.

The volunteers have a range of skills. Some have never picked up a hammer; others are builders. A roofer from a Methodist church in Los Gatos, California, has put thirty-four new roofs on houses damaged by Katrina, three of those roofs for Annie. He told his wife that he would like to stay until he does forty-five, one shy of his age. A Colorado church group arrived with tools and the skills to use them. These skilled workers arrive as if summoned. She could use more. The college students bring enthusiasm and heart. They need instruction. Volunteers have come from Oberlin College, Stanford, the University of Missouri, MiraCosta College near San Diego, and Franklin Pierce College in New Hampshire. They make friends unlike those they have at school. Many volunteers tell Annie that this was their best vacation; they want to come back. The high school kids from Andover give up a half-day in New Orleans' French Quarter to keep working on Mr. Leonard Cook's house. The young men from the Detroit YouthBuild program talk of moving down here and starting a construction company. They have never felt so safe. "You amaze us," Annie says to one. "We amaze ourselves," he answers. "We didn't think we could do anything."

～

On this Friday in April, the first two completed houses are dedicated. In a small ceremony, Tammy stands with the homeowner and welcomes reporters and officials from the local government and the Red Cross. Miss Frozine Culberson accepts her house, saying, "Thank you to every one of you for being here to help us out. It's truly uplifting for me. This is a neighborhood that we were raised and born in and that we love. And I'm glad to see it up and beginning to run again. I'm very grateful." The sixty-six-year-old grandmother adds, "I hope someday one of my grandbabies will want to live here and keep this in the family another generation." After her pastor offers a blessing, a volunteer hands her a welcome mat.

At the next house, Mr. Leonard Cook offers thanks and a prayer. He's eighty-three years old, living alone since wife died fifteen years ago, and other than having had a quadruple heart bypass and gall bladder surgery, he's doing fine, he says. After the hurricane he lived behind his house in a FEMA trailer while he reclaimed his house, room by room. He lost everything he had. He rebuilt his bedroom, kitchen, and bathroom and moved back in. Everyone flees their FEMA trailers at the first moment, preferring to live in their own home even in the midst of construction.

100 Homes in 100 Days helped him to finish his last two rooms. He accepts a welcome mat as the Andover High School students and the Los Gatos Methodists applaud. "I am thankful for what they've done," says Mr. Cook. "I pray that they have a safe journey back home."

Where do you start on that first day when you return to your destroyed home? I ask him.

"You don't start nowhere," he answers. "You just thank the Lord you're still living and He'll make a way for you. And that's what happened. He made a way for me. I've come a long way with this house. It turned out pretty nice."

Three more houses are dedicated this day. Every Friday until July they will be dedicating houses in this neighborhood.

⁓

Miss Annie brings help to many people. They call it a blessing and they want to thank her. They do this by asking if she's been saved. Think of it as a complimentary relief effort. It seems that she can't buy a few sheets of plywood without being pulled into a circle to pray.

She grew up in a large Catholic family in Connecticut and has since lapsed into New England's leading religion, a pragmatic compassion. In the houses, volunteer Methodists work alongside the born again and people who go to church only for weddings and funerals. It doesn't matter when the hammer hits the nail. The people of Pascagoula pray for them all and they let them know about it.

Miss Annie has a deep connection to those suffering in the storm's aftermath. She tells me about handing out food on the Red Cross trucks right after the hurricane. She met a young man in his early twenties who was living in an old Chevy. He was a roofer with no tools, no one to hire him, no money for gas. The storm had wiped it all away. He had been living with his family, but he did not want to be a burden so he lied to his mother, telling her that he was staying with friends. "I don't want to ask for help," he said. He was sick—"he had yellow stuff coming out of his eyes," which may have been from swimming through the flood waters when they rescued his mother. He had no money to see a doctor and wasn't asking for anything more than a peanut butter sandwich from the Red Cross. Annie gave him what she had in her pocket, twenty or thirty dollars. She looked for the young man again, but never found him. "There wasn't anybody to help him," she says. Her eyes fill with tears. "We're all just kids inside." She can't talk. We sit silently. It's no wonder that here in the Bible Belt when people look her in the eye, they see faith.

∾

We go visit Miss Sabrina Williams. She comes out to the porch and throws her arms around Miss Annie in a short, powerful embrace. Her youngest daughter, eight-year-old Tyra, is at home. They give Miss Annie a present that they've been holding on to since Christmas. It's an angel just like the one they had before Katrina. The angel lights up and the wings move.

"That's what we think of you!" Sabrina says.

"You crazy girl!—that's beautiful!" Annie says. In her time in Mississippi she's been given many angels.

I ask Miss Sabrina about recovering after the storm. It must have been hard. "It was, but I had an angel," says Sabrina, looking toward Annie.

On the evening before the hurricane hit Pascagoula, Sabrina and her family evacuated to her grandmother's house in the country, away from the coast. Then they struggled to get back home. "We waited in line eight hours at night to get gas. And then when we got to the pump, we could only get $50 worth at a time, each person. And as it started getting later and later, and the gas is going lower and lower, they start chalking it down to a certain amount, a certain amount. And I was just lucky that we rented a car and it was one of those compacts.

"We were on dirt roads, back roads. Oak trees had fell in the road and we had to wait until the people come with chains and saws to cut them up and pull them to the side to get back out. So it took us two days to get back home.

"It didn't even look like life was living here. No. Everything at the beach, every home down there just wiped out. And it really looked like a hand been in some of those buildings and just tore stuff back out. . . . We come back, our vehicles had been under water. When we opened the doors, the water just poured out. Everything.

"When we left, we didn't think of this type of destruction. We know a storm was coming, okay. It might be a little damage, you know. But never, never, never in a million years to think that you would come home and not have—people not having their own houses, just a slab or their front porch steps, you know.

"When we first come back, we couldn't find no water. We couldn't find no food. We couldn't get gas. Nothing. You would have to go somewhere to Alabama to get gas and there you were in line four and five and six hours." They stayed with her mother. Sabrina, her six children, and one of her son's friends, crowded into two rooms. They were without electricity for two and a half weeks. "We stayed there five months before we got a FEMA trailer.

"I mean many tears, many tears because you get frustrated. You don't know what to do. How you're going to rekindle this. You know you're getting a little bit of governmental help. But you know, and not to be saying it to sound like it's greedy, but it's never like where you started from. What you had, you know. Starting all over. Like I told my children, you're just going to be thankful that we are here, still living.

"You know people still aren't back together. I'm just blessed. Yep, we were blessed with an angel," she says. Miss Annie is sitting on the porch holding Tyra. "I was able to come home. I have family that was in New Orleans. They're still not able to go home." She has cousins who moved away and have "been through more torment than what you think."

"I seen people pull together. I seen people rip each other apart due to the storm. I seen people take it and use it as it should have been used. And I have seen people misuse it." The hurricane "changed everybody's life whether you were out or wasn't out, whether you had or didn't have. Because you've actually seen what your neighbor might have went through, which might have been a little bit worse than you, or they might have been okay. I flooded here; across the street they didn't flood. I don't understand.

"The house over there, they got damaged; she was okay a little bit. But they say the way it come through it didn't touch everybody. Maybe my touching was a blessing. Because it makes me value life more. And if I can value life, I can teach them the same thing. My children know what it's like to have and not to have. To sacrifice and not to sacrifice. To help somebody else or to help us through."

She has seen the community "come together, pulling together like it should have been, like we were once before." And she is thankful for all the help that came from out of state. "It makes you say: wow, we're loved. Because you kind of think you're forgotten."

She welcomes us inside to see some furniture she's cleaning up.

As we leave, Miss Sabrina says, "Y'all have a blessed day."

⁓

"There's no overstating what the human cost of this was after the hurricane," Annie says as we return to the neighborhood to check on the volunteers. There is a "strain on marriages, a strain on any relationship you can imagine." Many people are stuck with relatives out of state. "We all love our families, but I don't want to live with my family again. It's a strain on the family who used to only see their brothers and sisters on Christmas and always had a wonderful reunion, but now they took up their brother's invite to stay with them. The brother thought it's going to be a couple of months. Now a year and a half later there's this insane and sometimes irreparable damage to an extended family.

"There are all sorts of judgments by outsiders and even within families: 'Well, you're not trying hard enough. Boy, if it happened to me, I'd already be back in my house.'

"Now that you've been down here, you can see how difficult it is to get your life back, your house, your job, your car. Couples split. FEMA checks come; sometimes the husband or the wife took off with it. A marriage is a compromise. We had people who had anywhere from two feet to ten or twelve or twenty feet of water in their houses, or over their roofs. And the husband or the wife decides, I love it here, hon; I want to rebuild. The partner does not want to rebuild. How do you compromise? One of them wants to leave. And I'm talking about hundreds, maybe thousands like that."

Children are hostage to this dilemma. "The kids are afraid to still live here.

The parents said no: 'This is where we grew up; this is where we're going to stay.' These are the kinds of discussions that are still happening. They're not discussions—they're fights. There's this horrible strain. It's not resolvable. And I'm not saying every family is like this. There's other families that have rebuilt their houses and they're doing it as a team and they're excited to move back in." But it's not easy for the go-getters either. She knows one family where the father has a good job at the shipyard, and they're handy, but "they were struggling to buy a few pieces of sheetrock or some flooring. They do a little bit, a part of a room a time.

"These people have dealt with all the biggest strains there are in life, all at the same time. We can choose to move—I can choose to move to another house and be doing that because I want to and still dread it because I hate moving. It takes forever. It's so stressful to pack everything up. These people were moved without any choice, and into FEMA trailers.

"Everybody thinks: You've got a FEMA trailer. They're fine. What's the big deal?" says Annie. She and Tammy share a small travel trailer that took on over a foot of flood water. The families in the trailers face double utility bills for the trailer hook-up and the electricity and water running to the house they're try-ing to repair. Most people's utility bills have jumped 50 to 100 percent.

"They're very careful when they talk. Most of them are," Annie says. "'It's hard living in this FEMA trailer.' And then they'll catch themselves and say, 'We don't want to sound ungrateful. We're glad to get the FEMA trailer. We needed it. We're blessed that we got it.' So then you have somebody scram-bling because they know they're being portrayed as ungrateful.

"For over a year and a half they've read headlines that called them lazy and fraudulent and living off unemployment checks. They've been abused on every level in a very public way. The media has basically put a stamp on these people as being incapable, irresponsible, whiners—all of those things. And that's damning, too.

"I just feel like they keep getting hit by debris."

As we drive down School Avenue one more time, she says, "A lot of those houses that are empty were not empty before the hurricane. The neighbors got washed away, washed to wherever they went. A lot of the elderly people, the storm took a toll on them. Many, many people have died since the hur-ricane. Some people died from being tired; from being worn out."

~

Hurricane Katrina is a disaster we cannot face. It is the most destructive natural disaster in American history. The statistics are numbing, the aerial photos of houses reduced to pick-up sticks and cars tossed about are too distant. The storm was too vast, too powerful to comprehend, and also too intimate.

Katrina destroyed sixty-five thousand houses in Mississippi. More than another one hundred thousand houses were not habitable, not fit for dwelling. They were the walking wounded: houses left standing, flooded, moldy, missing parts of roofs, windows. They were outlines of houses—a sodden mess that was once your home. With another hurricane season approaching, one hundred thousand people are still living in trailers.

For a year and a half these people have led a life that "none of us ever want to live," says Annie. "All the people we are helping have such tough days. Every day." The hurricane was personal.

When Miss Annie goes home, people ask her: How's everything down there? Is it okay?

Well, no. It's a year and a half later and people are still lacking beds and houses.

There are billions unspent at the state, hundreds of millions unspent at the Red Cross, and these people still need help. Too many charities are operating out of habit, following old models that no longer apply. Too many donors are doing what they think should be done, not what needs to be done, she says. We need to be imaginative, to find new ways to respond. The usual ways won't do.

Annie was living in the FEMA-sponsored tent city in Pass Christian the first Christmas after the hurricane. The television news show *Good Morning America* arrived in Pass Christian and the Poster Child syndrome hit. The show's co-anchor, Robin Roberts, grew up in "The Pass" and had family there. When she was asked about her family, she broke down and cried, not something she wanted to do on the air. Viewers "adopted" the town. Tractor-trailer loads of toys were delivered. They had more bicycles to give out than there were children.

"That Christmas, convoys bought hundreds of thousands of dollars of toys," Annie says. "They don't want toys. Ask them what they want and they say: 'I want mama to stop crying.' Ask them to draw what they want and they draw a house." They don't want a dollhouse. They want a house; they want to go home again.

It's what everyone wants. The Mississippi Gulf Coast is like the Land of Oz. Everyone is trying to go home again. There *is* no place like home. But after Hurricane Katrina your home is like no place you have ever known.

DWELLING IN POSSIBILITY

Why should beauty emerge from the world of the ordinary?
The answer is, ultimately, because that world is natural.

☙ Soetsu Yanagi, founder of the Japanese
folk craft movement

✤ Counting Houses ✤

The LQ and OLQ of Americans

Early in the twenty-first century, I swore an oath to defend our constitution and took part in something Americans have been doing since 1790: trying to keep track of each other. I went out to see where my fellow Americans were dwelling. They were living in LQ and OLQ—Living Quarters and Other Living Quarters. This is the lingo of the Census Bureau for houses and apartments. I had been hired as a census taker, or more accurately, I was an Update/Leave Census Enumerator working in the Decennial Management Division. I was one of 1.4 million temporary workers hired in the country's "largest peacetime mobilization."

I have said that I could go from house to house clear across the country, knocking on doors to ask if could I come in and look around—*What's your favorite room? Your latest house project? I'd like to see them all*—and here was a job that paid me to do that. I was deputized to be nosy, but I was nosy about my own particular questions.

According to my census training, Americans were living in apartments, student dorms, nursing homes, jails, group homes, homeless shelters, hospitals, residential treatment centers, convents, monasteries, abbeys, migrant worker camps, construction camps, hotels, and motels. We were living in single-family houses, townhouses, row houses, duplexes, mobile homes, RVs, campers, boats, tents, fairgrounds and carnivals, railroad cars, and even caves. When you run through the list of where Americans live, it seems a little crazy, as if we were a people who had just fallen to earth and crashed into whatever shelter was handy.

No matter where you're hiding out, the Census Bureau is determined to find you and make you sure you are counted, and thus—the theory goes—are fairly represented in Congress. I'm knocking on your door for your own good—if I can even find you. That's the $13 billion question (the cost of the 2010 Census). There were a surprising number of empty houses in the territory I canvassed. Were the homeowners gone or just gone to Florida for the winter? Had they walked away from their mortgage or were they snowbirds? It's difficult to keep track of all 309 million of us. It's not like we can all return to our ancestral villages on a pre-arranged day to be counted.

I had committed much time to counting houses. I had qualified for the job by taking the census test, which required sorting long numbers, alphabetizing, following a filing system code, choosing the shortest route in a neighborhood, and distinguishing Ann Maria Rodrigez from Ann Marie Rodriguez, as well as Allan Schmitt from Allan Schmidt. I had to sit through four days of training during which our cheerful crew leader read each word aloud, as she was required to, from a training manual the size of a city phonebook. "I like to think of us as the USS *Census*," she had said at the start of the first morning. "We're all on a ship and you are my crew."

We spent half a day filling out forms. There were forms about whom to contact if we lost our paperwork, forms so the government could award the remains of our lavish earnings of a few weeks should the USS *Census* go down at sea, forms upon forms.

The forms scripted each move we were to make once we put on our plastic ID badges. We were to introduce ourselves to a resident following the prompts on D-535(UL), hand them confidentiality statement D-31, then check their address on D-105A, or if they weren't home, to put the questionnaire D-1 in plastic bag D-217. Each day we were required to record our work on D-451 and file D-308 to be paid. If we encountered "difficult or threatening situations," we were to report it on D-225 INFO COMM. If we lost PII—Personally Identifiable Information—we were to refer to D-449(PBO) and within one hour call the Decennial CIRT—Computer Incident Response Team. The team might have to contact the FOSD, CLD, CL, FOS, and LCO—you really don't want to know. The organization chart looked like the management plan that got General Motors into trouble. If I was in doubt about any of this, I was to consult manuals D-648 and D-590.

And we were fingerprinted (for our own safety, of course). When I was having my fingertips rolled in ink twice—since two sets were required—the fingerprint takers were surprised that I had never had my fingerprints "captured." Ten of our group of fifteen were fingerprint virgins.

We stood up, raised our inky right hands, and "solemnly" swore an oath to "support and defend the Constitution of the United States against all enemies, foreign and domestic. . . . So help me God." All this to ask someone how many people live in his or her house.

∽

On the last day of our training we were sent out on a sample canvassing operation. With two other trainees, I covered a small triangle of an old village with houses that dated to the early 1800s.

A few houses were well-tended, but most were coming apart, as if they had been hit by invisible tall waves—storm doors with broken glass, porches piled with junk, porches kneeling to the earth, ready to pull away from the house. Paint long gone, bad repairs, windows covered with blankets, and home improvement projects given up so long ago that the plywood had grayed and the white Tyvek wrap was flapping in the breeze.

At each house, when someone answered our knock, I was impressed by the way people appear at the door: their whole being and presence arrives along with the breath of the house—the house's odors exhaling on you. On these late winter days, it was like seeing a turtle sticking his head out of his shell.

I've had this experience before. I have worked as a door-to-door salesman; I have delivered the mail. Knocking at a stranger's door, you are at the threshold of other lives, right at the line of privacy.

Two people told us that they had sick people in the house. One woman was a little too quick to tell us that she didn't have any additional apartments. (We all thought that she did. There were several cars there and an extra entrance on a large back wing.)

Each home was a mystery. Just what were people doing in there?

∽

In truth, I had signed on wishing to conduct my own private census. What I wanted to ask the people who came to the door was: So how's it going with you? I mean really—not income, not the size of your house, but how is it going with your soul? The census that I wished to take was Gaston Bachelard's. The philosopher would remind friends and students to dream well.

I tried to judge houses on what I called the Bachelard Index: Are the people here dreaming well? Are these houses nourishing the souls dwelling there?

We should be building good places for dreaming. After basic shelter, this is what matters. The rest is home décor.

~

We were working in Mud Season, that time of year in northern New England when the Ice Age slowly recedes. The dirt roads were frozen or muddy and puddled, depending on where you were. The dirt driveways were ice, slush, and mud. The snowbanks were piled so high that you couldn't see if you were backing out of a driveway.

I locked the wheels on my old pickup truck into four-wheel drive, provisioned myself with a snow shovel, snowshoes, a walking stick, a road atlas, and dog biscuits. I used them all. In my Bean boots and gaiters, I slopped through icy-muddy water, climbed over snowbanks and stood in snow up to my thighs. I sidled past barking dogs straining their chains, dogs who were not won over by my dog-biscuit diplomacy. I parked my truck at the end of roads where the plow had piled up a mountain of snow and snowshoed in a half mile to isolated cabins. I explored private roads I had always wondered about; I poked around lakes and hilltops.

"My territory" was the shaggy north end of a blue-collar town where it gave out to dirt roads that trailed away into abandonment in the woods, where there were low-slung log cabins favored by those seeking isolation on long private roads winding into the trees. There were sketchy, home-built A-frames, geodesic domes, vinyl-clad slap-'em-down suburban ranch houses. There were more examples of arrested home improvement: At one house, paint color samples—those strips of four colors—were tacked by a front door, faded, curling in the weather. There were rotting porch floors as thin as Saltines, and many houses fronting wide mucky expanses given over to cars, trucks, and snowmobiles. In their mid-day slumber these houses suggested a confused mind, a hurried life, anxiety in suspended animation.

I canvassed my first houses with the crew leader assistant. She had grown up in the town and she had her own neighborhood map. She posted the landmarks as we drove by: foreclosure . . . suicide . . . stoned schemer . . . and skinny-dipping teenage girls by the roadside. This is the type of PII—Personally Identifiable Information—that stays local.

~

My census devolved into many censuses: The dead truck and junk census, the dog census, the grumpy old man census, the startled woman census, and the inventory of closed summer cabins, some of which were sublime. A few findings:

The Old Truck Census

What a heap of dead machinery "my people" in "my territory" are holding on to. Old plow trucks, plow blades, cars, snowmobiles, bulldozers, trailers, ATVs, chainsaws, and who knows what else is under the snow. People can't believe that their tools no longer work and aren't worth something. They can't bear to part with them. It's as if they were awaiting the messiah of seized pistons and blown head gaskets to come resurrect their beloved rusting machines.

I spent a half hour or more trying to correct the address of a dead-end homestead that was one family's junkyard. All along the dirt road was a traffic jam of dead vehicles: old pickup trucks with smashed windows, rusting bulldozers, a dump truck holding a pile of flattened gas tanks. These trucks had gone on to the next stage, their paint dulled and marked by streaks, more like lichen on a granite boulder. There was a white school bus carcass—just the passenger compartment. A big square of sheet metal had been cut out of the roof. Another truck was piled with bicycles. A Day-Glo pink kiddie bike caught my eye.

The house was surrounded by more old trucks, buses, ATVs, and dirt bikes, some of which may have been working. Two rubber tractor treads led to the door. The ground had that oily smell of junkyards and I saw the rainbow swirl of oil in the water.

I was alone in the wilderness of machines. I had gone forth to find dwellings and I found machines in the woods. It's so telling, so obvious, so like a freshman-year honor's thesis that I turn away from it: here dwell devices.

This is the end of the line for the Gross Domestic Product. Here the assembly line, showroom, and pride of purchase gave way to rust, mud, and decay. Imagine the assembly line and shrink-wrapped newness ending up here. Imagine the assembly line spilling out into the woods.

Once in these hills we lived with animals—horses, oxen, cows, sheep, goats, and chickens. We defended them with the gun. All the other critters— fox, bears, beaver, fisher—have returned since we gave up farming. Used to be if you saw a wild animal around, you grabbed your gun and shot it, one woman who grew up here told me.

Except for dogs, I saw a horse or two, and one little flock with three ducks, two white hens, and a cat. The machines, the old beat trucks, the dented and picked-apart cars stand in for the missing farm animals.

The Grumpy Old Man Census

We had been warned that we might meet with some hostile "respondents." ("Be confident. . . . When you introduce yourself, say it like you expect co-operation.") Over in Maine, census workers had been assaulted. "They'll have doors slammed in their faces and (in very rare cases) guns put in their faces," said a Census Bureau spokesman in another state. But "ultimately we have no choice but to finish this job."

Since I was working the back roads, I thought that I might encounter some people who didn't want to be bothered by anyone. (A founding principle of the republic. George Washington had to put a good spin on the first returns, saying that the nation's population would be "far greater" than 3.9 million if you could count all the refuseniks.) They were not looking for someone with a plastic badge to come along and tell them that their government wanted to count them in. They had counted themselves out, thank you.

I had visited a few places that were menacing, like the private road guarded by eight signs: Posted: No Trespassing; Keep Out; DANGER, Do Not Enter, Authorized Personnel Only. And other variations on the theme. I drove in. A long narrow road looped around into a mess of a gravel pit and muddy staging area. No one around; no house.

And I had been spooked by a snowshoe hike to an abandoned dark gray mobile home with four dead cars entombed in the snow. Laundry was hanging out on the line—fitted sheets and towels. The wind had blown them about for months, but they still hung there. This person left in hurry, maybe when the first snow started falling. I opened the door a little on the windowed-in porch. It was piled with faded boxes and smelled strongly of mildew. I caught the quick motion of a rodent diving under a corner of the house. Rats move like that.

At a couple of houses I was received with a look of wary forbearance, as if I had set up a three-cup-and-a-pea con game on their doorstep. I'm watching you, their look said. You won't pull one over on me. *The United States of What? America? How long has that been going on?* But once I said hello, I watched them seesaw between wariness and the desire to chat.

I had expected to meet the tribe of *No!*, but I found people just piecing it together, hanging on to their little scrubby patch of the American Dream.

I did come upon one swearing, anti-government man. He was a cartoon and I welcomed the entertainment. At a little house, a man with an old-fashioned white chin beard answered the door.

"You have to talk to my wife. I don't want to have anything to do with you. *Goddamn* government gets its nose stuck in my business. *Goddamn* president—" he said and walked past me out the door toward the mailbox.

I didn't egg him on for my own amusement, though I was tempted: "That's Goddamn *Mr.* President to you."

I waited for his wife. "Don't listen to him; it's not you," she said.

I smiled, gave her the census and checked their address.

He stormed back in. "Why'd you take that thing?" he was saying as I left. She was shushing him.

I also met a couple of angry younger men. At the end of a road, I was driving down yet another long private driveway when I saw a pickup racing up behind me. I waved—what else could I do? I pulled in and the truck pulled in right beside me. The truck bed held some cordwood, a gas can, bits and pieces from working in the woods.

A guy in his thirties with work-roughened hands got out and stood with his truck between us. He was not welcoming.

I introduced myself. He told me that he had just filled out something last year. I told him that was a special census survey. I paused and looked across the valley.

"Nice spot you've got here," I said.

"Yeah. Can't beat it. Too bad I still can't get away from this shit."

Americans live far apart—as far apart as we can manage. The Puritans preached against "outlivers" and some towns levied heavy fines on those refusing to live next to their neighbors, but it's where we've been headed almost since the Europeans arrived. The 1980 census showed that Americans were living farther and farther apart from one another. This is proof of the centrifugal tendencies of American life, the impulse to migrate to the farther reaches of whatever precinct we inhabit. (A quick primer of the types of American space: 1. Cabin in the woods. 2. Car as cabin in the woods. 3. iPod on city street as cabin in the woods.)

I thought about this as I trespassed on official business, bouncing along rutted private roads to clearings where a geodesic dome stood, or a shed, or that kind of brown backwoods cabin with a yellow *Don't Tread on Me* flag hanging on the small second floor porch.

You're still free to live your dream. And if your dream is confused, well then, welcome to America.

The Census of Houses Awaiting Summer's Return

There were a few houses where I lingered. Well-sited old farmhouses with views of the hills, sheltering under big thick maples. Old cabins that even in winter held their summer poise. In deep snow, I trooped around on snowshoes among a group of rustic shingle-style cottages by a small lake. No one was around but me and the ghosts of a century or more of summers. On broad and saggy porches worn wicker chairs and tall-backed rockers sat gathered in a circle as if still in conversation. There were faded paper lanterns, abandoned mosquito coils, and bug spray. My favorite cabin was sheltered in a grove of birches. From the porch, the lake revealed itself, demurely, glinting between the trees.

The summer houses, humming to themselves the tune of another season, had an arresting grace. They were at ease. This began to trouble me. They posed an entirely different set of census questions. Why do summer places have the signs of home—big trees, prospect, repose—but "daily" houses look worn and beat? Is this a chicken-and-egg question? Were these houses chosen as summer places because they were special? Or are they just curated differently? Someone's pet, someone's dream of New England?

Do we trample the gentler qualities of a home place with our daily comings and goings? Or are modern houses just graceless? The old houses belong unquestionably to their place. The new houses are just set down.

What I learned from my many censuses is that all houses are provisional. No matter how much brick, stone, and wood we erect, no matter how much family history we wrap ourselves in, a dwelling is a temporary encampment.

The houses that seem the least temporary are the ones that are settled each day—in which each activity binds the people to the place, planting or building or being in a way so that house, land, and people seem to be breathing at the same rate. But if we're not here, then our homes are not here. The old farmhouses surely were here—they had no choice—and it's that *hereness* that is pleasing. But these days it seems we are running short of *here*. We have a heap of *now*—but it's a placeless *now*. Old houses are brimming cups of *here*.

As I walked around, I came to wonder about the possibility of dwelling in the ordinary. What would it take? Why is it that the ordinary is so hard for us? Not the nine-to-five daily slog, but the grace of the ordinary. The world is a cup running over with grace, and we walk about parched.

∼

I also worked another census operation: NRFU—Non-Response Follow-Up, in which we tried to ferret out WHUHE's (pronounced *who-ee*)—Whole Household Usual House Elsewhere. We were visiting those who hadn't mailed in their questionnaires. (About one-third of the country.) In the NRFU operation I stood with people a long time, asking them about the age, birthday, and race of everyone in the household in tedious detail as I filled out the EQ—Enumerator Questionnaire. I handed them a menu of races and Hispanic points of origin and asked them to choose as if they were placing an order for ancestors.

It reminded me of hitchhiking: the car door opens and you enter someone else's life at an oblique angle that bounces you right out again, like a spaceship skipping through the atmosphere on the wrong trajectory.

Here I was moments after knocking on a door, asking someone if they own their house with a mortgage or "free and clear." Asking them if their children were "biological" or "adopted." Here I was asking a Korean woman married to a white man how she wanted to characterize the race of her children. I felt as if I were an advance man for some new Jim Crow regime.

After such personal questions, it seemed like I could slip in my own questions: "Would you say this is a good house for dreaming?" "How much does this house feel like home? Very much so? Somewhat? Not at all?"

But based on my two tours of duty with the Census Bureau, I couldn't consistently apply the Bachelard Index. I tried other measures, asking myself if a house was *heimlich* or *unheimlich*, familiar and welcoming or alienating. Again, I have inconclusive results, but I suspect that a national census would report a falling Bachelard Index and a rising *unheimlich*. I can't prove it; I can only say that our houses are as troubled—or as peaceful—as their dwellers.

But one measure of a dwelling's fitness did prove true. The architect Christopher Alexander says that we can immediately feel when a place makes us feel more alive. "We become happy in the presence of deep wholeness," he says. Our souls reach out for what's nourishing, he says. Those summer cabins were like that. "When a building works, when the world enters the blissful state which makes us fully comfortable, the space itself awakens. We awaken. The garden awakens. The windows awaken. We and our plants and animals and fellow creatures and the walls and light together wake."

In his masterful poetic book *The Timeless Way of Building*, Alexander called this animating spirit "the quality without a name." "There is a central quality which is the root criterion of life and spirit in a man, a town, a building, or a wilderness. This quality is objective and precise, but it cannot be named." He considers some descriptions—alive, whole, comfortable, free, exact, egoless, and eternal—but while that's partly it, no single word captures this quality.

"The search which we make for this quality, in our own lives, is the central search of any person, and the crux of any individual person's story," Alexander writes. "It is the search for those moments and situations when we are most alive."

This has been Alexander's search as an architect. With his colleagues he wrote *A Pattern Language* to give people a way to build places that had "the quality without a name." Well-built places are made of patterns—parts—in the right relationship, like that imperiled footpath on the Main Street of my town. "The more living patterns there are in a place—a room, a building, or a town—the more it comes to life as an entirety, the more it glows, the more it has that self-maintaining fire which is the quality without a name."

But in the hands of the first recipients, *A Pattern Language* didn't produce the "self-maintaining fire." The book gave people a language they were not ready to speak. In the 1970s when bootlegged early drafts of *A Pattern Language* were circulating, Alexander would go visit houses that people had built with his language and they were awful. They weren't what he had intended at all. He kept seeing "funky, ungainly" buildings with too many alcoves, columns, and different-sized windows. People picked up his language and spoke weirdly. They didn't build calm spaces of "limpid beauty." He was appalled.

He has worked for more than twenty-five years to correct what he had seen. He dug down deeper and looked at the structure beneath the patterns, coming to understand something he calls "living centers"—the basic geometry that can be found in nature, in great Turkish rugs, in old mosques. When a place makes us feel more alive, we are responding to these "living centers," the geometry that imbues a place with soul. Each "living center" amplifies the next center. He insists that we need to understand this complex, interlaced geometry before we can build robust places that have nature's wholeness.

"Wholeness" sounds like a squishy New Age idea, but to really understand how to make something with that quality is difficult, he told an interviewer. "Let's say . . . we're trying to figure out how to build the windows in that room, so as to make the room as good as possible," he said of an unfinished room. "Now, the thing that's going to get us furthest in making that attempt is painstaking observation of our feelings as we are in the room. . . . And whether we do it through mockups in the full size or whether we make models or we even try little sketches or whatever it is we're doing . . . what we're trying to read is what depth of feeling comes into being because of the window being such and such a size, shape, position, and so forth. Now, this is hard work, very hard work.

"Every time we build a building, it is the degree of participation in the greater wholeness of the world around it, which will determine its success, harmony, and degree of life."

When Alexander begins a design, he asks himself: "What will bring real life to the conditions of a building, or garden, or street, or town? What kinds of events make us feel close to our own wholeness? . . . Which kinds of centers will do the most to produce real spiritual life in people: Which things, events, moments, kinds of centers, will create a spiritual awakening in a person or a person's life?

"I am trying to find those aspects of sight, sound, smell, the sandwich eaten on the back of the truck, the sun's rays on the bedroom floor, which will illuminate existence and make a person come in touch with his eternal life."

∾

Alexander's books are about asking the right questions. This is harder than it first appears. We are trapped by the questions that we know to ask.

Bachelard, the poet of dwelling who started out as a historian of science, said that good science is about asking good questions. No questions, no science.

A new set of questions—a new census—can set society on a new course. The women's movement in the 1970s is a good example. June Arnold recalls that time. She started a "consciousness raising" group with her friends. They began to realize that they were asking the wrong questions. "As a group we would refuse to consider the charge that we were personally inadequate, neurotic or not pretty or smart enough.... Where then did the charge originate?" They asked themselves how had they come to be defined by these words.

"We asked the question everywhere during the week and discovered that once you have changed the question you have changed the world. There was no way to un-see what we had begun seeing."

Change the questions; change the world. That's the start. Change your mind; change the world—eventually, maybe, in time. To build soulful places, first we need to believe that it is possible. That's what Christopher Alexander asks of us.

We know that certain places are powerful, he says. "We find ourselves bewitched, affected, moved. These are the spaces to which we gravitate. We come back to them again and again. This is similar to the experiences we have in nature. In a grove of trees on a hilltop, in a canyon next to a broad river, or in a gentle valley, or along the shore of a quiet lake. The same feeling can come from a door which has wide frames or borders, a long table for six to twelve people, a niche where people sleep, a window seat, an avenue, a gate, a small tree which stands purposefully and collects people, gatherings, meetings, music...."

"How many such places exist in the environments you know? It is rare to find such places." His "deepest wish" is to help people build places in which they will find well-being. "I think most people have given up hope for realizing beauty. They assume it's not available, and yet paradoxically find it too painful to admit to this assumption. But it is possible," he says. "If we try our best to make all the places in our contemporary world with such vivid depth of feeling, surely then something will happen that changes our lives."

But first we have to recalibrate our sight and learn to see the grace of the ordinary.

~§ Sheds ð~

Where I live, we really have only one kind of building, old and new, big and small: the shed. From woodsheds to barns, to houses, meetinghouses, and covered bridges, they are all sheds. New England has never gotten much beyond the shed and we're the better for it. In fact, it's what tourists respond to, though they certainly won't say, "We've come to see the sheds." But they love covered bridges, and the way that the houses lining the common seem like the little brothers of the bigger meetinghouse, or the way the connected sheds and barns trailing behind a house stand there like a third-grade class lined up for its photo.

Sheds are utilitarian. Sheds contain small things—wood and tools—and big: summers, winters, solitude, festivity. The smallest sheds can be liberating: a bob house on a frozen lake, a summer cabin. They can shelter dreams.

Sheds are reticent. They stand back; they're demure, easily adaptable. They let life flow on through.

A shed is the shortest line between need and shelter. It's a trip from A to B. It's often built of found materials; it's built with a distilled practicality.

The best sheds house this contradiction: they are built according to accepted rules and thus they are free.

Here's a small tour, near and far, of sheds:

Covered Bridges

Covered bridges are the stars. These sheds spanning the water are beloved for the beautiful pictures they make.

Devoted "bridgers"—as enthusiasts are known—talk about the "bygone horse-and-buggy days": "prancing hoofbeats" on the wooden boards, "the fragrance of the aging wood," kids swimming under the bridge or fishing off the bridge, young swains stealing a kiss with their "best girl," and the ghosts that might be seen in the terrifying dark on moonless nights. Bridgers keep the nostalgia mills turning.

But the strongest appeal of covered bridges, I think, lies in the surprising feeling of shelter they arouse in people. Passing into the bridge's shadows, a traveler is enclosed and suspended, and in many bridges, open to the water—looking through the trusses or windows, or down through the boards of the roadway. This sudden enclosure and suspension reawakens the senses.

Covered bridges are like tree houses in that way—you're high up, hidden, and have a view. For a moment you are hiding out. The English geographer Jay Appleton says that people are drawn to shelters that offer "prospect and refuge." Evolving as hunter-gathers, humans naturally sought out places where they could see without being seen. Passing through a covered bridge offers a quick taste of our old affinities. The bridgers' stories are tales of refuge.

But covered bridges weren't built to star on calendars. They weren't built to be pretty. They were built with roofs to protect the bridge's support, the trusses you see on the side scissoring by. Twenty different truss designs, most of them patented, were used in the nineteenth century. Philadelphia built the country's first covered bridge in 1805 at the insistence of a local judge who said, correctly, that the bridge would last much longer if its trusswork were protected from the weather. This innovation was quickly adopted across the country with great success. Bridges that once had to be replaced frequently now could serve for a century—or more, in the case of several bridges. Across the country, about 850 covered bridges survive, due in part to the vigilance of the bridgers. These calendar stars are sheds for trusses.

Barns

On our old barn there's a big rusty pulley hanging under the eaves on a back corner with a big rusty hook below, big blocks on three of the corners that were once useful, the outline of one or more vanished sheds on the rear wall, and, on one side, cut boards showing where the house once joined the barn, before the barn was dragged off to rest beyond the house.

A barn is tool. It's like a big workbench bearing the marks of many projects: saw bites, clamping dents, drilled holes, paint drips, and burns. The workbench takes on a topography, a work history.

Our old barn has a similar topography. It's been changed many times and, like most barns, openly shows the signs of wear and change. Houses tend to hide their changes under clapboards, plaster and paint, but a barn is all bones. It's right out in the open. And actually, the degree of openness, or shelter, is one of the qualities that changes over time as the barn's occupation changes.

This small barn has about a dozen doors. On the front, under the gable, are two closed hay doors. We enter through a big red sliding door, which has, in the center, a small door that was added later. We never use the small door. The right side has two small, square doors, now closed. One is under the eaves, and the other, perhaps newer, is on the second floor. On the ground floor are two big sliding doors, entrances for our pig pen, our chicken coop, and the cool, dark, dirt-floored space—a former "manure basement"—where we store hay, feed, and a "library" of old fencing: chicken and turkey wire, metal poles, wooden pallets. Upstairs, the right side has one old window, and an open window-space with loose fitting boards for a cover. Touching the ground are either two more hatches or maybe just patches near the rock foundation. There are two more square doors on the back, one likely added to pitch out manure.

Barns are really best thought of as a semi-shelter, more like a lean-to, open to the weather and the bats, birds, squirrels, mice, rats, and cats who come and go.

Inside, toward the back, the old floorboards have been worn by hooves into smooth hills and valleys, and a long-gone horse has chewed ("cribbed") a beam. There are old heavy hooks, rings, and generations of nails stuck into the timber frame. I can always find a place to hang up a tool, or to hoist a riding lawnmower with a come-along. The timber frame itself is steadfast. The joists and floor of the hayloft are gone. Part of the second floor was added later, framed in with weathered lumber from another shed or house. Our old barn has passed through many hands and hoofs, claws and paws.

Work Sheds

Tilting is a small Newfoundland town of sheds, or "stores" as they are called. There are wood stores, grub stores (for bulk food), general stores (for all-purpose tools and supplies), stages (built out over the harbor to store boat gear and clean fish), twine stores (for mending nets), flakes (wooden platforms for drying fish), slide storage (for horse-drawn sleds), carpentry shops, coal houses, outhouses, garages, milk houses, hen houses, pig pounds, stables, and cabbage houses (old rowing punts, turned upside down and covered with earth).

Quite a few of these sheds are "launched just as boats are launched"— moved from place to place once one owner is done with them. Some sheds are pieces of houses that have calved like a glacier; an old "back kitchen" will be launched to continue life as an outbuilding elsewhere. In this way sheds—

ephemeral, a built tool—have nine lives, a surprising resiliency.

Houses, too, may be "launched." The houses are tough but loose-jointed, growing with the family, adding back-kitchens, bedrooms, back porches, wash houses. Built of trees felled on the island, the houses are tight enough to withstand wind-driven rain and the salt air. They don't mar the land with a foundation or a basement. They sit on "shores"—posts like those used to support docks. When a house is sold, the land stays in the family, and the house is launched, pulled across the ice, or floated across the harbor. Horses once did the pulling, and before that a team of seventy-five to eighty men. Today a tractor is used. (A house once went through the ice. They dug a channel and pulled it out. The house was in fine shape, only the wallpaper "spoiled.")

If you drove through Tilting without an introduction (after the fifty-minute ferry crossing from the mainland and a forty-five minute drive across Fogo Island), it might strike you as a stark, treeless place with angular, boxy houses bobbing on a rocky landscape, jouncing up against each other. But in his fine book about the town, architect Robert Mellin teaches us to see Tilting's rough beauty.

The town took its name from the splitting and salting of fish, or from the sheds set up to do that, the "tilts . . . temporary wooden structures, constructed with vertical log walls and log roofs covered by birch rinds and sods." So Tilting is a town that may be named for a temporary shed.

Mellin has visited and measured every house in the small town of 350. (He also bought one.) The population is down by a third since the collapse of the cod fishery, due to overfishing by large off-shore draggers. Ashore, Tilting folks were once busy hunting, berry picking, and hauling fresh water until it was connected to a public water supply in 2001. In winter, woodcutting used to be a full-time job, the men working in small groups to "slide haul" wood across the island on horse-pulled sleds. "Tilting's traditional way of life was in balance with its available resources," Mellin wrote. It's still a hardworking place. Tilting "never stops working. If they are not fishing or farming, they are making repairs or trying to get ready for the long winter ahead. Tilting's out-buildings are a testament to the diverse and difficult work of the community."

Once a shed is set in motion, it, too, never stops working. "Gilbert Dwyer's twine loft was originally a house built by John Ellsworth around 1872. Before it became a twine loft, it was a store and then a cod liver oil factory. It was also used for pit-sawing lumber and for building boats; Phonse and Joe Dwyer built twenty-five boats in it. The building was moved three times, and its roof was cut down from a gable roof to a flat roof."

The brightly painted houses and sheds are "a formal architecture of resistance," but also "a fragile architecture that ultimately acknowledges that circumstances change, families get larger and then smaller, people move around or they move away, but life still goes on." Mellin has identified an important mixture—the temporary and permanent, the soft and hard qualities that animate shelter.

In the many sheds "there are contrasts of light and dark, closed and open, dry and humid, quiet and noise. The fishing shed with its open floor of spaced beams, or longers, is open to the air and the sound of the water below, producing a slight feeling of exposure or vulnerability. The stage offers variations in light—the daylight of the open flake or bridge, to the dark stage interior with its small windows, to the brightness of the stage head with light reflecting off the water. The stable is enclosed, dark, soft with hay, and muffled in sound. The root cellar is dark, humid, cool, and silent. You have to feel your way around in the dark. The twine-mending loft and carpentry shop is bright, dry, and warm, and the crackle of softwood burning in the makeshift oil barrel stove provides the background to the sound of conversation and work. In each outbuilding, what you notice first and what predominates in memory is the smell of fish, hay, earth, twine, or wood."

None of these buildings have what we would consider a proper foundation. "It is this aspect of Tilting's construction that's remarkably fragile: houses, outbuildings, stages, and flakes constructed with wood foundations that carefully supported and balanced the superstructure over rugged, irregular terrain, and left no traces."

A shed is more fragile than, say, a cathedral or a big box store, but because of its fragility it may outlive both. Fragility may equal flexibility. This is the chief distinction of the shed: it is flexible. It can be rebuilt, moved, taken apart, reassembled, restored, renewed. Sheds are workshops for life.

Connected Farm Sheds

In the spring of 1850, Tobias Walker, a Maine farmer, used forty oxen to pull his large woodshed from behind his house to the barnyard. Later that year he took

down two old barns to replace them with one larger barn. Many of his neighbors were busy with similar projects. Northern New England, a tough place to
farm, was losing out to bigger farms out west. Farmers like Walker responded
by moving their sheds and barns, lining them up, and joining them to their
houses. They were looking to modernize, to make their farms more efficient.
And they were looking for a touch of grace, detailing their barns with the same
elegant restraint as their houses. When Walker's new barn was finished three
years later, he painted the clapboards white with red and yellow trim. He had
let his old barns blacken in the weather. "Improvement is now the order of the
day; improved stock, improved buildings, improved implements, improved or-
chards, gardens, mowing, pastures, improved everything," one Maine farmer
reported to his state's agricultural board in 1858.

The unique connected farm sheds, a sign of progressive agricultural reform, became a "conspicuous and remarkable aspect of the New England
countryside," said architect Thomas C. Hubka in his study of the form. A
children's verse from the nineteenth century captured the new setup: "Big
house, little house, back house, barn." Some old-timers could even recall the
games they played to this rhyme. The connected farm buildings flourished
for almost a hundred years, as common and as nameless as a stray cat. The
childhood refrain is the only known regional description. "This is surprising
to a visitor from outside New England because elsewhere the connected farm
building organization is extremely unusual," said Hubka.

The "big house" was the family's home; the "little house" included the
kitchen, which was the hub of daily life, the summer kitchen, and a small
woodshed (to feed the stove); the "back house," which connected to the barn,
was a workshop and storage space for tools and a wagon. The privy was usually in the corner of the back house, closest to the barn. The little house and
back house were called "the ell" because they formed the longer part of an L-
shape with the big house. The connected sheds were lined up to shelter a work
yard—the dooryard—from the north or west winter winds. The dooryard
and the barnyard usually faced south or east. (There were as, well, at least a
half-dozen outbuildings on most farms, housing cows, pigs, sheep, chickens;
crops like corn, hops, apples, a root cellar; a sugarhouse to boil maple sap; a
well house, and an icehouse, among others.)

Connecting the houses with the barn was a way to bring order to the endless work required to raise several crops and small livestock; cut firewood; repair tools, fences, and the house; cook, wash, and sew. "The task of describing work on the farm is staggering simply because it includes almost everything that everyone did, all the time," said Hubka.

The farmers worked hard, improved their farms time and again, followed the latest advice from their state agricultural agents, the Grange, and the farming periodicals. It was a brave, century-long battle, but they lost. "Today even a casual observer is struck by the dynamic force of these rhythmic, unified compositions. It took an undaunted collective will to improve the farm and to conduct such an optimistic building experiment in the face of a stiff struggle just to continue farming," said Hubka. "The dogged persistence of their labor and the grandeur of their dreams are still evident in the design of their farmsteads."

Anti-Shed I

Electricity killed the work shed; it was no longer needed. The small retinue of sheds around the farmhouse vanished. "Gone were the smokehouse, the blockhouse, outdoor privy, the open well with rope and bucket, the cistern and gutter system to catch rainwater on the roof and the rain barrels under the corner eaves of the house," wrote historian D. Clayton Brown. "In many instances the garden disappeared as refrigeration enabled housewives to store fruit and vegetables." Yards were tidied up. With washing machines replacing hard days of scrubbing on a washboard, "backyards were no longer cluttered with kettles and ashes from last week's laundry."

Zoning ordinances finished the job, outlawing backyard chickens and pigs and even, sometimes, laundry drying on the line.

Worship Sheds

Meetinghouses were not sacred places. The Puritans wanted nothing to do with the pomp and theater of other denominations. They had simple requirements: a room, a pulpit, and a table. They built plain, large houses for worship in early New England. Meetinghouses were anti-churches—they had no spire, tower, bell, clock, stained glass, statues, frescoes, or altar. They were oriented in an un-churchlike direction: the front door was on the long side (not the narrow gable end). They were just minimal shelters for prayer. (Quite minimal.

They had no lighting and no heat. "Bread was frozen at the Lord's Table," noted Samuel Sewall in January 1716.)

These Sabbath Day tools were roughly treated. They were moved, burned, and discarded; they were converted to ugly churches or useful barns. (The Third Meetinghouse in Hatfield, Massachusetts, later served as a tobacco barn.) Thousands were built; few survive. Of the 337 "first period" meeting-houses built between 1622 and 1770, only 15 are left, or about 4 percent. Of the 1,156 built later in the "second period" (between 1699 and 1820), just about 190 remain, roughly 16 percent. The last 603 meetinghouses built, in the short "third period" (1790-1830), fared better, with more than half still standing. In the early periods, the least likely structure to be left standing after fifty years was the meetinghouse, said historian Peter Benes, who provides the count. Fashions in faith brought changes; towers and spires were added, buildings were rotated to a more churchly position, entrances and pulpits were moved, pews and furnishings grew ornate. Today they are venerated as symbols of continuity and repose, great white ships of faith, but the meetinghouse re-mains a barn with a spire.

Dream Sheds (Summer Cabins)

"In Finland, life is dictated by the seasons; summer holds the promise of leisure time and, in a sense, of liberation from the community—from school or work," write Jari and Sirkkaliisa Jetsonen. "People construct dreams for the summer—often a cottage built with their own hands."

Finnish summerhouses are small, one-story, and often modern. Usually the sauna is built first, followed over time by a series of cabins or rooms. They are arranged to shelter the inhabitants from the wind and to separate guests from the kitchen.

It may be the sauna that keeps the houses close to the earth, keeps them honest, suggest the Jetsonens. Each house is informal, even the modern ones. Each is built to drink in the most daylight, to get the most out of a fast-passing summer. They are summerhouses in the true sense of the word—to dwell there is to dwell in summer.

Over the years I have passed the time in a number of summer cabins. New Hampshire has many lakes and ponds, each with its own loyal protectors. Each lake and pond is some family's secret holy land, and they fear the day it might be overrun and overbuilt. The most satisfying cabins are the most unhouse-like in their shambling informality. They have not been "improved" into a state of stultifying airlessness. They are imperfect and static. Summer after summer has been allowed to settle like dust. Odd gatherings of old furniture, yellowing nautical maps, hoofs and horns, found bones and shells all form a narrative, a memory map of past summers, a family history of grandparents, great-greats, aunts, uncles, cousins, children, and close friends. The stop-time, deep-family time, eternal childhood summer of these cabins is alluring. This is your place, your people's place, now and forever.

These small cabins are a promise: summer waits. After the long winter, the story will resume.

Everyman's Shed
The A-frame was "the quintessential postwar vacation retreat," wrote Chad Randl. The tent-shaped houses were everywhere, with their steeply pitched roofs forming the walls, and the all-glass gable ends facing a lake, beach, or ski slope. "The A-frame was the right shape at the right time. It was the era of the 'second everything,' when postwar prosperity made second televisions, second bathrooms, and second cars expected accoutrements of middle-class American life. Next, signs at the hardware store and ads in popular magazines declared, 'Every family needs two homes! . . . one for the workweek, one for pure pleasure,'" wrote Randl in his homage to the triangle that took over America.

The small cottages with cathedral pretensions—a six-hundred-square-foot shed with twenty-foot high ceilings—were cheap and easy to build. Some cost no more than a new car. "For about $2000 you can whip up a small, beguiling shack from a jack-straw-heap of logs, boards, or plywood sheets delivered on your some—day doorstep—or as near it as a truck can go," said *Life* magazine in 1963. The aspiring builder could order a precut kit to build his "leisure house," or build one from the "Care-Free Living" plan books published by the Homasote Company, or the plans in magazines like *Popular Mechanics, Woman's Day, House Beautiful,* and *Mechanix Illustrated.* They all promised that the weekend home handyman, and a few friends, could build an A-frame in a few days (or so). The foundation required only some concrete footings below the frost line. The identical triangles of the frame could be assembled on the ground, hoisted into place, and joined with lightweight plywood, Masonite, or Homasote panels. "Tricky gable roof framing is eliminated," said *Popular Science*. For those who left the building to others, developers filled resorts with A-frames, some quickly raised in just two days after purchase.

The A-frame was a Dream Shed for the middle class. "Plan now to use your off hours and vacation time to build one of these uncluttered little cottages, made better, easier and more economically with fir plywood," said the Douglas Fir Plywood Association vacation home plan book in 1958. "A little later you'll be swimming and boating with the kids, hunting, fishing or skiing, or just plain loafing in headquarters of your exact choice."

War Sheds

The homeowner who was ready to spring for an A-frame kit in the 1950s and 1960s was often a veteran who may have slept and worked in another prefabricated shed, the metal Quonset Hut. Shaped like half of a can, the Quonset Hut, like the Jeep, became a symbol of America at war. It was "a kind of heroic icon," wrote Tom Vanderbilt, "a Coca-Cola of the landscape."

"The world's largest housing project" was born on the run. In 1941 the Navy contracted the George A. Fuller Company to design and produce temporary, movable shelters. The company's architects redesigned a British World War I all-metal shed, the Nissen hut. But the T-Rib Quonset was a little more hospitable, with Masonite interior walls, wood floors, and paper insulation. The basic structure was a sixteen-foot diameter steel arch frame that supported corrugated metal panels. As in the A-frame, there was great strength in carrying the roof right to the ground. (And like the A-frame, its interior was compromised by the lack of vertical walls.) Within two months the Rhode Island company was producing thousands of huts at Quonset Point.

Quonsets were flexible, serving as barracks, mess halls, offices, latrines, showers, hospitals, and bakeries. The Navy designed eighty-six different floor plans for the standard longhouse that was erected in lengths of twenty, thirty-six, and forty-eight feet, and the much larger warehouses. A hut was shipped in ten crates—less shipping space than tents with wood floors and frames. It could be erected in one day by ten men. Quonsets served in the tropics, following the American advance across the Pacific, and in the arctic. Between twenty thousand and thirty thousand were shipped to Alaska. In their first winter, the huts were tested by a raging storm in Iceland: "A night gale of hurricane proportion that wrecked shipping in the harbor, tossed crumpled PBYs [sea planes] on the beach like paper hats, and ripped the covering completely off of many British Nissen huts, left the Quonset huts practically undamaged," said the Fuller Company.

Wartime redesigns of the first T-Rib Quonset Hut created versions that were lighter and less expensive to produce, gave the hut some useful vertical walls, and reduced assembly time in the field by substituting much of the nuts-and-bolts construction with the brute force of hammers and nails. Anyone, the thinking went, could drive a nail home. In all, with the various redesigns, some 153,000 Quonset Huts were launched into the world.

After the war, this temporary shed refused to retire. The returning vet might find himself living in a can once more due to the severe housing shortage, or taking classes in one at a university that was overrun with veterans returning to school on the GI Bill. One manufacturer, Stran-Steel, tried to convince consumers that the huts would make ideal homes. ("You are looking at a revolution in low-cost home design!" said one ad.) House Beautiful, admitting that a Quonset wasn't a dream house, dressed up the hut with white clapboards, a picture window, and a fireplace. Some vets, including former Seabees who had spent the war erecting the huts, became Quonset dealers. But there were plenty of war surplus Quonsets around. As the cans were sold off, they became grocery stores, restaurants, bars, movie houses, churches, hospitals, schools, music studios, and hay barns. Stran-Steel counted 257 different uses.

On Seward Peninsula, Alaska, which had a plentiful supply, the arching metal ribs made good fish racks. "Everybody in the family can reach some of the racks. Kids can hang up the salmon at the lower end. It's a good system," said Cathleen Doyle. "And if you take out walls [at each end] then you get an ideal way for the air to move through and dry the salmon. And, easy to close it off and smoke it out, too."

The Quonset Hut has inspired a new generation of designers looking to create prefabricated, modular housing. Shipping containers have become the new building blocks of lower-cost housing. There are seventeen million of the sturdy, all-metal containers, most in two standard sizes: eight feet tall, eight feet wide, and either twenty or forty feet long. In Amsterdam they have been stacked into an apartment block to house one thousand students. In Odessa,

Ukraine, the stacked containers form the largest market in Europe, housing sixteen thousand vendors on 170 acres. In the United States, due to our trade imbalance, there were at one time seven hundred thousand empty containers piling up at the docks, some available for as little as $1,200. They are being converted for housing, with windows, decks, and spray-on insulation, and, to come full circle, as ISBUs (Intermodal Steel Building Units), movable metal housing for the military.

Bob Houses

When winter begins to close in on me, when I feel as if I were wearing a groove indoors, I head out to a nearby lake to talk with the men ice fishing. (It's mostly a guy thing.) It's a relief to get outdoors, to drink in the horizon, to look straight across the expanse of flat ice for miles. I set out on snowshoe or ski or foot, depending on the conditions, to visit the small settlements of bob houses, the sheds that the ice fisherman pull out on the ice. On this lake they are mostly small, with just enough room for a bench to catch a catnap, a small woodstove, a hole or two in the floor so you can bore right into the ice and fish, and a window so you can see your "tip-ups"—the flags that signal you have something on one of your other lines. "It's a man house," said my friend Eric Aldrich, an outdoorsman. "You want one big enough to sleep in." (That is, in case you're in trouble at home, which he emphasized he wasn't—not at the moment.)

Bob houses are built mostly of plywood, often of scrap, and painted, if they are, with what's on hand. This is strictly "what's on hand" construction. No one runs their table saw overtime confecting a little Parthenon. You don't want to get too fancy; it adds weight. A bob house has to be portable; it has to fit in a pickup truck bed or on a trailer. Lighter is better. Simplicity is achieved by subtraction.

None of them are beautiful, but on the ice they seem like they belong. Out of season, out by the woodpile or by the pile of things-that-could-be-useful-one-day, they seem crude, like a plywood privy. But on the ice their roughness is a match to the below-zero winds that get moving on the lake.

We call them bob houses in New England. (So named for the bobbing of a fish line through an open hole in the ice.) Out in the Midwest they favor ice house, fish house, or ice shanty, but shanty has that wrong-side-of-the-tracks, Hooverville connotation.

Fishing seems to be a little beside the point (except for a famous fishing derby). The number of tip-ups you can have is limited, and fish are lethargic in winter. On some lakes you can fish all winter and not catch a thing. "You can be out there all winter and not a see a flag go up. All winter," said Aldrich. "And some doofus gets out there at 11 a.m., sets out a tip-up, and he gets a twenty-inch lake trout right off the bat."

On New Hampshire's big lake, Winnipesaukee, home of the famous ice-fishing derby, some bob houses have gone beyond "what's-on-hand" construction. Some have generators, propane heaters, camping toilets, and satellite television. Some are finished with clapboards and even have drapes in the window. Some guys just set up their camping trailers. Years ago there was a village out on the ice that even had its own post office with mail delivered right to your bob house.

Other big lakes have also seen the supersizing of bob houses. On Mille Lacs Lake in Minnesota there may be five thousand ice shanties, some of which have bloated to dry-land excess: cathedral ceilings, custom kitchen cabinets, sound systems, DVD players, satellite television, underwater cameras to watch fish, "auto jiggers" that tend the fishing line, one house with Brazilian cherry inlaid floors, and another with a stainless-steel urinal (a finishing touch that would have escaped Martha Stewart).

Aldrich, who worked for the state's Fish and Game Department, once spent a few days visiting bob houses on Winnipesaukee. The oddest one he saw was this big white plastic dome with a door cut in the side. What the heck was that? The big plastic tank belonged to a septic field designer. While everyone else was struggling to get their bob house on the ice, he just turned his dome on its side and rolled it out. It was perfect. A septic yurt.

On Aldrich's tour he saw some "shaky stuff," he said. "Some guys with teeth and some without teeth." A few guys from the city moved out of their apartments for the winter. "It's free lakefront," he said.

Bob houses may be the last free housing in America. No one inspects them; no one will tell you that you have to build them to meet "code." New Hampshire's rules are few: put your name and address on the outside and some reflectors so a snowmobile won't crash into it at night, and get it off the ice by April Fool's Day.

All the ice fishermen I've ever talked to are happy to be out there, sitting in a meager shed on the ice. Why come to the lake when it's freezing out? I once asked an ice fisherman. He was wearing a dirty tan one-piece coverall. He had a red face from sun and wind, and probably drink.

"Good time to be *he-ah*," he said. "Mosquitoes aren't a *baw-tha*."

Bread Truck
"Hermie Newcome lived in a bread truck on the edge of Bear Swamp."

> *He had a bunk up front where the seats used to be*
> *so in the morning he could wake up and look out*
> *the windshield at the day.*

He had a small woodstove in the back, a table and chairs, and "some crates for cupboards," wrote Vermont poet David Budbill in "The Chainsaw Dance."

> *It was always neat in there.*
> *It was a good place and cozy.*
> *Hermie didn't need anything big as a bus.*

Before the bread truck, Hermie lived in a shack with "his woman, Florence." But Hermie "flew into a rage, which he did about twice a week" and burned down his shack:

> *"Burn! Goddamnit!*
> *Burn! you wuthless place.*
> *You never was no goddamn good!"*

He and Florence moved on to a shack by the cemetery.

> *Hermie liked it there,*
> *said it was the first place he ever lived*
> *where he had decent neighbors.*

Someone went by one Saturday night and saw Hermie and Florence "dancing with the chainsaw going in the middle of the floor." Hermie adjusted the carburetor so that it ran rough, and "would sputter, bounce with a rhythm worthy of a good musician." But he burned that shack, too, and Florence left him.

> *Then he moved alone into the bread truck in the swamp.*
> *Hermie spent his life looking for the perfect place.*
> *That's what all those fires were about.*
> *And in the end he found that place.*
> *The bread truck wouldn't burn.*

Hermie inhabited his craziness. He was at home. Was he askew, or was the world askew, or both? Yeah, probably both.

As I read the poem, Hermie is clear-eyed and crazy. Spot-on and off-kilter. He's living truthfully—by the crooked measure of his madness. "To thine own self be true" is Shakespeare's famous advice. But what if that truth is madness?

For Hermie the bread truck was a Dream Shed.

Subterranean Dreamspace

If you drive through the curving lanes of suburbia, everything you see is tucked in. It's a landscape with "hospital corners." But you can't see all the basement workshops, model railroad layouts, home handyman-built bar/entertainment, all-in-one rooms.

A few neighbors might work on cars in the driveway, but this is a weekend-only event. No one gives up their driveway to a continuing hulk-in-progress (or they will invoke their neighbors' ire).

Any unfinished space can be a dreamspace. It's the place people fill with their plans—that will be the guest room, the kids' hangout, the place where we'll host parties. It will be a playroom now, a family room later, and then my study. All that can fit in a few hundred square feet of a damp cement basement.

Unfinished spaces are where houses flex. In the past, big New England houses went from sheltering families of a dozen or more in one era to a nuclear family in the next. Big old houses were divided into apartments and then reunited.

Houses, like people, live in many ages. Even suburban houses can bend and flex.

A Shed of One's Own

If there is a utopia built of small cabins, it is the MacDowell Colony in Peterborough, New Hampshire. There are thirty-two studios for artists hidden on 450 acres. The little houses are tucked into the woods or stand at the edge of a field. The Colony is a happy contradiction—a neighborhood of hermits, group solitude. Walking down a country road, a dirt lane winding through the forest, and coming upon a cabin is reminiscent of a fairy tale—but which one? Hansel and Gretel? Little Red Riding Hood? Cinderella? Many fairytales take place in a kind of remembered European landscape of dark forest enveloping a little cottage. And all fairytales seesaw between enchantment and entrapment. Most "Colonists," as they are called, are enchanted; a few, up from the cities, are spooked by the dark and the green, silenced by the quiet.

Each cabin is a distinctive, diminutive house, a short essay about dwelling: a room, porch, bathroom, fireplace. There are cabins impersonating a classical temple and a Swiss votive chapel, cabins that have come down with a touch of Tudor or German cottage fever, cabins in clapboard, shingles, stucco, granite block, stone, brick, logs, and white-pine bark, but simplicity prevails. Most were built before the 1930s in a sort of North Country Craftsman style, a sturdy boots-on, outdoorsy, rough-and-ready spirit that is just right. (It implies that a birch bark canoe is nearby, ready to take you trout fishing.) Marian MacDowell, who founded the Colony in 1907, called her collection of studios "little boxes."

The Colonists are grateful for the gift of "a room of one's own," in Virginia Woolf's phrase, for the time to think, to dream, to create. They speak of finding a "world within a world," "a deep well," "pure time." There are no interruptions from breakfast to dinner. A lunch basket is quietly deposited at their door. They are amazed at the amount of work they can get done, and they are proud to add their name to those of the other artists who have worked in that studio and signed one of the studio's small wooden "Tombstones."

"It's like one of Plato's universals," poet Howard Moss said. "The ideal place to work, to rest, to concentrate, to think, to be." Privacy is the last luxury.

It's ideal, except, of course, when it's not—when the novel or concerto or film or sculpture is going poorly. Then they are not enchanted by this fairy tale of artists in the woods. Then the wolf is at the door. And "MacDowell can be Hell," wrote novelist Peter Cameron. "For an artist, there are few fates worse than being stuck in a cabin in the woods with a putrefying canvas, or manuscript, or idea. There are only so many walks (and naps) you can take, books you can read, only so many times you can check for mail or messages— you must keep returning to the small lonely room that seems to contain your inept mediocrity. And knowing that the woods are alive with the sounds of artists creating, creating, creating is enough to drive you mad. . . .

"It can get a bit creepy, late at night, looking at the names on those wooden plaques bearing former Colony Fellows' names, some disappearing beneath the bruise of time," writes Cameron. "So much of art is futile—unappreci-ated or unacknowledged, forgotten or unseen. But, oh—to be given a place to be alive in and create art, a place in the woods, a fireplace, a screened porch, a window, a birch tree iridescent in a stand of pines, a field of snow."

Saunas

Saturday night was sauna night when Ralph Kangas was growing up. Around one in the afternoon, his father would say, "Ralphy, time to lug the water and get the wood in—get the sauna going." His Finnish grandfather had built their sauna the old way, with a wood fire and water hauled in by the bucket.

Everyone in their community of Finns got their saunas going on Saturday. His family, like other Finnish families in town, had come to New Ipswich, a small New Hampshire town on the Massachusetts border, in the early twen-tieth century, taking up farms that the Yankees had abandoned. Most of them settled in a part of town that was soon called Finn Country. On Saturdays they danced polkas at the "Cracker Box" to the Lampi family's accordion, and they visited family and friends for a sauna (which is properly pronounced *sow*—as in pig—*na*).

"It was always open to your closest friends. You didn't call. There was never a Saturday night without a sauna," said Kangas. Afterward, in his fam-ily, the adults sat around talking over coffee and *nisu,* Finnish coffee bread. "There wasn't much to watch on TV, just test patterns a lot. People just sat around and shot the breeze." Other Finnish families in town mixed in a Yan-kee custom, a frank and bean supper.

"All the Finn farmers had saunas." None of the Yankees, who lived in the center of town, had them. In his class at school, at least half of the twenty-five kids had saunas at home. "It was the only way you could keep clean because there was no shower," he said. The old farmhouses did not have indoor bath-rooms until the mid-to-late 1950s. (A hand pump in the kitchen sink brought water into the house.) Most of the people Kangas knew had outhouses. Theirs was in the back shed—the shed linking the barn to the house. His father added an indoor bathroom with a shower in 1956. Before that they washed three times a week, once in a galvanized metal tub and twice in the sauna, Satur-day and Wednesday nights, which was not a time for visiting. To wash in the sauna, they mixed two buckets of water, a cold water bucket on the floor and a hot water bucket heating on the stove.

His grandfather built a series of saunas on their farm. The first was in the back shed, the next was behind the barn on a knoll (but that was damaged by the great hurricane of 1938), and finally the one that the family still uses, just behind the house.

Construction was simple: two-by-fours, no insulation, and a poured ce-ment floor, which was sloped toward a drain. This was all do-it-yourself work. There were no sauna contractors, no cement trucks. They got a cement mixer, or just used a "mud tub," and poured the slab themselves. To wire the sauna for a light, they hung a wire from the barn to the side of the sauna. "There were no building inspectors and permits. You just built it. You didn't go to the selectmen to get permission—no tax on it."

The sauna shed was the size of a one-car garage, "if you drove the car in the gable end." That's the way most of them were built in town. There were two rooms—a changing room with a small window, and the sauna room itself, with an upper and lower bench (the higher up you sit, the hotter it is) and a woodstove attached to an outside cement-block chimney. The walls were tongue-and-groove knotty pine. "The pine pitch blistered out and gave it a nice smell." No one used cedar like they do today. The one flourish his grand-father, a good carpenter, allowed himself, was a "pigeon stool"—the molding that follows the slope of the gable returns a short way across the front, as it does in Greek Revival houses, to suggest a formal temple-like pediment.

In front, the Finns planted flowers, usually hollyhocks, said Kangas, and a lilac or two, which would thrive on the ashes from a woodstove. "The Finns love lilacs," he said.

The woodstove was the heart of the sauna. A sauna woodstove has an open box on top to hold stones. Kangas's father used smooth, round stones from the beach. "They were just better. You never saw a rough stone." A bucket of water poured over the stones provides the steam. "It's a dry heat at first and then the water goes on the stove, and all of a sudden that blistering humid air just grabs on your skin and, wow, you could feel it." The sauna would heat up to between 140 and 180 degrees—heat and humidity that will do in most beginners, he said. In winter Kangas would sprint up to the top of the field and jump in a snowbank. "Even if it was ten degrees out, it was like a summer's day." No one he knows continued the Old World practice of switching themselves with a bundle of leafy birch twigs.

Today almost all the sauna sheds are gone. Kangas can count only maybe ten old sauna sheds when he drives around town. They were lost to fires— on Saturdays the fire engines were always going out—and to rot—there was no pressure-treated lumber back then—and they were lost to changing times.

Saunas have moved indoors. They have electric stoves that heat up quickly after a twist of the timer. Many are built from kits, set up in basements or garages or the house itself. They're like furniture, said one Finnish sauna salesman. You can take your sauna with you when you move.

To someone raised with a wood-fired sauna, it's a diminished experience. "I've been in electric heat at the health club I go to. Not the same. Everything's fake on it," he said. Pouring water over the fake rocks doesn't jolt you with that "blistering humidity."

When the sauna moved indoors, some of the sociability was lost, too; some of the heat went out of visiting. "It's a sad thing. People don't go out to other people's houses as much," Kangas said. "Everyone is locked up in their TV/computer world."

Anti-Shed II

Peter Eisenman's House VI is meant to upset us. An upside-down staircase hangs over the dining room table, a column breaking up the dining room denies dinner conversation, and a column outside dangles from the roof, with no support from below. In the small master bedroom, a slot cuts the room in two, making it impossible to fit in a double bed. "This forced us to sleep in separate beds, which was not our custom," said Suzanne Frank, who with her husband, Richard, commissioned the weekend house in Cornwall, Connecticut. Eisenman refused the necessity of a roof and instead substituted another flat wall with windows. The non-roof leaked and has been replaced three times since the house was finished in 1975.

Eisenman's House VI is "a high point in his disdain for function," said the *Encyclopedia of 20th Century Architecture*. "These constructions of complex geometrical systems are not meant to fulfill any needs; Eisenman's aesthetic mannerism brushes aside the client's expectations in order to criticize them." His defenders concede that his architecture is not "user friendly." The Franks had to fight to get a bedroom included in their new home. The bathroom is accessible only by walking through the bedroom; the kitchen is awkward. The architect insisted on having only a half-refrigerator, until Richard Frank, a cook and food photographer, said that was "ridiculous." Frank had also wanted a fireplace, but that reeked of nostalgia. Eisenman has said that he treats his clients like this in order to "shake them out of those needs." The homeowner is an "intruder."

His mission is to "destabilize the idea of home," to disabuse us of the old ideas of architecture—that columns support and that roofs shelter, that architecture is a way to order our lives. Such notions are tired and outmoded in our "futureless present." He wants to "alienate the individual from the known way in which he perceives and understands his environment" and "dislocate the house" from the "comforting metaphysic and symbolism of shelter," he has said. "The house may once have been a true locus and symbol of nurturing shelter, but in a world of irresolvable anxiety, the meaning and form of shelter must be different . . . such symbols are today meaningless and merely nostalgic." The Rubik's Cube of House VI can be turned upside down—the top and bottom are interchangeable—because "our culture has been turned upside down."

Eisenman has gone on to win big commissions for apartment buildings, offices, museums, schools, and a convention center. At the Aronoff Center for Design and Art at the University of Cincinnati, the school's main space is twisted and cut up. "The result is unnerving: what ought to be the apex of spatial synthesis becomes a sequence of visual antigravities that untethers expected behaviors," said one admiring architecture critic. His Greater Columbus Convention Center, designed to mimic the curving trains that once used the trainyard there, unnerved and untethered the AARP conventioneers seated at a ballroom dance there in 1998. They "began vomiting and collapsing due to a vortex of conflicting grids, age, and alcohol."

Michael Pollan, the noted writer about our industrial food complex, once lived in the same town as House VI and went to visit. At the time, Pollan was building a shed of his own, a writing studio on his farm. He was learning to build a level floor, a snug roof, and a sunny, inviting room. Visiting House VI, Pollan said, "took me deep into the very heart of architectural unreality." His first impression of the house was that it "resembled some sort of spiny gray-and-white spaceship hovering several feet above the lawn." ("The ground is cut away from the front corner, eliminating it as a datum for the house," said one architecture book.)

The Franks were welcoming. They love their house; they have spent all their savings and twice increased their mortgage to rebuild the house almost entirely. They have feuded with Eisenman over adding a slope to the non-roof and they have since spanned the bedroom trench with a double bed. The house, a modest fifteen hundred square feet, took three years to build. "He was somewhat cynical about practical construction matters in general," Suzanne Frank said of her architect. He was casual about flashing to seal the non-roof—it leaked from the start—which led to the house rotting out after only twelve years. And yet, she said of living and raising a child in House VI, "generally I could not ask for a lovelier experience." She loves the quality of light and the way "the house awakens my intellectual curiosity."

House VI, Pollan concluded, is "a kind of anti-primitive hut for our time . . . the purpose of the primitive hut was to shelter us, to minister to our needs." House VI wants us to live as if we had outgrown shelter. It stands against the common sense of building. It stands against the colorful worksheds of Tilting, Newfoundland, against the summer cabins, A-frames, bob houses, covered bridges, barns, and meetinghouses.

Anti-Shed III

The Austrian architect was enjoying his visit to a lakeside mountain village "where everything breathes beauty and peace" when he came across a new building. "What's this then? A false note disturbs the peace. Like an unnecessary screech: among the peasant's houses which were not made by them but by god [his lower case], there is a villa. The work of a good architect, or a bad one? I don't know. I know only that peace and beauty have fled," Adolf Loos wrote in 1909. "Why is it that every architect, whether he is good or bad, harms the lakeside?

"The peasant does not. Nor does the engineer, who builds a railway to the lake, or plows deep furrows in its bright surface. They create in another way. The peasant has pegged out a patch of green meadow on which the new house is to stand, and dug a trough for the foundations. If there is clay in the neighborhood, then there will be a brick kiln to supply bricks; if there isn't, the stone round the edge of the lake will do equally well. And while the mason lays brick on brick, stone on stone, the carpenter has set up his rig. He is making the roof. Will it be a beautiful roof or an ugly roof? He doesn't know. A roof.

"The peasant wanted to build a house for himself, his kin and his cattle, and he has succeeded. As his neighbor and his ancestor succeeded. As the animal succeeds, guided by its instincts. Is the house beautiful? Yes, just as beautiful as the rose and the thistle, the horse and the cow. I therefore ask again, why does the architect, be he a good or a bad one, harm the lakeside? Because the architect, like practically every townsman, has no culture. He lacks the security of the peasant, who does have a culture. . . . I call culture that harmony between the inner and outer man which alone guarantees sensible thinking and acting. . . ."

Storage Sheds

They have become a defining characteristic of the roadside, wedged in among the malls and fast food franchises, barrack-like rows of buildings with small garage doors, surrounded by a fence. A gated enclave for excess stuff.

There are 2.3 billion square feet of "self-storage" space in America, or more than seven square feet for every, man, woman, and child in the country. It's now "physically possible that every American could stand—all at the same time—under the total canopy of self-storage roofing," boasts the Self Storage Association. There are about fifty-one thousand storage facilities in the country—more than four times the number of McDonalds. The storage shed may be our most common shed, worthy of a commemorative stamp. One in ten households rents a unit.

Surveying these mute buildings, a friend's child was curious about what they were. After they were identified, he asked, "So—some people have a house just for stuff—but some people don't have a house?"

Teahouses

We don't have teahouses in America. Teahouses are anti-storage sheds. We have one and not the other. The small garden teahouse was introduced to many in the West by *The Book of Tea*. Written in 1906 by a Japanese art scholar who was a curator at Boston's Museum of Fine Arts, it stands out as one of the earlier reports of Japanese traditions. *The Book of Tea* is a record of artful simplicity; it is about carefully selecting a few things, about deliberateness. It is, of course, the opposite of clutter and noise, two constants in our lives and homes.

The author, Kakuzo Okakura, proceeds by beguiling contradictory epigrams—"Teaism is the art of concealing beauty that you may discover it." He tells us how the tea ceremony was lost and found and changed over the centuries of different dynasties, invasions, and restorations. "We find a Ming commentator at loss to recall the shape of the tea whisk mentioned in one of the Sung classics," he wrote about aftermath of the thirteenth-century Mongol invasion of China that interrupted the evolution of the tea ceremony.

Tea spread through China with Buddhism. Zen monks took up tea, sharing "a bowl before the image of Bodhi Dharma. . . . It was this Zen ritual which finally developed into the tea ceremony of Japan in the fifteenth century." The great Japanese tea master Rikyu perfected the ritual in the late sixteenth century, defining the four principles of the Way of Tea as harmony, respect, purity, and tranquility.

"Tea with us became more than an idealization of the form of drinking; it is a religion of the art of life," wrote Okakura, "a sacred function at which the host and guest joined to produce for that occasion the utmost beatitude of the mundane." The tea ceremony "shows comfort in simplicity rather than in the complex and costly; it is moral geometry, inasmuch as it defines our sense of proportion to the universe."

Okakura, who wrote *The Book of Tea* in English, calls this "Teaism." Its roots are in Taoism and in Zen, which, he said, recognized "the mundane as of equal importance with the spiritual." "The whole ideal of Teaism is a result of this Zen conception of greatness in the smallest incidents of life." From Zen, an awareness of life's evanescence entered the tea ceremony. The body is but "a hut in the wilderness," grasses tied together, he wrote. Release the binds and the body returns to "original waste." "In the tea room fugitiveness is suggested in the thatched roof, frailty in the slender pillars, lightness in the bamboo support, apparent carelessness in the use of commonplace materials."

The teahouse is "an ephemeral structure built to house a poetic impulse." Smaller than the smallest Japanese houses, it is crafted with "immense care and precision" by carpenters who are "a distinct and highly honored class among artisans." It is "consecrated to the worship of the Imperfect, purposely leaving something unfinished for the play of the imagination to complete."

Each teahouse has a small tea room, an anteroom where the tea utensils are washed and arranged before they are bought in, and a shelter at a distance down a garden path, where guests wait until they are summoned. The path is meant to shake off the daily world and put the guests at ease. "One who has trodden this garden path cannot fail to remember how his spirit, as he walked in the twilight of evergreens over the regular irregularities of the stepping stones, beneath which lay dried pine needles, and passed beside the moss-covered granite lanterns, became uplifted above ordinary thoughts."

Showing their humility, guests enter the teahouse by crawling through a low doorway, not more than three feet high. The colors are muted, the light subdued. The tea is on the boil and there is a flower arrangement or one art object. One thing at a time. The guests quietly wait for the tea, attend to each detail. Time is slowed; attention is paid. Here and now is given its due respect.

"The host will not enter the room until all the guests have seated themselves and quiet reigns with nothing to break the silence save the note of the boiling water in the iron kettle. The kettle sings well, for pieces of iron are so arranged in the bottom as to produce a peculiar melody in which one may hear the echoes of a cataract muffled by clouds, of a distant sea breaking among the rocks, a rainstorm sweeping through a bamboo forest, or of the soughing of pines on some faraway hill."

Flower arranging is an adjunct art. Great respect is paid to cut flowers; only a few are displayed at a time. Sometimes a monument is erected in memory of the flowers, Okakura said. "Entering a tea-room in late winter, you may see a slender spray of wild cherries in combination with a budding camellia; it is an echo of departing winter coupled with the prophecy of spring. Again, if you go into a noon-tea on some irritatingly hot summer day, you may discover in the darkened coolness . . . a single lily in a hanging vase; dripping with dew, it seems to smile at the foolishness of life." The tea master orders his life by the high standards of the teahouse. He maintains serenity. "Until one has made himself beautiful he has no right to approach beauty," said Okakura. "Thus the tea master strove to be something more than the artist—art itself." He lives by Rikyu's four principles of harmony, respect, purity, and tranquility.

The Way of Tea is simple, said Rikyu.

> *First you heat the water,*
> *Then you make the tea.*
> *Then you drink it properly.*
> *That is all you need to know.*

We will be on a path to a happier life when we begin to trade in storage sheds for small garden teahouses.

The Exalted Ordinary—A Peasant's Bowl

An old peasant's bowl isn't a shed, but it has the ordinary qualities that make a shed ordinary. This one is a lopsided brown ceramic bowl with a bad finish, the kind of thing that might be left behind at the end of a garage sale. It's easily overlooked; it's only three-and-a-half inches high and six inches across. No one knows who made it. There were thousands upon thousands of bowls like this once: unseen in their daily use, broken at the some point, discarded, forgotten.

Not long after this bowl was made in Korea in the sixteenth century, it was shipped to Japan, one piece of crockery among hundreds unloaded on the dock. The first person who saw it—who was he?—saw something special in it: the bowl was ordinary, perfectly ordinary.

In time this bowl was declared a "meibutsu," Japanese for masterpiece, "literally 'thing with a name.'" This anonymous bowl was given the name of its owner, Takeda Kizaemon, an Osaka merchant. Today, the Kizaemon Bowl, chipped and repaired, dirty from centuries of use, is honored by the Japanese government as a national treasure and is considered to be the finest tea bowl in the world, the essence of the Way of Tea.

When it was discovered on the dock, there was not much pottery being made in Japan. Shipments from Korea and Southeast Asia were eagerly awaited by a small band of a few hundred enthusiasts: nobles, monks, temple officials, warriors, doctors, and wealthy merchants. "These men knew one another, met regularly for tea, and competed intensely on issues of taste and ownership of utensils," wrote Louise Cort, a curator of ceramics at the Smithsonian Institution. They developed a language of appreciation, a way of seeing these ordinary bowls. They classified the Kizaemon and other bowls of this shape as an "Ido" bowl, because looking into the deep bowl as they drank tea from it was like looking into an *ido*, a well.

In particular they admired the Kizaemon's failed firing, the way the glaze had "crawled," pulling away from the clay in "beadlike globules." They called this "plum-blossom bark" after the shark skin used in sword fittings. "The appearance of the coarse and abundant crawling is interesting beyond my powers to express," said one admirer.

The Kizaemon was treasured, passed on through the centuries, and used in tea ceremonies. It was "a duty of ownership" to cultivate "the patina of use and age," wrote Cort. The true nature of a thing can be known only by using it. "In properly venerated Ido bowls, brown tea tannin has been allowed to sink into the cracks and pits of the glaze. Oil from caressing hands has given a luster to the surface. Rough edges have been worn down . . . breaks and repairs are openly acknowledged," wrote Cort.

And like some treasures, it gathered a legend of extracting a high price for possessing beauty. A number of owners were cursed with "a plague of boils" and death.

Very few people got to see these honored Ido bowls. "The tea masters guarded their treasures with religious secrecy," said Okakura. "Rarely was the object exposed to view, and then only to the initiated." The Kizaemon was enshrined in boxes within boxes, five in all. It was bedded in wool and wrapped in purple silk.

Soetsu Yanagi, the founder of the Japanese folk craft movement, wanted to see the Kizaemon. He had seen only the fuzzy black-and-white photos that were available in the early years of the twentieth century. Yanagi used his connections to gain an audience. Finally, when the day arrived, he was ushered in and stood by as box after box was removed and the silk unwrapped.

"I had expected to see that 'essence of Tea,' the seeing eye of Tea masters . . . the embodiment in miniature of beauty, of the love of beauty," wrote Yanagi. "When I saw it, my heart fell. A good Teabowl, yes, but how ordinary! So simple, no more ordinary thing could be imagined. . . . It is just a Korean food bowl, a bowl moreover, that a poor man would use everyday—commonest crockery."

It was carelessly made—"the work had been fast; the turning was rough, done with dirty hands; the throwing slipshod"; the firing in a wretched kiln was haphazard. "No one invested the thing with any dreams," said Yanagi. But, he said, this is "as it should be." He saw the essence of the bowl. "More than anything else, this pot is healthy. Made for a purpose, made to do work. Sold to be used in everyday life. If it were fragile, it would not serve its purpose. By its very nature, it must be robust. . . . Only a commonplace practicality can guarantee health in something made."

He saw the Ido bowls as the tea masters saw them. "The tea masters liked the fine netting of crackle on Ido bowls for the warm, fresh friendliness it gives. They found a charm when the glaze skipped in firing, and when a 'landscape' formed in the pattern of mended cracks. . . . [T]hey developed a high appreciation for the internal volume and curves of bowls; they looked to see how green tea settles into them. They were particular how the rims of bowls feel to the lips and how the endless ring is varied. They embraced the shape and kissed the thickness. And they knew what heart's ease there was in a gentle deformity."

Yanagi was grateful to them because "they saw things directly." "From my heart I am thankful for those discriminating eyes," he said. "The early tea masters apprehended the profundity of normal things. . . . If what the masters had marveled at had been something merely unusual, they would have been nothing exceptional. Anyone could have done that. But the masters' eyes were more penetrating. They did not see the extraordinary in the extraordinary. Therein lies their merit. They did not draw their cherished treasures out of the valuable, the expensive, the luxurious, the elaborate or the exceptional. They selected them from the plain, the natural, the homely, the simple, and the normal. They explored the uneventful, normal world for the most unusual beauty. Can anything be more uncommon than to see the uncommon in the commonplace?

"Most of us today have grown so commonplace that we cannot see the extraordinary save in the exceptional." But Yanagi was hopeful. He believed that we could become connoisseurs of the commonplace. "In actuality we today have more opportunities of seeing, of finding crafts of this order than the old tea masters had. Were they be amongst us once more, their tears would fall with delight, and they would be collecting newly seen things of Tea and adapting them for a new Way of Tea for all people."

Seeing and handling the Kizaemon Bowl convinced him that this revival was possible. "I shall strive to find the way for such things to be made again," he vowed. He had been inspired by his visit. This "commonest crockery" was beautiful, he said. "Why should beauty emerge from the world of the ordinary? The answer is, ultimately, because that world is natural. In Zen there is a saying that at the far end of the road lies effortless peace. What more can be desired? So, too, peaceful beauty. The beauty of the Kizaemon Ido bowl is that of strifeless peace."

∼

The Kizaemon Bowl left Japan for the first time in 1991. It was exhibited in a sprawling blockbuster show at the National Gallery of Art in Washington, D.C., lost among the hundreds of objects from Europe, Africa, the Americas, and Asia. Curator Cort came upon it unexpectedly and revisited it many times. "On more than one occasion I found myself defending this lopsided, cracked and scarred brown bowl against the skeptical comments of unimpressed viewers."

The bowl was smaller than she had expected and cut off from the Way of Tea. It had suffered. "It was dried out and lusterless after its ordeal in the brightly-lit case. Upon its return to Kyoto, I was reassured, it would be soaked in water to revive it."

What Makes a Good Shed?—Some Concluding Principles for Shed Making

1 Sheds are flexible and fragile. They live in this paradox: they are strong enough to bend. If they break, they can be fixed with common knowledge and common tools. A shed is a simple form, easily rebuilt.

2 They are temporary and yet they last. (The paradox continued.)

3 They evolve and devolve as needed. They can take the accretion of style—a steeple, a gable, a dormer, fish-scale shingles, and shrug them off. Steeples have been a part of meetinghouses for about two hundred years, and yet in their essence the meetinghouse is unchanged.

4 They are part shelter and part tool. We change them to fit the job at hand.

5 They are permeable. Each shed is partly shelter and partly open to the day, each to a different degree. The measure of enclosure changes; the mix of

darkness and light, warmth and coolness, dampness and dryness. This quality of indoor/outdoorness is one that we have trouble understanding. Sheds, and old houses in particular, suffer when people try to shut down this permeability.

The best sheds are like summer cabins and lake houses. They are just enough shelter—more summer than cabin, more lake than house. They are alive to the season.

6 They can bear, at least, one metaphor. Sheds are like our lives—not the grandest building or the most graceful. Sheds are ordinary—and in that they are exalted.

❧The Beginner's Book of Dwelling ❧

To dwell we need peace, silence, and dreams. We need places that have the "quality without a name." But where does that quality reside and what cuts us off from it?

The Divide

There is a stark divide between the way we build our dwellings now and the way they were built for thousands of years. When did it happen? Some say it happened in the nineteenth century with the coming of steel and plate glass and the elevator and the professions of architecture and planning. Building was no longer strictly a local craft, a unique creation of a time and place. We could choose many dates to mark this divide—and a shelf of polemics aim to do just that—but let's place it here in Pessac, France, near Bordeaux, on June 13, 1926.

On that day Henry Frugès, owner of the local sugar refinery, dedicated fifty-one modern houses he was building for workers. The crisp, flat-roofed houses were designed with the best of intentions, using modern materials and methods to build "low-cost housing." At the dedication, Frugès's architect, Le Corbusier, a high priest of the Machine Age, spoke: "We approached the problem in the way many problems have been approached by industry: aeroplanes, motor cars, etc. . . . are machines to fly in, machines to drive in. We have tried to produce a *machine to live in.*" That statement became famous: *machine-à-habiter*. His next sentence is seldom quoted: "But since men also have hearts, we have also tried to ensure that men with hearts would be able to live happily in our houses."

And there stands our great challenge. We have to house the heart; we need to build good, low-cost housing. We have not solved the problem posed by Pessac.

The locals didn't like the houses, calling them "sugar cubes." "These houses have no roofs," they said. Frugès computed the reaction at the dedication: 1 percent "enthusiastic," 40 percent "worried and stupefied," 55 percent "concerned that I had gone mad." The sales brochure was defensive, insisting that while Le Corbusier's functional Cubist concrete may not look pleasing at first, the eye adjusts. The Bordelaise were comfortable in their own "lean-to" houses—a gable-roofed cottage with a long sloping back (like a saltbox roof on a New England Colonial). They had a tradition of adding to their houses and building sheds as needed. Not one house in the "Quartiers Modernes Frugès" sold. They were eventually rented to the poor. Another two sections with about fifty more houses were never built.

Not long after the houses were dedicated, the critics declared them a failed experiment. And years later, after seeing how the inhabitants had altered the houses and let them decay, they again called them failed: Le Corbusier's pure forms were ruined.

"I expect modern design to be clean, orderly, and impeccable," said one resident. "If it is not impeccable, it is worthless."

It would take a lot of maintenance to keep these cubes in their pristine, machined glory. They seem to have been designed for the full-on sun of the Mediterranean, but instead the "sugar cubes" have melted in the rains of Bordeaux. The locals may have been right when they said the flat-topped houses were better suited for Morocco. All buildings change over time, but these were supposed to be beyond style and history, a clean edge to defy time and slice right through it.

The houses pictured in Philippe Boudon's study of Pessac, *Lived-In Architecture*, are a motley collection. Having lost their colors like a bird without its plumage, they are gray, cracked, water-stained. They look like the bottoms of empty, drained pools. They wear an array of windows. A few even have shutters. Many of the roof terraces have been covered, as have the open ground floors where the villas sat on "stilts." The whole place seems, in the black-and-white photos, as if people had come along and converted military bunkers to a domestic use and done it with whatever they could scavenge.

When old wooden houses slump and are changed over time by the weather and their inhabitants, we feel that the houses are more authentic; they are more a part of the earth. Aging gives a house authority; it belongs in that place. A really good house could exist only there; a great house defines the place. And a very few houses, the best, ennoble a place. They translate the place. They are that place.

Pessac, at age forty-five, looks like a car up on blocks, like tractors and tools left to rust in the rain. But that's not the truth, says Boudon. The buildings have proved to be durable, the interiors flexible. Almost every resident makes a distinction between the exterior—"I didn't like it at all"—and the interior—"I saw its potential at once . . . you could introduce all manner of combinations." And no one, it seems, uses the roof terrace to garden. They just don't live that way, even if Le Corbusier thought that terrace living was charming.

Assessing all the changes the residents had made to his sleek machine for living, Le Corbusier confessed, "You know, it is always life that is right and the architect who is wrong."

Tradition

"Traditional Samoan canoe builders sang a song which, line by line, told them what to do, in order to build their canoe," writes Christopher Alexander in *The Nature of Order.* "The song begins 'First find your tree,' and then goes on to describe, line by line, what must be done next—cut down the tree, strip the branches, hollow the trunk, shape the prow—all the way to the carving of the traditional ornaments which will appear on the canoe.

"The design is not done on paper. The design emerges from the process, which is described, step by step." By following simple steps in the prescribed order, they build a unique canoe. "The song guarantees that the operation being performed always fits beautifully and naturally into the gestalt of the canoe. . . . The whole becomes alive."

Tipis are built in a similar way. The step-by-step process creates the form: leaning the long poles against each other in a rough circle, tying the poles together where they cross at the top, and then stretching animal skins over the poles. "Again, this process defines the building. There is no design."

The same is true for weaving a traditional carpet—each step arises from the previous step—or for raising a timber-framed dwelling. The builder selects the best site and outlines the foundation by pacing it off. (Literally, step by step.) "The foundation is built as an extension of the ground. The walls are built as extensions of a nearby mountain or a street. The roof and its overhang are built as an extension of the wall."

Following basic steps, the builder of the canoe or tipi or timber frame—or the weaver of the rug—creates a "lovely harmony" that is "simple, well adapted, and profound. We see it and feel it in the constructed details."

Alexander points to larger examples that have unfolded over centuries as builders followed their tradition step by step: the building of the Duomo

in Florence from the thirteenth to the fifteenth centuries, Chartres cathedral, a
Chinese palace. "In the case of a big city—Prague, St. Petersburg, Kyoto, Cairo,
Lhasa, Amsterdam—the result was that hundreds of millions of actions, tak-
en one by one over several centuries, together created a living whole. . . . The
tradition told the builders how to do this, and told them that they must do
this. . . . What is done next always has a natural and comfortable relation to
what existed before."

We feel alive in these places. "Plants and flowers bloom. Cows, dogs, horses,
cats, fish, birds, and insects are all there in their well-being. The air is fresh.
The storm blows. The water runs. Shadows glide over the fields. Evening red
light colors the bushes. Tiles crack. Plums fall on the ground."

But we don't sing songs to build canoes. We are no longer peasants in our
valley, members of a tribe on the beach. The world has knit together. We're
mobile, global, and post-industrial. We build by committee, by regulation,
with an eye on liability.

Christopher Alexander and others are trying to find a new, old way to
build. He wants to find the true process from which the design will unfold,
just as life develops in nature, by unfolding, with small changes from step to
step. If the process is right, he says, the design will be good. But he says this is
very hard to do, and we need to do it over and over, thousands of times, if we
are to save ourselves. Can we unite new materials and technology with old
feeling and find the steps to build our canoe today?

"It is not an elaborate thing," says Alexander. "Just common sense, shap-
ing every tiny part within the whole." Or as Le Corbusier said, it is always life
that is right.

Still Life: Pueblo Pottery in Drosscape

One evening we went to hear a neighbor, Martha Yates, lecture about Pueblo
pottery. When she's back East in the summers, Martha lives quietly nearby in a
small cabin on a pond. Out West, as Dr. Yates, she has been the district archeol-
ogist for the Santa Fe National Forest in New Mexico and has taught at UCLA
and elsewhere. She showed us pictures of some fabulous pottery. These pots are
alive, she said. Each pot is a living vessel, just as our bodies are sometimes said
to be vessels. Clay is a living being. The vessels are living; they hold a spirit. The
Pueblo Indians break the pots so the spirits can be released.

Their pottery reminded me of the living spirit in Shaker furniture. "The peculiar grace of a Shaker chair is due to the fact that it was made by someone capable of believing that an angel might come and sit on it," said Thomas Merton.

Earlier in the day I'd been reading a book that characterizes what's happening to America in a word: *drosscape*. Dross is leftover industrial wastelands, wasted space like huge parking lots and waste itself—sewage, dumps, federal Superfund sites. Dross is what we produce. Dross is inevitable, says author Alan Berger. No economic growth without dross.

There are pages of aerial photos of all that stuff you see when you fly across the country: regional malls with 1.8 million square feet of space, failed malls, power lines, pipelines, gated communities on artificial lakes, landfills, abandoned arsenals, railroad switching yards, chemical plants, strip mines, brown weedy and woody closed factory lands, and on and on.

Drosscape has no spirit; drosscape isn't alive. Drosscape is vast and ugly. It's what this country is becoming. "As America rapidly deindustrializes, it is simultaneously urbanizing faster than at any other time in modern history," says Berger. We are rapidly remaking America with a myriad of landscapes we haven't yet named. We live with a vast churning of places, the mixing of the global market.

Drosscape comes into focus from above. It's built on a massive scale. This is not a walker's world, a turtle's world. Drosscape is a megastructure; it's the horizontal, linear city. It's the city everywhere. Once this kind of industrial squalor was found only in cities near factories and railroads. It had its own zone, its habitat. But now drosscape is all enveloping. All previous ways of building and being, all the graces, are threatened with becoming, at best, an island in the drosscape.

This Frankenstein landscape is the monster that stalks all efforts at landscape preservation, that threatens to make every river, natural spot, and saved building an island in drosscape, a roadside curiosity. It can pop up anywhere. Bam! A fifty-thousand-square-foot warehouse, another snaking subdivision, cell towers and windmills, stores and stores, industrial parks and new toxic waste sites.

"All locations have been converted into interchangeable parts and parcels that are traded in international markets," writes the architecture critic

Grady Clay. "Nature is now abstracted for world data-banking and trading. All places are now designated, and we are going through the painful process of deciding which shall be saved, which used, which exhausted, and to whose benefits or loss."

Drosscape is the landscape of appetite, of getting and spending, of consuming, of trash. It's the land we shape with our commerce, with millions of individual choices. But it's writ so large that everyone can disown it. We are all responsible for a part of the refineries and coal-fired power plants and the highways thick with tractor-trailers. Dross is us.

But Martha's lecture that evening offered a way out of the labyrinth. I looked at an eight-hundred-year-old ceremonial pot in the shape of a turning snake. It has life, has snake movement and snake poise. I looked at pots of vivid color with snakes, parrots, and dragonflies. It all has life. No dross.

Power Without Wisdom

Marge Bruchac, the brilliant Abenaki scholar and storyteller, told me this story about Jesus and the Mikmaq trickster Gluskabe. They had heard of each other.

"Jesus was curious to meet this Indian god. And so he traveled to the shores of Nova Scotia to meet this man. And as they stood on the shores, looking out across the ocean, they talked. Jesus said, 'Let me show you how powerful I am.' He said, 'You see that island out there?' And Gluskabe said, 'Yes, I see that island.' Jesus said, 'Watch this.' And he prayed to the heavens. He reached his hands out and he asked God to bring that island. And that island came right into shore.

"Gluskabe said, 'Oh-ho! That's pretty good.' And he said, 'Now let me show you how strong I am.' And Gluskabe called to all four directions, he called to the birds and the trees and the water, and then with one little *wahhhh!* he put that island back where it belonged. And Jesus said, 'Anyone could do that.'

"'Oh no! *Anyone* could move an island. But only an Indian would know enough to leave it where it belonged in the first place.'"

In Praise of What Cannot Be Named

What matters most cannot be named. What persists is eternal and elusive. Try to name it and it's gone. We can speak with allegory and example, and then bravely admit that to get ourselves in the vicinity of this "quality without a name" we need to simplify. We have to restore the ordinary—the ordinary that lives in the shadows, quiet, talk, the hearth. It lives in the spaces in between—which the Japanese call *ma*—not in clutter. We need to give ourselves room to be. We need less. These are old arguments, but more urgent than ever.

We have to start over as beginners at dwelling. To have a beginner's mind is a good thing, says Shunyru Suzuki in the well-known book of his teachings, *Zen Mind, Beginner's Mind*. "In the beginner's mind there are many possibilities; in the expert's mind there are few."

There is no magic formula. ("Schedule spontaneity," advises one "lifestyle" magazine.) There is no handy checklist you can fold into your wallet. The "quality without a name" can never be a polished monument. It can't be a bumper sticker slogan or a sound bite. But it can become our guide and practice. It's not too late. The qualities await us.

⤙ Bibliography ⤚

BOOKS ABOUT HOUSES AND HOME

Abbott, Philip. *Seeking Many Inventions: The Idea of Community in America*. University of Tennessee Press, 1987.

Andrew, Elizabeth J. *On the Threshold: Home, Hardwood, & Holiness*. Westview Press, 2005.

Benedikt, Michael. *For an Architecture of Reality*. Lumen Books, 1987.

Benjamin, Walter. *A Berlin Childhood Around 1900*. Belknap Press of Harvard University Press, 2006.

— "One Way Street" in *Reflections*. Peter Demetz, ed. Schocken Books, 1986.

— *Selected Writings Volume 2, 1927–1934*. Michael W. Jennings, ed. The Belknap Press of Harvard University Press, 1999.

Busch, Akiko. *Geography of Home: Writings on Where We Live*. Princeton Architectural Press, 1999.

Chandler, Marilyn R. *Dwelling in the Text: Houses in American Fiction*. University of California Press, 1991.

Chow, Renee Y. *Suburban Space: The Fabric of Dwelling*. University of California Press, 2002.

Donald, Elsie Burch. *The French Farmhouse: Its History, Construction, and Regional Styles*. Abbeville Press, 1995.

Doty, Mark, ed. *Open House: Writers Redefine Home*. Graywolf Press, 2003.

Flint, Anthony. *This Land: The Battle Over Sprawl and the Future of America*. The Johns Hopkins University Press, 2006.

Gallagher, Winifred. *House Thinking*. HarperCollins, 2006.

Goldstein, Carolyn. *Do It Yourself: Home Improvement in 20th-Century America*. Princeton Architectural Press, 1998.

Gordon, Alastair. *Spaced Out: Radical Environments of the Psychedelic Sixties*. Rizzoli, 2008.

Gowans, Alan. *The Comfortable House: North American Suburban Architecture 1890–1930*. The MIT Press, 1986.

Hale, Jonathan. *The Old Way of Seeing*. Houghton Mifflin, 1994.

Handlin, David P. *The American Home: Architecture and Society, 1815–1915*. Little, Brown and Company, 1970.

Hayden, Dolores. *Seven American Utopias: The Architecture of Communitarian Socialism, 1790–1975*. The MIT Press, 1976.

Holleran, Michael. *Boston's "Changeful Times." Origins of Preservation & Planning in America*. The Johns Hopkins University Press, 1998.

Jackson, J. B. *Landscape in Sight: Looking at America*. Helen Lefkowitz Horowitz, ed. Yale University Press, 1997.

Jacobs, Karrie. *The Perfect $100,000 House*. Viking, 2006.

Kawashima, Chuji. *Japan's Folk Architecture*. Kodansha International, 1986.

Khan, Lloyd. *Homework: Handbuilt Shelter*. Shelter Publications, 2004.

Kis-Jovak, Jowa Imre, ed. *Banua Toraja: Changing Patterns in Architecture and Symbolism Among the Sa'dan Toraja, Sulawesi Indonesia*. Koninklijk Instituut Voor De Tropen, 1988.

Laird, Ross A. *Grain of Truth: The Ancient Lessons of Craft*. Walker & Co., 2001.

Manning, Richard. *A Good House: Building a Life on the Land*. Grove Press, 1993.

Messer, Sarah. *The Red House: Being a Mostly Accurate Account of New England's Oldest Continuously Lived-in House*. Viking, 2004.

Moore, Charles W., Kathryn Smith, and Peter Becker. *Home Sweet Home:American Vernacular Architecture*. Rizzoli, 1983.

Morgan, William. *The Cape Cod Cottage*. Princeton Architectural Press, 2006.

Norberg-Schulz, Christian. *The Concept of Dwelling: On the Way to Figurative Architecture*. Rizzoli, 1984.

— *New World Architecture*. The Architectural League of New York/Princeton Architectural Press, 1988.

Olmert, Michael. *Kitchens, Smokehouses, and Privies: Outbuildings and the Architecture of Daily Life in the Eighteenth-Century Mid-Atlantic*. Cornell University Press, 2009.

Pallasmaa, Juhani. *Encounters: Architectural Essays*. Rakennustieto Oy, 2005.

Perec, Georges. *Species of Spaces and Other Pieces*. John Sturrock, trans. Penguin Books, 1997.

Porte, Joel, ed. *Emerson in His Journals*. Belknap Press of Harvard University Press, 1982.

Porteous, J. Douglas, and Sandra E. Smith. *Domicide: The Global Destruction of Home*. McGill–Queen's University Press, 2001.

River. *Dwelling: On Making Your Own*. Freestone Publishing Co., 1974.

Rybczynski, Witold. *Last Harvest: How a Cornfield Became New Daleville*. Scribner, 2007.

— *The Most Beautiful House in the World*. Viking, 1989.

Sartwell, Crispin. *Six Names for Beauty*. Routledge, 2004.

Schoenauer, Norbert. *6,000 Years of Housing*. Rev. ed. W. W. Norton & Co., 2000.

Sparkes, Stephen, and Signe Howell, eds. *The House in Southeast Asia*. RoutledgeCurzon, 2003.

Tung, Anthony Max. *Preserving the World's Great Cities: The Destruction and Renewal of the Historic Metropolis*. Clarkson Potter, 2001.

Woodward, Christopher. *In Ruins*. Pantheon, 2002.

DWELLING IN THE ORDINARY

Pages from an Ice Storm Journal

Banham, Reyner. *The Architecture of the Well-Tempered Environment*. 2nd ed. University of Chicago Press, 1984.

Beecher, Catherine E., and Harriet Beecher Stowe. *American Woman's Home*. (1869) Library of Victorian Culture, American Life Foundation, 1979.

Braudel, Fernand. *Civilization and Capitalism, 15th–18th Century.* Vol. 1. Harper & Row, 1982.

Brewer, Priscilla T. "'We Have Got a Very Good Cooking Stove': Advertising, Design, and Consumer Response to the Cookstove, 1815–1880." *Winterthur Portfolio.* Spring 1990.

Clark, Clifford Edward, Jr. *The American Family Home, 1800–1960.* University of North Carolina Press, 1986.

Cowan, Ruth. *More Work for Mother: The Ironies of Household Technology from the Open Hearth to the Microwave.* Basic Books, Inc., 1983.

Crowley, John E. *The Invention of Comfort.* The Johns Hopkins University Press, 2001.

Demos, John. *A Little Commonwealth: Family Life in Plymouth Colony.* Oxford University Press, 1970.

Dickens, Charles. *American Notes for General Circulation.* (1842) Penguin Books, 1972.

Downing, A. J. *The Architecture of Country Houses.* (1850) Dover Publications, Inc., 1969.

Freese, Barbara. *Coal: A Human History.* Perseus Publishing, 2003.

Gideon, Siegfried. *Mechanization Takes Command.* Oxford University Press, 1948.

Hedrick, Joan D. *Harriet Beecher Stowe: A Life.* Oxford University Press, 1994.

Ierley, Merritt. *Open House: A Guided Tour of the American Home, 1637–Present.* Henry Holt and Company, 1999.

NEI Electric Power Engineering. *New Hampshire December 2008 Ice Storm Assessment Report.* October 28, 2009.

Nye, David E. *Electrifying America.* The MIT Press, 1990.

Nylander, Jane C. *Our Own Snug Fireside: Images of the New England Home, 1760–1860.* Alfred A. Knopf, 1993.

Public Service of New Hampshire, *New Hampshire Ice Storm 2008: Record Outage, Record Recovery.* 2009.

Rubel, William. *The Magic of Fire: Hearth Cooking.* Ten Speed Press, 2002.

Rugoff, Milton. *The Beechers.* Harper & Row, Publishers, 1981.

Schenone, Laura. *A Thousand Years over a Hot Stove.* W. W. Norton & Co., 2003.

Steinmetz, Charles P., "Electricity and Civilization." *Harper's Monthly Magazine.* January 1922.

Strasser, Susan. *Never Done: A History of American Housework.* Pantheon Books, 1982.

Townsend, Gavin. "Airborne Toxins and the American House, 1865–1895." *Winterthur Portfolio.* Spring 1989.

Weins, Janine. *Renovation Reflections.* Janine Weins, 2005.

The Age of Clutter

Aslett, Don. *Clutter Free! Finally & Forever.* Marsh Creek Press, 1995.

— *Clutter's Last Stand.* 2nd ed. Adams Media, 2005.

Atkin, Ross. "Going from Pack Rat to Clutter Cutter." *The Christian Science Monitor.* June 20, 2001.

Blumenson, John J.-G. *Identifying American Architecture.* American Association for State and Local History, 1977.

Bruno, Dave. "100 Thing Challenge." http://www.guynameddave.com.

Cathers, David, and Alexander Vertikoff. *Stickley Style*. Simon & Schuster, 1999.

Clean Sweep. *Conquer the Clutter: Reclaim Your Space, Reclaim Your Life*. Meredith Books, 2005.

Conover, Kirsten A. "In the Scramble to Simplify, Organization Is Big Business." *The Christian Science Monitor*. November 9, 1995.

Cook, Clarence. *The House Beautiful*. Scribner, Armstrong and Company, 1878.

Downing, A. J. *Furniture for the Victorian Home; from A. J. Downing, American: County Houses (1850) and J. C. Loudon, English: Encyclopedia (1833)* Reprinted: American Life Foundation, 1968.

Duchscherer, Paul, and Douglas Keister. *The Bungalow*. Penguin Studio, 1995.

Dudley, David. "Conquering Clutter." *AARP The Magazine*. January/February 2007.

Fenner, Elizabeth, and Stephanie Booth. "Too Much Stuff." *Real Simple*. April 2008.

FlyLady. http://www.flylady.net.

Freud, Sigmund. *Das Unheimliche [The Uncanny]*. 1919. Reprinted: Penguin Classics, 2003.

Gilman, Charlotte Perkins. *The Yellow Wallpaper*. Small & Maynard, 1899.

Great Brook School Fifth Grade Students. *Hancock Then and Now*. Great Brook School, Antrim, New Hampshire, 2003.

Greene, Lauren A., and Rita Emmett. "Get Organized!" *Cosmo Girl*. December 2005/January 2006.

Grier, Katherine C. *Culture and Comfort: People, Places, and Upholstery 1850-1930*. The Strong Museum, 1988.

Gutierrez, Lisa. "The Stuff of Life, Part 2: What Do You Part With? Your Memorabilia or Your Partner? Hmm. Tough Decision." *The Kansas City Star*. October 16, 2007.

Kaplan, Wendy, ed. *"The Art that is Life." The Arts & Crafts Movement in America, 1875-1920*. Bulfinch Press, 1987.

Larkin, Jack. *Where We Lived*. The Taunton Press, 2006.

Logan, Thad. *The Victorian Parlour*. Cambridge University Press, 2001.

Maddex, Diane, and Alexander Vertikoff. *Bungalow Nation*. Harry N. Abrams, Inc., 2003.

Merton, Thomas. *My Argument with the Gestapo: A Macaronic Journal*. New Directions Publishing, 1975.

Peterson, Harold L. *Americans at Home: From the Colonists to the Late Victorians*. Charles Scribner's Sons, 1971.

Pittman, Kyran. "Writer Goes on a Clutter Diet." *Good Housekeeping*, April 2009.

Schlereth, Thomas. *Victorian America: Transformations in Everyday Life, 1876–1915*. HarperCollins Publishers, 1991.

Seale, William. *The Tasteful Interlude: American Interiors Through the Camera's Eye, 1860–1917*. 2nd ed. American Association for State and Local History, 1981.

Shi, David E. *The Simple Life*. Oxford University Press, 1985.

Smallin, Donna. *Seven Simple Steps to Unclutter Your Life*. Storey Publishing, 2000.

Stevenson, Louise L. *The Victorian Homefront*. Twayne Publishers, 1991.

Stickley, Gustav. *Craftsman Homes*. 1909. Reprinted: The Lyons Press, 2002.

Sweeney, Kevin M. "Furniture and the Domestic Environment in Wethersfield, Conn., 1639–1800." In Robert Blair St. George, ed., *Material Life in America 1600–1800*. Northeastern University Press, 1988.

Vidler, Anthony. *The Architectural Uncanny*. The MIT Press, 1992.

Wagner, Charles. *The Simple Life*. McClure, Phillips & Co., 1901.

Walker, Lester. *American Shelter*. The Overlook Press, 1981.

Wharton, Edith, and Ogden Codman, Jr. *The Decoration of Houses*. 1902. Reprinted: W. W. Norton & Co., 1978.

Wright, Gwendolyn. *Building the Dream: A Social History of Housing in America*. Pantheon Books, 1981.

Finding Heaven in the Most Hated House on the Block

House and Home. "Merchandising." April, 1956.

— "This Rich and Rhythmic House Expresses 32 Simple and Basic Design Ideas of Frank Lloyd Wright." September, 1956.

Levine, Neil, Hetty Startup, and Kurt J. Sundstrom. *A Work of Art for Kindred Spirits: Frank Lloyd Wright's Zimmerman House*. Currier Museum of Art, Manchester, N.H., 2004.

Lind, Carla, ed. *Historic Structure Report for the Isadore J. and Lucille Zimmerman House*. Tilton and Lewis Associates, Inc., 1989.

Maddex, Diane. *Wright-Sized Houses: Frank Lloyd Wright's Solutions for Making Small Houses Feel Big*. Harry N. Abrams, 2003.

Pfeiffer, Bruce, and David Larkin, eds., *Frank Lloyd Wright, Master Builder*. Universe Publishing in association with the Frank Lloyd Wright Foundation, 1997.

Sergeant, John. *Frank Lloyd Wright's Usonian Houses: The Case for Organic Architecture*. Whitney Library of Design, 1976.

The Perilous Career of a Footpath

Adams, Henry. *History of the United States of America During the Administrations of Thomas Jefferson*. 1889. Reprint, Library of America, 1986.

Alexander, Christopher. "An Early Summary of 'The Timeless Way of Building,' 1970," in Jon Lang, et al., eds. *Designing for Human Behavior: Architecture and the Behavioral Sciences*. Dowden, Hutchinson & Ross, 1974.

— "Empirical Findings from *The Nature of Order*." 2007. www.livingneighborhoods. org/library/empirical-findings.pdf.

— *The Linz Café*. Oxford University Press, 1981.

— *The Nature of Order. Book One: The Phenomenon of Life*. The Center for Environmental Structure, 2002.

— *The Nature of Order. Book Two: The Process of Creating Life*. The Center for Environmental Structure, 2002.

— "Perspectives: Manifesto 1991." *Progressive Architecture*. July 1991.

— *The Timeless Way of Building.* Oxford University Press, 1979.

— and Randall Schmidt, *The Brookings Plan: The Generative Masterplan for Harbor Hills, Near Brookings, Oregon. A Model Creation Process for 21ˢᵗ-Century Cities.* Center for Environmental Structure and PatternLanguage.com, 2005.

— et al. *The Mary Rose Museum.* Oxford University Press, 1995.

— et al. *The Oregon Experiment.* Oxford University Press, 1975.

— et al. *A Pattern Language.* Oxford University Press, 1977.

— et al. *The Production of Houses.* Oxford University Press, 1985.

Bennett, Richard O. "Highway Safety: The Case of the Pedestrian, Cyclist, and Horsedrawn Vehicle," in Jean Labatut and Wheaton J. Lane, eds. *Highways in Our National Life: A Symposium.* Princeton University Press, 1950.

Bryant, Greg. "Alexander Visits the Oregon Experiment." *Rain Magazine.* Summer 1994.

— "The Oregon Experiment After Twenty Years." *Rain Magazine.* Spring 1991.

Environmental Working Group. *Mean Streets: Pedestrian Safety and Reform of the Nation's Transportation Law.* Environmental Working Group, 1997.

Davis, Howard. *The Culture of Building.* Oxford University Press, 1999.

Fisher, Thomas, and Ziva Freiman. "The Real Meaning of Architecture." *Progressive Architecture.* July 1991.

Grabow, Stephen. *Christopher Alexander: The Search for a New Paradigm in Architecture.* Oriel Press, 1983.

Jackson, Kenneth T. *Crabgrass Frontier: The Suburbanization of the United States.* Oxford University Press, 1985.

Kohn, Wendy. "The Lost Prophet of Architecture." *Wilson Quarterly.* Summer 2002.

Ladd, Brian. *Autophobia.* University of Chicago Press, 2008.

Mansfield, Howard. "An Almost All Right Main Street." *New Hampshire Home.* May/June 2010.

— *A Pattern for the Next Hundred Years. Celebrating the Centennial of the Jaffrey Center Village Improvement Society.* Jaffrey Center Village Improvement Society, 2008.

Manual on Uniform Traffic Devices, Federal Highway Administration, 2003.

Maryland State Highway Administration Bicycle and Pedestrian Design Guidelines. www.marylandroads.com/.../Chapter%209%20-%20Sidewalk%20Design.pdf.

Mumford, Lewis. *The Urban Prospect.* Harcourt, Brace & World, Inc., 1968.

NewsHour. "Transportation Secretary Discusses Concerns About National Infrastructure." Interview with Gwen Ifill. PBS, August 15, 2007. http://www.pbs.org/newshour/bb/transportation/july-dec07/infrastructure_08-15.html.

O'Connell, Kim A. "The Battle for Ordinary Human Existence in Our Time." Interview with Christopher Alexander. *Traditional Building.* n.d. www.livingneighborhoods.org/library/battle-for.pdf.

Progressive Architecture, "Revisiting Mexicali." March 1991.

Rifkind, Carole. *Main Street: The Face of Urban America.* Harper Colophon Books, 1971.

Steil, Lucien, ed. "New Science, New Urbanism, New Architecture?" *Katarxis No. 3.* September 2004.

Stollof, Edward R., et al. *Pedestrian Signal Safety for Older Persons*. AAA Foundation for Traffic Safety, 2007.

Tanizaki, Junichiro. "In Praise of Shadows," in Phillip Lopate, ed. *The Art of the Personal Essay: An Anthology from the Classical Era to the Present*. Doubleday, 1994.

Transportation Research Board. *Highway Capacity Manual. (HCM 2000)* National Academy of Sciences, 2000.

Vanderbilt, Tom. *Traffic: Why We Drive the Way We Do (and What It Says About Us)*. Alfred A. Knopf, 2008.

DWELLING IN DESTRUCTION

The Hut on Fire

Huts

Cline, Ann. *A Hut of One's Own: Life Outside the Circle of Architecture*. The MIT Press, 1997.

Rykwert, Joseph. *On Adam's House in Paradise: The Idea of the Primitive Hut in Architectural History*. The Museum of Modern Art, 1972.

Thomas, Elizabeth Marshall. *The Old Way*. Farrar Straus Giroux, 2006.

Vietnam

ABC Radio National Australia. "The Media Report Reflects on the Vietnam War." June 3, 1999. www.abc.net.au/rn/talks/8.30/mediarpt/mstories/mr990603.htm.

Bates, Milton J., ed. *Reporting Vietnam: American Journalism 1959-1969 (Part One)*. Library of America, 1998.

Brush, Peter. "What Really Happened at Cam Ne?" *Vietnam Magazine*. August 2003. www.historynet.com/what-really-happened-at-cam-ne.htm.

Charen, Mona. "Kerry's Past." *Jewish World Review*. April 2, 2004.

Critchfield, Richard. *Villages*. Anchor Press/Doubleday, 1981.

Donovan, Robert, and Ray Scherer. *Unsilent Revolution: Television News and American Public Life, 1948–1991*. Cambridge University Press, 1992.

Ellsberg, Daniel. *Secrets: A Memoir of the Vietnam War and the Pentagon Papers*. Viking, 2002.

Ferrari, Michelle. *Reporting America at War: An Oral History*. Hyperion, 2003.

Gibbons, William C. *The U.S. Government and the Vietnam War*. Princeton University Press, 1995.

Gibson, James William. *The Perfect War: Technowar in Vietnam*. Atlantic Monthly Press, 1986.

Griffiths, Jim. "Zippo Raids, Burning Villages, and Morley Safer—Another Side of the Story!" www.11thcavnam.com/education/zippo_raids.htm.

Halberstam, David. *The Powers That Be*. Alfred A. Knopf, 1979.

Hallin, Daniel C. *The "Uncensored War": The Media and Vietnam*. Oxford University Press, 1986.

Hammond, William M. *Public Affairs: The Military and the Media, 1962-1968*. Center of Military History, U.S. Army, 1988.

Hersh, Seymour M. "Uncovered." *The New Yorker*. November 10, 2003.

Kifner. John. "Report on Brutal Vietnam Campaign Stirs Memories." *The New York Times*. December 28, 2003.

Neener, Bob. "Assault on Cam Ne: Golf 2/9 'Hell in a Helmet.'" www.3rdmarines.net/Vietnam_Assult_on_Cam_Ne.htm

Prochnau, William. "When the World Began Watching." *APF Reporter*, Vol. 11, No. 3, 1988. www.aliciapatterson.org/APF1103/Prochnau/Prochnau.html.

Roberts, Craig. "Fact, Fantasy and Film at Eleven." www.riflewarrior.com/Cam Ne.htm.

Safer, Morley. Cam Ne Report. *CBS Evening News*. August 5, 1965. http://xroads.virginia.edu/~MA05/burnette/thesis/consensus2.html.

Sallah, Michael D., Joe Mahr, and Mitch Weiss. "Buried Secrets, Brutal Truths." *The Toledo Blade*. October 19-22, 2003.

Sheehan, Neil. *A Bright Shining Lie*. Random House, 1988.

Solomon, Norman. *War Made Easy: How Presidents and Pundits Keep Spinning Us to Death*. John Wiley & Sons, Inc., 2005.

Terry, Wallace. *Bloods: An Oral History of the Vietnam War by Black Veterans*. Presidio Press, 1985.

Turse, Nick. "Swift Boat Swill. From the National Archives: New Proof of Vietnam War Atrocities." *The Village Voice*. September 21, 2004.

— "The Vietnam War Crimes You Never Heard Of." *History News Network*. November 17, 2003. http://hnn.us/articles/1802.html.

— Deborah Nelson, and Janet Lundblad. "Verified Civilian Slayings." *The Los Angeles Times*. August 6, 2006.

Yates, Ronald. "A Viet Nam Village: Death Comes at Dusk." *Chicago Tribune Press Service*. http://yates.ds.uiuc.edu/new/articles_books/v-1975_01_31.html.

Young, Marilyn C. *The Vietnam Wars*. HarperCollins, 1991.

Zuckerman, Ethan. "Children's Voices from Drafur." Global Voices Online. www.globalvoicesonline.org/2005/04/29/.

World's Fair

The Queens Museum, New York. *Remembering the Future: The New York World's Fair from 1939 to 1964*. Rizzoli, 1989.

Samuels, Lawrence R. *The End of Innocence: The 1964–1965 New York World's Fair*. Syracuse University Press, 2007.

Smith, Michael L. "Representations of Technology at the 1964 World's Fair." *The Power of Culture*. Eds. Richard Wightman Fox and T. J. Jackson Lears. University of Chicago Press, 1993.

Young, Bill. *New York World's Fair, 1964/1965*. www.nywf64.com.

Keep the Home Fires Burning

Dehousing

Beck, Earl R. *Under the Bombs: The German Home Front 1942–1945*. University Press of Kentucky, 1986.

Boll, Heinrich. *Missing Persons and Other Essays*. McGraw-Hill Book Co., 1977.

Botting, Douglas. *From the Ruins of the Reich: Germany 1945–49*. Crown Publishers, Inc., 1985.

Fischer, Josef. *Koln '39–'45. Der Leidensweg einer Stadt Miterlebt*. J. P. Bachem Verlag, 1970.

Flanner, Janet. "Letter from Cologne: March 1945." *Reporting World War II: American Journalism 1944–1946*. Library of America, 1995.

Hewitt, Kenneth. "Place Annihilation: Area Bombing and the Fate of Urban Places." *Annals of the Association of American Geographers*. Vol. 73, No. 2. June 1983.

Orwell, George. *The Collected Essays, Journalism and Letters of George Orwell. Vol. 3. As I Please 1943–1945*. Penguin Books, 1970.

Webster, Sir Charles, and Noble Frankland, eds. *The Strategic Air Offensive Against Germany 1939–1945. Vol. IV. Annexes and Appendices*. Her Majesty's Stationery Office, 1961.

Building Better Fires

Center for Land Use Interpretation. "Nevada's Dixie Valley: A Drive-thru Enemy Landscape." *The Lay of the Land*. Summer 2004.

Davidson, Lee. "'German Village' May Soon Crumble." *Deseret Morning News*. April 7, 2006.

Davis, Mike. *Dead Cities*. The New Press, 2002.

Fieser, Louis F. *The Scientific Method: A Personal Account of Unusual Projects in War and Peace*. Reinhold Publishing Co.,1964.

Historic American Engineering Record. *Dugway Proving Ground, German-Japanese Village, German Village, South of Stark Road, in WWII Incendiary Test Area, Dugway, Tooele County, UT*. HAER UT-92-A.

— *Dugway Proving Ground, Dugway, Tooele County, UT*. HAER UT-35.

Noyes, W. A., Jr., ed. *Chemistry: A History of the Chemistry Components of the National Defense Research Committee 1940–1946*. An Atlantic Monthly Press Book/Little, Brown & Co, 1948.

Raymond, Antonin. *Antonin Raymond: An Autobiography*. Charles E. Tuttle Co., 1973.

Zanetti, J. Enrique. *Fire from the Air*. Columbia University Press, 1942.

Hamburg

Bond, Horatio, ed. *Fire and the Air War*. National Fire Protection Association, 1946, 1974.

Nossack, Hans Erich. *The End: Hamburg, 1943*. University of Chicago Press, 2004.

The Arithmetic of Devastation

Bess, Michael. *Choices Under Fire: Moral Dimensions of World War II*. Alfred A. Knopf, 2006.

Burleigh, Michael. *Moral Combat*. HarperCollins, 2011.

Davidson, Eugene. *The Death and Life of Germany: An Account of the American Occupation*. Alfred A. Knopf, 1961.

Diefendorf, Jeffry M. *In the Wake of War: The Reconstruction of German Cities After World War II*. Oxford University Press, 1993.

— ed. *Rebuilding Europe's Bombed Cities*. St. Martin's Press, 1990.

Dor-Ner, Zvi et al. *The Bombing of Germany*. American Experience. PBS, February 8, 2010.

Dyson, Freeman. *Disturbing the Universe*. Harper & Row, Publishers, 1979.

—*Weapons and Hope*. Harper Colophon Books, 1985.

Feltus, Pamela. "The Role of Bombing in World War II." *Centennial of Flight History*. U.S. Centennial of Flight Commission. www.centennialofflight.gov/essay/Air_Power/Bombing/AP27.htm.

Grayling, A. C. *Among the Dead Cities*. Walker & Co., 2006.

Hastings, Max. *Bomber Command*. The Dial Press, 1979.

Knell, Hermann. *To Destroy a City*. Da Capo Press, 2003.

Levine, Alan J. *The Strategic Bombing of Germany, 1940–1945*. Praeger Publishers, 1992.

Lindbergh, Charles A. *Autobiography of Values*. Harcourt Brace Jovanovich, Inc., 1977.

— *The Wartime Journals of Charles A. Lindbergh*. Harcourt Brace Jovanovich, Inc., 1970.

Mierzejewski, Alfred C. *The Collapse of the German War Economy, 1944–1945*. The University of North Carolina Press, 1988.

Overy, Richard. *Why the Allies Won*. W. W. Norton & Co., 1995.

Wohl, Robert. *A Passion for Wings: Aviation and the Western Imagination, 1908–1918*. Yale University Press, 1994.

—*The Spectacle of Flight: Aviation and the Western Imagination, 1920–1950*. Yale University Press, 2005.

Tokyo

Boot, Max. *War Made New: Technology, Warfare and the Course of History, 1500 to Today*. Gotham Books, 2006.

Boyer, Paul. *By the Bombs' Early Light*. Pantheon Books, 1985.

Coffey, Thomas M. *Iron Eagle: The Turbulent Life of General Curtis LeMay*. Crown Publishers, 1986.

Crane, Conrad C. *Bombs, Cities, and Civilians: American Airpower Strategy in World War II*. University of Kansas Press, 1993.

Johnson, Lyndon B. "Remarks upon Presenting the Distinguished Service Medal to Gen. Curtis LeMay. February 1, 1965." The American Presidency Project. www.presidency.ucsb.edu/ws/?pid=27096.

Kozak, Warren. *LeMay: The Life and Wars of General Curtis LeMay*. Regnery Publishing, Inc., 2009.

Lashmar, Paul. "Killer on the Edge." *New Statesman & Society*. September 15, 1995.

LeMay, Curtis E., with MacKinlay Kantor. *Mission with LeMay: My Story*. Doubleday, 1965.

McNichols, Charles L. and Clayton D. Carus. "One Way to Cripple Japan." *Harper's Magazine*. June 1942.

Meilinger, Phillip S. "Curtis E. LeMay." *American Airpower Biography: A Survey of the Field*. Air University Press, 1995.

Ralph, William. "Improvised Destruction: Arnold, LeMay, and the Firebombing of Japan." *War in History*, Vol. 13, No. 4, 2006.

Rhodes, Richard. *Dark Sun: The Making of the Hydrogen Bomb*. Simon and Schuster, 1995.

— "LeMay's Vision of War." *Race for the Superbomb. The American Experience*. PBS February 9, 1999. www.pbs.org/wgbh/amex/bomb/filmmore/reference/interview/rhodes07.html.

— *The Making of the Atomic Bomb*. Simon and Schuster, 1986.

Schaffer, Ronald. *Wings of Judgment: American Bombing in World War II*. Oxford University Press, 1985.

Sherry, Michael S. *The Rise of American Air Power: The Creation of Armageddon*. Yale University Press, 1987.

Wolk, Herman S. "The Twentieth Against Japan." *Air Force Magazine*. April 2004.

Flash Blindness

The New Yorker, Talk of the Town. December 11, 1943.

Learning to Dwell Again

Eliade, Mircea. *The Sacred and the Profane*. Harcourt Brace Jovanovich, 1987.

Praz, Mario. *An Illustrated History of Interior Decoration: From Pompeii to Art Nouveau*. Thames & Hudson, 1981.

Dwelling

Clark, Timothy. *Martin Heidegger*. Routledge, 2002.

Farias, Victor. *Heidegger and Nazism*. Temple University Press, 1989.

Faye, Emmanuel. *Heidegger: The Introduction of Nazism into Philosophy in Light of the Unpublished Seminars of 1933–1935*. Yale University Press, 2009.

Guignon, Charles. *The Cambridge Companion to Heidegger*. Cambridge University Press, 1993.

Heidegger, Martin. "Building Dwelling Thinking." *Poetry, Language, Thought*. Albert Hofstadter, trans. Harper Colophon Books, 1971.

— "The Fieldpath." Berrit Mexia, trans. *Journal of Chinese Philosophy 13*. 1986.

— "Hebel—Friend of the House." Bruce V. Foltz and Michael Heim, trans. *Contemporary German Philosophy, Vol. 3*. Eds. Darrell E. Christensen, Manfred Riedel, et al. The Pennsylvania State University Press, 1983.

— "Letter on Humanism." (1947) Miles Groth, trans. www.wagner.edu/departments/psychology/filestore2/download/101/.

— ". . . Poetically Man Dwells. . . ." *Poetry, Language, Thought*. Albert Hofstadter, trans. Harper Colophon Books, 1971.

— "The Thing." *Poetry, Language, Thought*. Albert Hofstadter, trans. Harper Colophon Books, 1971.

Malpas, Jeff. *Heidegger's Topology: Being, Place, World*. The MIT Press, 2006.

Otto, Hugo. *Martin Heidegger: A Political Life*. Basic Books, 1993.

Petzet, Heinrich Wiegand. *Encounters and Dialogues with Martin Heidegger, 1929–1976*. University of Chicago Press, 1993.

Sharr, Adam. *Heidegger for Architects*. Routledge, 2007.

— *Heidegger's Hut*. The MIT Press, 2006.

Sheehan, Thomas. "Heidegger and the Nazis." *The New York Review of Books*. June 16, 1988.

— "A Normal Nazi." *The New York Review of Books*. January 14, 1993.

Vycinas, Vincent. *Earth and Gods: An Introduction to the Philosophy of Martin Heidegger*. Martinus Nijhoff, The Hague, 1961.

Wolin, Richard, ed. *The Heidegger Controversy: A Critical Reader*. The MIT Press, 1992.

Young, Julian. *Heidegger's Later Philosophy*. Cambridge University Press, 2002.

The World Without Silence

Atchison. Liam. "Sucked into the Vortex of Rationalism: Picard's Tableau of *The Flight from God*." *Mars Hill Review*. Premier Issue. 1994.

Bennett, David H. *Demagogues in the Depression*. Rutgers University Press, 1969.

Godman, Stanley. "Max Picard: The Man and His Work." *The Dublin Review*. Spring 1949.

Marcel, Gabriel. *Awakenings: A Translation of Gabriel Marcel's Autobiography*. Peter S. Rogers, trans. Marquette Studies in Philosophy. Marquette University, 2002.

— *Man Against Society*. Henry Regnery Co., 1952.

Merton, Thomas. *Thoughts in Solitude*. Doubleday, 1968.

Picard, Max. *The Flight from God*. (1934) Henry Regnery Co., 1951.

— *Hitler in Our Selves*. (1945) Heinrich Hauser, trans. Henry Regnery Co., 1947.

— *The World of Silence*. (1948) Henry Regnery Co., 1952.

Regnery, Henry. *Memoirs of a Dissident Publisher*. Regnery Publishing, 1985.

Walker, Susan, ed. *Speaking of Silence: Christians and Buddhists on the Contemplative Way*. Paulist Press, 1987.

The Right to Dream

Alexander, Ian W. "The Phenomenological Philosophy in France. An Analysis of Its Themes, Significance and Implications." *Currents of Thought in French Literature: Essays in Memory of G. T. Clapton*. Basil Blackwell, 1965.

Babich, Babette E. "Philosophies of Science: Mach, Duhem, Bachelard." *Twentieth-*

Century Continental Philosophy. Routledge History of Philosophy Vol. VII. Ed. Richard Kearney. Routledge, 1994.

Bachelard, Gaston. *Earth and Reveries of Will.* Kenneth Haltman, trans. The Dallas Institute Publications, 2002.

— *Lautremont.* (1939) Robert S. Dupree, trans. The Pegasus Foundation, 1979.

— *On Poetic Imagination and Reverie: Selections from the Works of Gaston Bachelard.* Ed. Colette Gaudin. The Bobbs-Merrill Co., 1971.

— *The Poetics of Reverie.* (1960) Daniel Russell, trans. The Orion Press, 1961.

— *The Poetics of Space.* (1958) Etienne Gilson, trans. Beacon Press, 1969.

—*The Psychoanalysis of Fire.* (1938) Alan C. M. Ross, trans. Beacon Press, 1968.

— *The Right to Dream.* J. A. Underwood, trans. The Orion Press, 1971.

— *Water and Dreams: An Essay on the Imagination of Matter.* (1942) Edith R. Farrell, trans. The Pegasus Foundation, 1983.

Casey, Edward S. *Spirit and Soul.* Spring Publications, 1991.

Chimasso, Cristian. *Gaston Bachelard: Critic of Science and the Imagination.* Routledge, 2001.

Kushner, Eva M. "The Critical Method of Gaston Bachelard," Northrop Frye et al., *Myth and Symbol.* Ed. Bernice Slote. University of Nebraska Press, 1963.

Macksey, Richard, ed. *Velocities of Change.* Johns Hopkins University Press, 1974.

Smith, Roch C. *Gaston Bachelard.* Twayne Publishers, 1982.

DWELLING IN POSSIBILITY

Counting Houses

Books by and about Christopher Alexander are listed under "The Perilous Career of a Footpath."

Arnold, June. "Consciousness Raising," in Sookie Stambler, ed. *Women's Liberation: Blueprint for the Future.* Ace Books, 1970.

Karp, Andrew H. "Counting Towards a More Perfect Union: Technology, Science, Politics and the Decennial Census." PowerPoint lecture. 2010.

U.S. Department of Commerce, Economics and Statistics Administration, U.S. Census Bureau. Census Employee Handbook for Enumerators, Recruiting Assistants, and Crew Leader Assistants. 2010 Census. D-590. April 2009.

— *2010 Census Nonresponse Followup (NRFU) Enumerator Manual.* D-547. July 2009.

—*Update/Leave Enumerator Manual.* D-648. July 13, 2009.

Sheds

Covered Bridges

Appleton, Jay. *The Symbolism of Habitat.* University of Washington Press, 1990.

Congdon, Herbert Wheaton. *The Covered Bridge: An Old American Landmark.* Alfred A. Knopf, 1946.

Evans, Benjamin D., and June R. *New England's Covered Bridges: A Complete Guide.* University Press of New England, 2004.

Knoblock, Glenn A. *Images of America: New Hampshire Covered Bridges.* Arcadia Publishing, 2002.

Marshall, Richard G., ed. *New Hampshire Covered Bridges: A Link with Our Past.* New Hampshire Department of Transportation, 1994.

McKee, Brian J. *Historic American Covered Bridges.* American Society of Civil Engineers, Oxford University Press, 1997.

Wiebel, Jerry, ed. *Life in the Slow Lane: Covered Bridges.* Reiman Publications, 1998.

Barns

Arthur, Eric, and Dudley Witney. *The Barn: A Vanishing Landmark in North America.* New York Graphic Society Ltd., 1972.

Visser, Thomas Durant. *Field Guide to New England Barns and Farm Buildings.* University Press of New England, 1997.

Vlach, John Michael. *Barns.* W. W. Norton & Co., 2003.

Work Sheds

Mellin, Robert. *Tilting: House Launching, Slide Hauling, Potato Trenching and Other Tales from a Newfoundland Fishing Village.* Princeton Architectural Press, 2003.

Tuttle, Peter. "Home from the Sea." *Yankee.* March/April 2012.

Connected Farm Sheds

Hubka, Thomas C. *Big House, Little House, Back House, Barn: The Connected Farm Buildings of New England.* University Press of New England, 1984.

Anti-Shed I (Electricity)

Brown, D. Clayton. *Electricity for Rural America.* Greenwood Press, 1980.

— "Farm Life: Before and After Electrification." *Proceedings of the Annual Meeting, the Association for Living Historical Farms and Agricultural Museums.* Vol. 2. ALFHAM, 1975.

Project Laundry List. www.laundrylist.org.

Urbina, Ian, "Debate Follows Bills to Remove Bans on Clotheslines." *The New York Times.* October 11, 2009.

Worship Sheds

Benes, Peter. *Meetinghouses of Early New England.* University of Massachusetts Press, 2012.

— ed. *New England Meetinghouse and Church: 1630–1850.* The Dublin Seminar for New England Folklife Annual Proceedings 1979. Boston University, 1979.

— and Phillip D. Zimmerman. *New England Meeting House and Church: 1630–1850.* A Loan Exhibition held at the Currier Gallery of Art, Manchester, N.H. Boston University, 1979.

Donnelly, Marian Card. *The New England Meeting Houses of the Seventeenth Century.* Wesleyan University Press, 1968.
Sinnott, Edmund W. *Meetinghouse and Church in Early New England.* McGraw-Hill Book Company, Inc., 1963.
Dream Sheds (Summer Cabins)
Clark, Francelia, Dave Robinson, and Alison Rossiter. *Lake Nubanusit (Long Pond/ Great Pond). Its History and Its People.* Nubanusit Lake Association, Inc., 2000.
Colt, George Howe. *The Big House: A Century in the Life of an American Summer Home.* Scribner, 2003.
Jetsonen, Jari and Sirkkaliisa. *Finnish Summer Houses.* Princeton Architectural Press, 2008.

Everyman's Shed

Randl, Chad. *A-frame.* Princeton Architectural Press, 2004.

War Sheds

Clark, Tim. "Living in a Quonset Hut Is Like Eating Spam." *Yankee.* November 1985.
Decker, Julie, and Chris Chiei, eds. *Quonset Hut: Metal Living for a Modern Age.* Princeton Architectural Press, 2005.
Lamm, Michael. "The Instant Building." *American Heritage's Invention and Technology Magazine.* Winter 1998.
Levinson, Marc. *The Box: How the Shipping Container Made the World Smaller and the World Economy Bigger.* Princeton University Press, 2006.
Myers, Steven Lee. "Seventh-Kilometer Market Journal; From Soviet-Era Flea Market to a Giant Makeshift Mall." *The New York Times.* May 19, 2006.
Naval History website, http://www.history.navy.mil/faqs/faq75-1.htm.

Bob Houses

Aldrich, Eric. Interview with the author, September 2009.
Breining, Greg. "Wintertime, and Fishing Is Easy." *The New York Times.* February 15, 2008.
Dalrymple, Byron W. *Ice-Fishing for Everybody.* Lantern Press, Publishers, 1948.
Walker, Lester. *Tiny, Tiny Houses.* The Overlook Press, 1987.

Bread Truck

Budbill, David. *Judevine.* Revised ed. Chelsea Green, 1999.

A Shed of One's Own

Carley, Rachel. *The MacDowell Colony: A History of Its Development and Architecture.* Peterborough, N.H., 1981.
Wiseman, Carter, ed. *A Place for the Arts: The MacDowell Colony, 1907–2007.* The MacDowell Colony, 2006.

Saunas

Kangas, Ralph. Interviews with the author, September 2009.

Anti-Shed II (Eisenman's House VI)

Branch, Mark Alden. "Critique: Queasy in Columbus?" *Progressive Architecture.* February 1994.

Davidson, Cynthia, ed. *Tracing Eisenman.* Rizzoli International Publications, 2006.

Davis, Douglas. "Real Dream Houses." *Newsweek.* October 4, 1976.

Eisenman, Peter. *Houses of Cards.* Oxford University Press, 1987.

Frank, Suzanne. *Peter Eisenman's House VI: The Client's Response.* Whitney Library of Design, 1994.

Lampugnani, Vittorio Magnago, ed. *Encyclopedia of 20th-Century Architecture.* Harry N. Abrams, Inc., 1986.

Pollan, Michael. *A Place of My Own: The Education of an Amateur Builder.* Dell Publishing, 1997.

Steil, Lucien, et al., eds. "Contrasting Concepts of Harmony in Architecture: The 1982 Debate Between Christopher Alexander and Peter Eisenman." *Katarxis No 3.* http://www.katarxis3.com/Alexander_Eisenman_Debate.htm.

Anti-Shed III—(Adolf Loos at the Lakeside)

Benton, Tim and Charlotte, eds. *Architecture and Design, 1890–1939.* Whitney Library of Design, 1975

Storage Sheds

Mooallem, Jon. "The Self-Storage Self." *The New York Times Magazine.* September 6, 2009.

Self Storage Association. "Fact Sheet." http://www.selfstorage.org.

Teahouses

Benfey, Christopher. *The Great Wave: Gilded Age Misfits, Japanese Eccentrics, and the Opening of Old Japan.* Random House, 2003.

Keane, Marc P., and Haruzo Ohashi. *Japanese Garden Design.* Charles E. Tuttle, Co., 1996.

Okakura, Kakuzo, *The Book of Tea.* (1906) Project Gutenberg Ebook. http://www.gutenberg.org.

Okakura Tenshin and the Museum of Fine Arts, Boston. Nagoya Bosuton Bijutsukan, 1999.

Soshitsu, Sen, XV. *Tea Life, Tea Mind.* Weatherhill, 1979.

Takei, Jiro, and Marc P. Keane—*Sakuteiki: Visions of the Japanese Garden.* Charles E. Tuttle, Co., 2001.

The Exalted Ordinary—A Peasant's Bowl
Cort, Louise. "The Kizaemon Teabowl Reconsidered: The Making of a Masterpiece." *Chanoyu Quarterly*, No. 71. 1992.
Yanagi, Soetsu. *The Unknown Craftsman: A Japanese Insight into Beauty*. Revised ed. Kodansha International, 1989.

The Beginner's Book of Dwelling

Berger, Alan. *Drosscape: Wasting Land in Urban America*. Princeton Architectural Press, 2006.
Boudon, Philippe. *Lived-In Architecture: Le Corbusier's Pessac Revisited*. The MIT Press, 1972.
Clay, Grady. *Real Places: An Unconventional Guide to America's Generic Landscape*. University of Chicago Press, 1994.
Davenport, Guy. *The Hunter Gracchus*. Counterpoint, 1996.
Hayden, Dolores. *A Field Guide to Sprawl*. W. W. Norton & Co., 2004.
Huxtable, Ada Louise. "Le Corbusier's Housing Project—Flexible Enough to Endure," *The New York Times*. March 15, 1981.
Speck, F. G. "Some MicMac Tales from Cape Breton Island." *Journal of American Folklore*, Vol. 28. American Folklore Society. 1915
Suzuki, Shunryu. *Zen Mind, Beginner's Mind*. Weatherhill, 1970.

❧ Acknowledgments ❧

The book's title is taken from Emily Dickinson, as many readers will recognize. ("I dwell in Possibility.")

I thank Eric Aldrich, Ken Chester, and Amy Markus for their help fielding my questions. My thanks to Hancock Director of Public Works Kurt Grassett and retired city planner Peter Ryner for their critical reading of "The Perilous Career of a Footpath"; to aviation expert Leo Opdycke and Beth Preston, professor of philosophy, for reviewing "Keep the Home Fires Burning"; architectural historian Will Morgan for reading "Sheds"; Peter Benes for sharing his scholarship on meetinghouses; and Christian McEwen for her close, careful reading of the entire manuscript. Thanks also to Andrew Shier for acting as a thoughtful and intuitive walking companion as we explored paths and sidewalks, and to Isabel Kangas Bredin, Ralph Kangas, and Elizabeth Durfee Hengen, who were generous guides to the history of New Ipswich's saunas. Andrew Spahr, Hetty Startup, and Kurt Sundstrom shared their understanding of the Zimmerman House.

My thanks and admiration go to Annie Card for welcoming me on my visit to her volunteer organization in Mississippi. Her relief work is a model of pragmatic compassion.

The translation of Basho's haiku used as the epigraph is by Jane Hirshfield and Mariko Aratani and is from Hirshfield's *The Heart of Haiku*. I thank Hirshfield for her permission to quote it.

The quotes from David Budbill's poem "The Chainsaw Dance" are used with permission from Chelsea Green Publishing (www.chelseagreen.com). The poem appeared in Judevine (copyright 1999 by David Budbill).

Part of the "Bob Houses" section of the "Sheds" chapter appeared in *Yankee*. A version of "The Perilous Career of a Footpath" appeared in Terrain.org: A Journal of the Built & Natural Environments. "Finding Heaven in the Most Hated House on the Block" appeared in *The Magazine Antiques*. And a small part of "The Age of Clutter" and "The Hut on Fire" ran in *New Hampshire Home*.

I owe a debt to the late Walter Clark for introducing me to Budbill's poem and for reading it, as he read all poems, with grace. I knew Walter through poetry. Walter was a powerful reader. When he read aloud, he inhabited the word. He was reading from the inside out—from within the poem.

Dwelling in Possibility is, for me, a sad landmark. This is the last book to be shepherded by my agent, Christina (Kit) Ward. Kit died suddenly at age fifty-nine a few days before Thanksgiving in 2012. We had worked together for twenty years. Her death was a shock. It is a continuing loss. I will miss her generous spirit. Kit was a hardworking agent and an astute editor, but above all, through the many challenges of publishing, she remained a reader who loved the magic of a good book.

Once again, my deepest thanks to my wife and editor, Sy Montgomery.

Book designed by Kirsty Anderson
and typeset in Robert Slimbach's Arno Pro
Cover design by Henry James

Manufactured by Versa Press, East Peoria, Illinois